CESARE PAVESE & ANTHONY CHIUMINATTO: THEIR CORRESPONDENCE

EDITED BY MARK PIETRALUNGA

Italian poet, novelist, literary critic, and translator Cesare Pavese (1908–1950) is widely recognized as one of the most important writers of his period. Between the years 1929 and 1933, Pavese enjoyed a rich correspondence with his Italian American friend, the musician and educator Anthony Chiuminatto (1904–1973). The nature of this exchange is primarily related to Pavese's thirst to learn about America: the culture, the latest books, the most important writers, as well as contemporary language and slang. This volume presents an annotated edition of Pavese and Chiminatto's complete correspondence.

Mark Pietralunga's introduction provides historical and cultural context for the letters and traces Pavese's early development as a leading Americanist and translator. The volume also provides an appendix recording Chiuminatto's detailed annotations and explanations of colloquial American terms and slang, including those drawn from the works of Sinclair Lewis, Sherwood Anderson, and William Faulkner. This lively and illuminating collection of correspondence ultimately corroborates critical opinion that Pavese's fascination with America was the igniting spark of his career as a writer and translator.

MARK PIETRALUNGA is the Victor B. Oelschlager Professor of Modern Languages in the Department of Modern Languages and Linguistics at Florida State University.

Cesare Pavese and Anthony Chiuminatto

Their Correspondence

EDITED BY MARK PIETRALUNGA

UNIVERSITY OF TORONTO PRESS
Toronto Buffalo London

Toronto Buffalo London
Printed in Canada
Reprinted in 2017

ISBN 978-0-8020-9294-6 (cloth)
ISBN 978-1-4875-8719-2 (paper)

Printed on acid-free paper

Toronto Italian Studies

Library and Archives Canada Cataloguing in Publication

Pavese, Cesare
Cesare Pavese and Anthony Chiuminatto : their correspondence / edited by Mark Pietralunga.

(Toronto Italian studies)
ISBN 978-0-8020-9294-6 (bound). – ISBN 978-1-4875-8719-2 (pbk.)

1. Pavese, Cesare – Correspondence. 2. Chiuminatto, Anthony L. (Anthony Lawrence), 1904– – Correspondence. 3. Authors, Italian – 20th century – Correspondence. I. Pietralunga, Mark II. Chiuminatto, Anthony L. (Anthony Lawrence), 1904– III. Title. IV. Series.

PQ4835.A846Z48 2007 853'.912 C2006-905663-3

This book has been published with the help of a grant from the College of Arts and Sciences and the Ada Belle Winthrop King Institute of Contemporary French and Francophone Studies at Florida State University.

University of Toronto Press acknowledges the financial assistance to its publishing program of the Canada Council for the Arts and the Ontario Arts Council.

University of Toronto Press acknowledges the financial support for its publishing activities of the Government of Canada through the Book Publishing Industry Development Program (BPIDP).

Cover photograph: Cesare Pavese, age 21. The photograph was taken for his graduation from the University of Turin In June 1930. Photograph courtesy Cesarina and Maria Luisa Sini.

Dedicated to the memory of
Professor Marziano Guglielminetti

CONTENTS

EDITOR'S NOTE

The correspondence between Cesare Pavese and Anthony Chiuminatto numbers seventy letters between 1929 and 1933. The transcriptions of Pavese's letters printed here are drawn from the 1966 Einaudi edition of the Italian writer's correspondence and from the handwritten rough drafts housed at the 'Guido Gozzano–Cesare Pavese' Center for the Study of Piedmontese Literature at the University of Turin. Some duplicates of these letters have found their way to the Einaudi Archives in Turin, but the collection at the Einaudi Archives includes no letters that are not already part of the collection at the 'Guido Gozzano-Cesare Pavese' Center. Instead, the transcription of Chiuminatto's letters are taken from originals, all typewritten, housed in the Chiuminatto folder at the 'Guido Gozzano–Cesare Pavese' Center.

A valuable part of this correspondence is Chiuminatto's exhaustive explanation of slang and idiomatic expressions from the novels of Sherwood Anderson (*Dark Laughter*), Sinclair Lewis (*Babbitt* and *Arrowsmith*), and William Faulkner *(As I Lay Dying)*. I have elected to include this rich material in its entirety in the appendix of this volume. This section will be of particular interest to the specialized, bilingual reader.

To preserve both Pavese's and Chiuminatto's letter-writing style, I have attempted to reproduce each letter as exactly as possible. No grammatical errors or inadvertent misspellings from Pavese's letters have been corrected. In the case of Chiuminatto's letters, only inadvertent typographical errors have been corrected. On a few occasions I have supplied a missing letter or word in brackets. In my annotations to Chiuminatto's letters, I have also attempted to identify only those instances when the underlining of a word or words clearly appeared to be added by Pavese.

I wish to acknowledge my indebtedness to the late Marziano Guglielminetti and to Mariarosa Masoero, past and present directors of the 'Guido Gozzano–Cesare Pavese' Center for the Study of Piedmontese Literature at the University of Turin. Their generosity, encouragement, and guidance have truly inspired me in the various stages of this endeavor. I am thankful to Ms. Suzanne Chiuminatto for her support and for the precious information about her father. I extend my appreciation to Cesarina Sini and Maria Luisa Sini Cossa for their gracious assistance. I am deeply grateful to Lorenzo Mondo, who, along with making key documents available, openly and graciously shared his rich editorial expertise with me. A special thanks goes to Roberto Cerati and Mauro Bersani of Einaudi Publishers for allowing me to feel at home in the Einaudi Archives. My thanks to Silvia Savioli, whose shared passion for Pavese's letters led to many an interesting discovery. I would like to thank Anthony Chiuminatto's friends and former colleagues at St Thomas for their encouragement and insight. I should also like to put on record my gratitude to the following: Anne Keane, Head of Special Collections at the O'Shaughnessy-Frey Library of the University of St Thomas; Mary Nelson, Special Collections/University Archives, at Wichita State University; and Sister Marian Voelker, OSF, Archives Consultant at the University of St Francis. Many thanks to Ron Schoeffel of the University of Toronto Press for his thoughtful support and generous advice. I wish to express my appreciation to Florida State University for providing me with a sabbatical and a summer research grant that greatly facilitated the completion of this manuscript and to the late Mrs Ada Belle Winthrop-King, whose generous bequest to the Department of Modern Languages and Linguistics at Florida State University has provided support for the book's preparation. A final expression of deep gratitude to Karen Myers, whose steadfast patience and grounded perspective served as fundamental ingredients to the completion of this book.

CESARE PAVESE AND ANTHONY CHIUMINATTO: THEIR CORRESPONDENCE

INTRODUCTION

'To my dear, dear Buddy in America, who let me in a new world.'[1]

Cesare Pavese's epistolary exchange with the Italian American musician and educator Antonio Chiuminatto represents an important chapter in the Piedmontese writer's development as Italy's leading Americanist and the pre-eminent translator of his generation.[2] The correspondence with Chiuminatto offers an eloquent testimony of Pavese's joy of discovery of America, his fascination with American language, and his insatiable curiosity to learn about American literature. In his first letter to Chiuminatto, Pavese thanks his friend for having initiated him 'to the mysteries of your language and nation,' and recalls the passion he felt for 'American things' (29 November 1929). And on 5 April 1930 Pavese shares with Chiuminatto his enthusiasm and admiration for America and its writers: 'You [America] are the peach of the world! Not only the wealth and material life but really in liveliness and strength of art which means thought and politics and religion and everything. You've got to predominate in this century all over the civilized world as before did Greece, and Italy and France.' Critic and translator Edwin Fussell describes these early years of Pavese's literary career as 'intense, communal, and

1 Dedication to Chiuminatto that accompanies Pavese's essay on Sinclair Lewis ('Un romanziere americano, Sinclair Lewis') for the journal *La Cultura,* November 1930. See Cesare Pavese, *Lettere 1924–1944,* ed. Lorenzo Mondo (Turin: Einaudi, 1966), 257.

2 The influence of Chiuminatto on Pavese's development as an Americanist has recently been treated by Valerio Ferme, *Tradurre e tradire: La traduzione come sovvversione culturale sotto il Fascismo* (Ravenna: Longo, 2002), 101–5.

in some ways as idyllic as [his] early essays on [Sinclair] Lewis and [Sherwood] Anderson.'[3] Fussell also recognizes the importance of Pavese's intense collaboration with Chiuminatto, who informed his Italian friend of the new literary works that appeared in the United States, sent books that were unavailable in Italy, explained and translated American idioms, and attempted, unsuccessfully, to have an early essay of Pavese's on Lewis published in an American journal.[4]

Throughout their correspondence, Chiuminatto also served as an important source of encouragement and support to Pavese in the latter's vigorous, yet frustrating efforts to come to America, most of them in connection with a teaching position at Columbia University.[5] Upon learning the news that Pavese might be coming to New York to teach Italian literature at Columbia, Chiuminatto was quick to respond in a letter of 30 June 1930:

> So you might be in Columbia this winter, eh? Boy, you can just expect a visit from yours truly, say at about Xmas time. I'll be there with bells on; and don't forget the drinks! You're good in English, there's no doubt about it – and if you keep it up, why, say, kid, you'll be getting to heaven some day with your shoes on! No kiddin'! If you ever should be asked to write your 'memoirs' some day for one of these syndicated magazines, please don't forget to give me a look-in on the immortality!

Even when Pavese's plans to teach at Columbia appeared to have fallen through, Chiuminatto was no less determined to make his friend's

---

3 Edwin Fussell, 'Foreword,' *American Literature Essays and Opinions*, by Cesare Pavese, trans. Edwin Fussell (Berkeley: University of California Press, 1979), xviii.

4 Pavese's previously unpublished essay on Sinclair Lewis for the American journal *Thought* has recently appeared in print, along with a detailed account of Chiuminatto's attempt to translate and publish the article. See Mariarosa Masoero, 'Parlare di Sinclair Lewis agli americani è un'impresa un po' forte,' *Sincronie* 7, 15 (January–June 2004), 31–46.

5 In June 1930 Pavese applied to Columbia University in the hope of obtaining a salaried position as a tutor. The sponsors of his application to Columbia were Arturo Farinelli and Ferdinando Neri, professors of German and French respectively at the University of Turin, and Augusto Monti, Pavese's former professor at the Liceo Massimo D'Azeglio in Turin. Pavese exchanged letters with Frank Diehl Fackenthal, then secretary at Columbia, and Giuseppe Prezzolini, who had just begun his twenty-year relationship with Columbia as professor of Italian literature and director of the university's 'Casa Italiana,' asking for information and clarification of his application, which turned out to be a grant that would enable him to study at the American university.

dream ('I dream, hope, long, die after America, I must come,' 2 April 1932) become a reality, even in the midst of the Depression. On 3 June 1932 he writes: 'If I find the least opening for you, I'll lay your name before the Italian consul Castruccio, and do all I possibly can to see you over here. We'll have to be patient, though, because these are not things that can be arranged over night. And with all the unemployment in America, the problem becomes just that much more complicated.'

Anthony 'Tony' Chiuminatto, who was born on 31 May 1904 in Rivarolo Canavese (province of Turin), was only four months old when he accompanied his mother to America to join his father, who had been an American citizen for several years and had settled in Green Bay, Wisconsin. In May 1925 Chiuminatto's mother, who longed to take a trip to Italy and visit her own mother, decided that Anthony would return with her and study music. He enrolled in a violin course at the Giuseppe Verdi Royal Conservatory of Music in Turin, where he studied with Maestro Riccardo Bellardi. While there he also took private lessons with the University of Turin musicologist and music critic Andrea Della Corte. Chiuminatto received his teaching diploma from the Verdi Royal Conservatory in June 1929 and the following October returned to his home in Green Bay.

In a letter dated 21 June 1965, Lorenzo Mondo writes Chiuminatto, by then chair of the Department of Music of the College of St Thomas[6] in St Paul, Minnesota, announcing that the publishing firm of Giulio Einaudi was collecting Pavese's letters with a view to publication and that a number of letters in rough draft had been found, 'all in the American language,' and addressed to the Italian American musician around the late 1920s to early 1930s.[7] Mondo asks Chiuminatto if he had kept any letters that he had received from Pavese; moreover, he poses a series of questions that would help in the task of annotating the edition of letters (How did he meet Pavese? How long did they associate with one another? Was it Chiuminatto who taught Pavese about slang?). On 25 June 1965 Chiuminatto responds to these queries:

> How did I meet Cesare? It seems to me that it was through another fellow university student, Dr. Guiscardo Tirotti. I believe that in 1926 or during

6 In 1990 St Thomas changed its name from College to University.

7 The letter is located in the Chiuminatto file at the Einaudi Archives in Turin.

> the early months of 1927 he told me that two students, a certain Massimo Mila[8] and Cesare Pavese, would like to meet me so that they might be able to practice their English. If I am not mistaken we met at the Cafe Mugna in front of the Porta Nuova train station. From that day until my departure in October 1929, I continued my friendship both with Mila as well as with Pavese; but perhaps I must add that our encounters always had as their sole aim the study of English. I don't recall ever spending an evening with them simply for pure pleasure. We would agree to meet at the Cafe Mugna; other times we would go to Mila's home, where I remember as if it were yesterday I read out loud Longfellow's *Hiawatha.* We would discuss how English pronunciation differed from American, then the usual grammatical and syntactic considerations. Then I had them read some prose and poetry. Now I'm sure Massimo would remember all this ... and particularly that week (or two?) when he was under house arrest for something having do with the black shirts! Yes, and I'm sure about this – I was the one who taught Cesare about American slang. This was a point that gave him a great deal of trouble and one could easily understand why, because at that time there was no dictionary of slang. At our meetings he would bring a list of slang phrases that I would explain to him one at a time until he could find its Italian equivalent. In addition, I would prepare a list of phrases for eventual use. I remember very well how at the end of each of these meetings his face would light up with great satisfaction ... With regard to Pavese's letters, I do not have any.[9]

Thanks to Pavese's habit of conserving the rough drafts of his own letters as well as those he received, especially in the early years of his literary formation, the reconstruction of the epistolary relationship with Chiuminatto, as the editors of the 1966 two-volume edition of the Piedmontese writer's letters have noted, can be accomplished in an exhaustive manner.[10] The correspondence between Pavese and Chiuminatto

---

8 Mila was a highly respected musicologist and critic, who was Chiuminatto's classmate during the latter's years of study in Turin. In later years, Mila provided his Italian American friend with valuable material for his doctoral dissertation on the eighteenth-century Venetian composer Baldassare Galuppi. Chiuminatto received his PhD from Northwestern University in June 1959.

9 The letter is in the possession of Lorenzo Mondo, who graciously provided me with a photocopy. A good portion of this letter appeared in Pavese, *Lettere,* 158–9. The translation is mine.

10 *Lettere,* v.

began in November 1929 and ended in March 1933. (Their strongly differing views on war debts and the U.S. depression may have been a factor in the abrupt end of the correspondence. It is more likely, however, that Chiuminatto's role as a teacher and important resource had run its course.) Nearly the entire *corpus* of the letters in rough draft addressed to Chiuminatto appeared in the 1966 Einaudi edition of Pavese's correspondence.[11] While collecting the letters for publication, Italo Calvino wrote Pavese's friend and collaborator Bianca Garufi[12] about the significance of the writer's epistolary: 'With regard to [Einaudi's] plans for the publication of Pavese's works, the project that will create a real stir is his epistolary. It's a very big deal in terms of quantity, quality, and importance, since Pavese was one of the last writers who knew how to express himself through his letters: in fact, there is much of Pavese that the letters and only the letters can give us.'[13] The thirty-one letters from Pavese to Chiuminatto, included in the 1966 edition, are considered to be among the richest contributions to the collection. Critic and translator R.W. Flint refers to Pavese's 'English' letters as 'certainly his quaintest, the sort of English the first really literate Italian computer will write after it has been liberally programmed with Americans from Walt Whitman to Damon Runyon.'[14] And A.E. Murch, the English editor and translator of Pavese's letters, highlights the 'youthful exuberance of this correspondence, its gay humour and optimism,' which is in marked contrast 'to the sardonic, pessimistic or introspective tone' that one often finds in 'letters to Italian friends and in his fiction.'[15]

Both the 1966 Einaudi edition and the English version of Pavese's let-

---

11 The rough draft of Pavese's letter of 22 February 1930 appears to have escaped the meticulous scrutiny of the editors of the 1966 edition. The draft is housed in the 'Guido Gozzano–Cesare Pavese' Center for the Study of Piedmontese Literature at the University of Turin. It has recently been published in a selection of letters between Pavese and Chiuminatto by Mark Pietralunga, 'L'amico del "Middle West": Lettere inedite di Antonio Chiuminatto e Cesare Pavese,' *Levia Gravia* 5 (2003), 267–300.

12 In 1946 Garufi collaborated with Pavese to write the novel *Fuoco grande* (1959), which was never completed.

13 The unpublished letter is located in the Bianca Garufi file at the Einaudi Archives in Turin. The translation is mine.

14 R.W. Flint, 'Introduction,' *Selected Works of Cesare Pavese*, by Cesare Pavese, ed. and trans. R.W. Flint (New York: New York Review Books, 2001), xiii.

15 A.E. Murch, 'Introduction,' *Selected Letters 1924–1950*, by Cesare Pavese, ed. and trans. A.E. Murch (London: Peter Owen, 1969), 8.

ters have long been out of print.[16] On the other hand, Chiuminatto's letters have never before been collected and edited, and are largely unpublished; consequently, these insightful documents, which provide a much more complete picture of an important resource for Pavese's exploration of American language and culture, have not been readily accessible to scholars and general readers of the Italian writer and translator.[17] Chiuminatto's letters include numerous pages of copious explanations of American slang and non-slang expressions drawn from the novels of Sherwood Anderson (*Dark Laughter*), Sinclair Lewis (*Babbitt* and *Arrowsmith*), and William Faulkner (*As I Lay Dying*). Both Chiuminatto and his responsive Italian pupil put the slang phrases and idiomatic expressions to immediate use in their letters. For a translator like Pavese, who was constantly seeking to bring 'new contributions to the texture of contemporary prose,'[18] these meticulous and detailed annotations offer precious insight into the early stages of his linguistic laboratory, as they prove especially fruitful for his future translations of Anderson and Lewis.[19] In his comments on Lewis's *Babbitt,* Chiuminatto expressed his astonishment with Pavese's curiosity and ability to probe a work that is so rich in American vernacular: 'I am surprised, though, that you were able to delve into him [Lewis] for he not only makes an almost 100% use of slang in his personages but has them speaking the most every-day common English, and he writes it just as they speak it and not as it should be written!'[20] Among the material that Chiuminatto included in his letters to Pavese, one also finds translations of grammar exercises in English, excerpts from as well as a complete transcription of articles on Sinclair Lewis by North American critics, and newspaper clippings related to American vernacular and slang.

In the early months of their correspondence, when Pavese had

16 It should be noted that the English edition did not include the entire corpus of Pavese's letters to Chiuminatto; moreover, a good portion of these letters were substantially abridged.

17 A small selection of Chiuminatto's letters have appeared in my article 'L'amico del "Middle-West."'

18 See Claudio Gorlier, 'Tre riscontri sul mestiere di tradurre,' *Sigma* 3–4 (December 1964), 73. The translation is mine.

19 Among Pavese's papers at the 'Guido Gozzano–Cesare Pavese' Center at the University of Turin, one finds block notes and loose sheets of paper full of slang expressions drawn from the Piedmontese writer's readings of Anderson's *A Storyteller's Story*, Jeffers's *Roan Stallion,* Hemingway's *The Sun Also Rises,* and Lewis's *The Job.*

20 See Chiuminatto's annotations to *Babbitt* in the appendix.

already received Chiuminatto's detailed comments on the slang phrases from the novels of Anderson and Lewis and had demonstrated an impressive competence in his use of American expressions, the Piedmontese writer began to contact Italian publishers offering his services as translator. In a letter dated 12 March 1930 he writes Gianni Dauli of the Modernissima publishing house and refers to the firm's book series of translations of contemporary foreign works, most notably those from North America.[21] After noting Modernissima's plan to 'build up in Italy a group of enthusiastic translators whose taste and efficiency are beyond question,' Pavese adds: 'I wish to inform you that I am available as a translator of North American novels, possessing a high degree of competence and the advantage of being able to obtain information direct from the United States ... I venture to draw your attention to the authors, who have been my special study, Sherwood Anderson and Sinclair Lewis, the first of whom you yourself have mentioned in your list of projects.'[22] Pavese concludes by stating that he would be open to other suggestions of the publisher within the field of North American contemporary literature. Failing to obtain the desired result from Dauli, Pavese had in the meantime entered into contact with Arrigo Cajumi, then director of the literary review *La cultura* and an editor at the Florentine publishing house Bemporad. Over the course of several months in 1930, Pavese and Cajumi discussed a number of possible translations, all of which figure prominently in Pavese's correspondence with Chiuminatto. Several of the translations proposed by Pavese, including of Anderson's *Dark Laughter* and Cabell's *Jurgen*, were deemed too literary for Cajumi's series. In November 1930, just days after Sinclair Lewis was awarded the Nobel Prize for literature, Cajumi writes Pavese, requesting a translation of a novel by the American author that was not too long and not protected by copyright laws. They ultimately agree on *Our Mr Wrenn*. On 26 November shortly after confirming he would undertake the translation, Pavese informs Chiuminatto of the project and alerts him that he may be seeking out his assistance in explaining the more difficult words: 'Do you know, my boy, I'm translating *Our Mr Wrenn*? The Nobel Prize's awakened Eyetalian publishers and I'm drudging now six hours a day about this book. New worries for you. Of course there is something here and there I'm afraid I don't quite understand, and so

21 This letter was originally attributed to Florentine publisher Bemporad by the editors of Pavese's *Lettere*. See Ferme, *Tradurre e tradire*, 106.

22 Pavese, *Selected Letters 1924–1950*, 83.

I'll send you someday the very book with all difficult words underlined ... will you then be so kind, as to send me, a last time, some of your thorough explanations? Honestly, let me know before, whether you have the time.' With his usual generosity, Chiuminatto is quick to offer his assistance: 'As for *Mr Wrenn*, my big opportunity as a friend has arrived, I guess! Whoopee! Say, Buddy, just send me the whole book, marked, and with it your translation – so that I can cross-examine the entire work, not to criticize your handling of it, understand, but to help you find the "perfect" translation' (18 December 1930).

As it happened, Pavese was forced to work under tight time constraints and did not have the opportunity to share the entire translation with Chiuminatto. Instead, he made good use of his American friend's previous lists of phrases.[23] Nevertheless, at the time of submission of the manuscript to Cajumi at the end of 1930, Pavese indirectly recognizes Chiuminatto's role in helping him deal with the slang expressions and in broadening his knowledge of American colloquial speech, which, in turn, he attempted to instill in his translation: 'It is somewhat of a problem to deal with slang words and phrases, but I have largely overcome the difficulty by communicating direct with an American authority. In some instances I have used terms borrowed from Italian dialects when these seemed appropriate. Throughout I have maintained a rather colloquial tone, bearing in mind the general atmosphere of the original work.'[24] Just a few months later, Pavese defends the colloquial tone of his translation of *Our Mr Wrenn* in a letter dated 4 April 1931 to the publisher Enrico Bemporad, who had accused him of presenting to Italian readers a work that contains 'pages that are absolutely incomprehensible': 'In this work I took considerable pains to ensure that Italian readers would get the same impressions, colloquially rendered in their own language, as American readers did from the original text. When necessary, I may have used unfamiliar or even harsh terms so as to bring home to Italian readers the realization that this is a *foreign* work, written from a point of view very different from their own.'[25]

23 In his letter of 28 April 1930, Chiuminatto informs Pavese that he was nearing completion of his comments on *Our Mr Wrenn.* It is uncertain whether Chiuminatto ever completed these comments on the Lewis novel. They are not found among Chiuminatto's letters in the Pavese archives at the University of Turin.

24 Pavese, *Selected Letters 1924–1950*, 101. Without mentioning Chiuminatto, the English translation of this letter is nevertheless more direct than the original in its reference to Pavese's American friend as his resource for the colloquial expressions in *Our Mr Wrenn.*

25 Ibid., 111.

Pavese's determination to give Italian readers 'a re-creation of the original novel' serves as an important step in a developing theory of language that he would eventually realize in his first mature collection of poetry, *Lavorare stanca* (Hard Labor). In the essay 'Il mestiere del poeta' (The Craft of the Poet), which appeared as an appendix to the definitive 1943 edition of *Lavorare stanca*, Pavese focuses on 'Mari del sud' (South Seas), the first groundbreaking poem in this collection that marks his creative maturity as a writer, and discusses those factors that enabled him to achieve his aims: 'My studies of American literature put me in contact with the reality of a developing culture, a culture "in growing pains." My experiments with fiction enlarged and sharpened my sense of human experience and rooted those interests in a real world. Finally, from a technical point of view, my work on the "pornotheca"[26] was crucial, teaching me the profession of art, the joy of resolving problems, the limits of a theme, the play of imagination and style, and also the mystery of felicity in a given style, which means coming to terms with the possible audience or reader.'[27] Each of these three areas allowed Pavese to enter into contact with a linguistic creation based on dialect or common speech. This linguistic discovery was the result of his studies of colloquial American and his use of Piedmontese or Turinese slang in his efforts to write naturalistic prose dialogue. For Pavese, both of these activities represented 'the adventurous projects of youthful enthusiasm, to which [he] had devoted sustained and serious thought, and both were integrated by the encounter with a theory in which poetry and language were identified.'[28]

It was in his 'youthful' years, not long before he enrolled in the university, that Pavese discovered his affinity with American culture and literature. First inspired by Walt Whitman, whose works were the subject of his thesis at the University of Turin in 1930, Pavese found in American literature a vehicle to free himself from an imposing tradition and to discover a new way of living and a new means of expression. In the introduction to the collection of the young Pavese's unpublished short stories, *Lotte di giovani e altri racconti (1925–30)*, Mariarosa Masoero notes that Whitman, in the years that predate the Piedmontese author's thesis,

26 An amateur collection of ballads, tragedies, lyrics, and poems written in collaboration with close friend Mario Sturani.

27 Cesare Pavese, *Hard Labor*, trans. William Arrowsmith (New York: Grossman Publishers, 1976), 99.

28 Ibid., 100.

had entered 'with force into his writings and with him, progress, the crowds, and urban "modernity."'[29] Whitman, along with the newfound American culture, represented a source of health ('sanità'), that is, a means to counterbalance the suffocating and decadent atmosphere of Pavese's creative and personal world with a surge of modernity, freshness, and vitality. In his thesis, Pavese argues that Whitman, through his celebration of one's individuality as a person and as a nation, severed the umbilical chord with the Old World and gave life to a truly modern expression by filtering through the self the joy of discovery.[30]

Years later, in a 1947 essay entitled 'Ieri e Oggi' (Yesterday and Today), Pavese recalls those fervent years when he, along with others, discovered American culture:

> Around 1930, when Fascism was beginning to be 'the hope of the world,' some young Italians happened to discover in their books America – an America thoughtful and barbaric, happy and truculent, dissolute, fecund, heavy with all the past of the world, and at the same time young, innocent. For several years these young people read, translated, and wrote, with a joy of discovery and of revolt that infuriated the official culture; but the success was so great that it constrained the regime to tolerate it, in order to save face.[31]

Pavese's brilliant translations and excellent essays on American authors, which reveal a sensitivity to the democratic spirit of discovery, the immediacy of expression, and the linguistic experimentation taking place in American literature during the 1920s and 1930s, helped contribute to the deprovincialization of Italian culture and make, as he observes in his 1947 essay, 'the first little hole in the wall to freedom.'[32] Pavese saw in the works of such writers as Whitman, Lee Masters, Anderson, and Lewis an alternative to the fossilized and autocratic culture of the Fascist establishment. He was struck by the rebellious

29 Cesare Pavese, *Lotte di giovani e altri racconti (1925–1930)*, ed. Mariarosa Masoero (Turin: Einaudi, 1993), xii.

30 Pavese's dissertation, entitled 'Interpretazione di Whitman,' is found in the Sini collection of the Pavese archives at the University of Turin. Pavese argues in his thesis that it is the figure of the pioneer who embodies this spirit of discovery and represents the generating force behind Whitman's monumental poem 'Song of Myself' (53).

31 Pavese, *American Literature Essays and Opinions*, 196.

32 Ibid., 197.

force and commitment of human existential values that emerged from the writings of the American authors he translated and studied. American culture provided Pavese with an ideal place, if only metaphorically, in which to work and study. America represented for him and other Italian intellectuals, such as Elio Vittorini and Giaime Pintor, a literary allegory, a spiritual ideal, and a political myth. For Pavese, the real lesson to be drawn from American culture was 'the continuing effort to readjust language to the new reality of the world, in order to create, in effect, a *new* language, down-to-earth and symbolic, that would justify itself solely in terms of itself and not in terms of any traditional complacency.'[33] An often cited passage from this 1947 essay captures the significant value Pavese placed on American culture in the years that corresponded with his intense epistolary exchange with Chiuminatto:

> It [American culture] became a sort of great laboratory where with another freedom and with other methods men were pursuing the same job of creating a modern taste, a modern style, a modern world that, perhaps with less immediacy but with just as much pertinacity of intention, the best of us were also pursuing ... During those years of study, it dawned on us that America was not 'another' country, a 'new' beginning in history, but only the gigantic theater where with greater freedom than elsewhere the drama of all was being acted out.[34]

Pavese admired the universality and originality of innovative Midwestern writers such as Lee Masters, Dreiser, Lewis, and Anderson, whose works, he believed, were able to transcend their regional and national boundaries. For Pavese, this was an unsatisfied need not only for his countrymen from Piedmont but also for his fellow European writers, as he notes in his 5 April 1930 letter to Chiuminatto: 'I'm in my earnestness when stating that a good modern European book is, generally speaking, only interesting and vital for the nation which produced it, whereas a good American one speaks to a larger crowd springing, as it does, from deeper wants and really saying new things not only queer ones, as we at our best are to-day doing.' In his subsequent letter of 17 April 1930, Pavese expresses to the Midwestern Chiuminatto his high

33 Ibid., 197.
34 Ibid., 197–8.

esteem for the writers of his region: 'You are filling the American Literature with Midwestern geniuses: Lee Masters from Kansas, Dreiser from Indiana, Lewis from Minnesota, Anderson from Ohio, Hemingway and Sandburg from Illinois, Wescott from Wisconsin: you've got to be new New England.'

The nature of the Chiuminatto–Pavese epistolary is primarily related to the young Italian writer's thirst to learn about American culture, its latest books, and its most significant contemporary writers. From Pavese's first letter to Chiuminatto, we learn how valuable his Italian American friend had become to his understanding of American slang:

> Perhaps you don't even assume what usefulness had for me your little lessons of American spoken. Yet I keep those jottings carefully, and scanty as the expressions and words are I could put down, yet as I read modern American authors, I feel more assured, bolder in understanding them, more in touch with their mood of living and thought. And all comes from your lessons of language.

Pavese is anxious to continue these lessons 'beyond the Ocean' and boldly includes in his letter a list of phrases from Sherwood Anderson's *Dark Laughter.* Half apologetically, he asks Chiuminatto to send the list back to him 'with your wanted so interesting explanations.' He then playfully adds: 'if you'll dedicate a little time, you'll do me a big, big gift. Think, 'tis for your own country's sake!' Chiuminatto's reply reveals the enthusiasm with which he accepts Pavese's proposal to exchange books and information about their respective literatures: 'As for the proposition you made me, why, I shall be glad to do anything and everything that I can for you. I am sure you know that I am always more than willing to lend you a little help where I know it is going to be of benefit, and with Mr. Pavese I shall be sowing seed on fertile ground!' (24 December 1929). Chiuminatto takes particular pleasure in his role as a teacher of slang and, in order to fill the lack of a dictionary on modern American speech at the time, he volunteers to be that book for his Italian friend: 'If ever I should hear of some book or other of this kind, I shall get it and send it for you; for the present, Mr. Pavese, send me a list of the phrases you do not understand and I'll be that book for you.' Upon receipt of Chiuminatto's thorough explanations of words and phrases from *Dark Laughter,* an exuberant Pavese is quick to thank his 'teacher' and to put his slang lessons to the test:

> I'm befuddled, all in a daze, with your titanic kindness. I'm now seeing the world only through a veil of pink sheets,[35] all bristling with slang-phrases which are meddling together, re-echoing and staring at me from everywhere. I've got now I can no more take a pull out of a bottle together with my gang, without thinking I'm going on the grand sneak. And how flip I get sometimes! And how many keen mamas I'm looking after! ... My whole existence has got a slang drift now. You could almost say I'm a slang-slinger (Ha!).

In this same letter Pavese seeks to arrive at a clear understanding of slang. He questions Chiuminatto's reference to slang as 'a special language or dialect, which exists by itself and is spoken only on certain occasions or places.' In addition, Pavese challenges the distinction Chiuminatto makes between a slang word and a classic one. He asks: 'But is not slang only the bulk of new English words and expressions continually shaped by living people, as for all languages in all times?' In other words, Pavese believes that a line must not be drawn between English (or better yet American) and slang, as if they were two different languages spoken by two different peoples. Pavese references Anderson's *Dark Laughter* to illustrate his point:

> That book you know, *Dark Laughter*, for instance, is written in English, but there are numberless slang-expressions in it and they are not as French words in an Italian book, but they are a natural part of language. And I said English, but I should have said American for I think there is not a slang and a classic language, but there are two diversified languages, the English and the American ones. As slang is the living part of all languages, English has become American by it, that is the two languages have developed themselves separately by means of their respective slangs. My conclusion is then that there are not a slang and a classic language but there is an American language formed by a perfectly fused mixture of both.

The reference to slang as 'the natural part of language' and 'the living part of all languages' is directly related to those qualities of freshness, primitiveness, and spontaneity that first attracted him to Whitman. For Pavese, Whitman's poetry 'is not a gallery of detached illustrations (or

35 Pavese refers to the color of paper on which Chiuminatto sent his explanations.

vignettes), but a Person, a sensibility, who moves in the real world.'[36] Whitman's idea of putting a real human being 'freely, fully and truly on record' captures what Pavese believes to be the true ambition of the modern American artist, that is, 'to attain to the true nature of things, to see things with virgin eyes, to arrive at that "ultimate grip of reality" which alone is worth recognition.'[37] Whitman's thoughts on language, as expressed in his essay 'Slang in America,' are derived from a similar organic view of the world. Calling slang 'the lawless germinal element, below all words and sentences, and behind all poetry,' Whitman believed that slang would strengthen an enfeebled English language.[38] For a young writer and translator like Pavese, who was seeking to infuse a moribund literary language with new, living models, this view of slang as an eternally active part of language unquestionably struck a chord. He would put this philosophy on language to an immediate test, as we noted above, in his translation of Lewis's *Our Mr Wrenn*.[39]

The correspondence with Chiuminatto allows us to witness the preliminary stages of a program of linguistic renewal of Italian prose that Pavese will articulate more fully in a series of essays on American contemporary writers, most notably those on Sinclair Lewis, Sherwood Anderson, and O. Henry. In these essays Pavese argues, as Italo Calvino has suggested, that these so-called 'provincial' writers succeeded in raising slang and the vernacular to the level of true poetry and a national language:[40]

> [On Sinclair Lewis]
> The true provincial nature of Sinclair Lewis is shown in the use of slang and the vernacular. This kind of jargon and dialect, the national expression of America, is understood by him, loved, and finally made into poetry, resulting in the true creation of a language – the American vernacular: a

---

36 Pavese, *American Literature Essays and Opinions*, 124.

37 Ibid., 124. The phrase 'ultimate grip of reality' is Sherwood Anderson's in *Dark Laughter.*

38 Walt Whitman, *Complete Poetry and Selected Prose and Letters*, ed. Emory Holloway (London: Nonesuch Press, 1967), 845.

39 For a close reading of Pavese's recourse to the spoken language in an attempt to render Lewis's use of slang in *Our Mr Wrenn*, see Ferme, who reads the translation as an act of subversion against the so-called 'official,' and conservative, literary language. *Tradurre e tradire*, 111–16.

40 Italo Calvino, 'Prefazione,' *La letteratura americana e altri saggi*, by Cesare Pavese (Turin: Einaudi, 1962), xvi–xvii.

> thing of which there has been no example since the times when the neo-Latin peoples stabilized their virgin idioms in works of art and life. Before Lewis, American slang was local color or journalistic improvisation.[41]

> [On Sherwood Anderson]
> Anderson's style! Not a crude dialect still too local – like that of dialect specialists who, even in the most distinguished instances, still retain something a little petty – but a new texture of English, entirely constructed of American idioms, a style no longer *dialect* but *language*, reworked in the mind, re-created, *poetry*. In a tale written by Anderson there is always heard an American speaker, *the living man*.[42]

> [On O. Henry]
> Finally, this literature that culminates in the 'prince' O. Henry has a new characteristic: it is a dialect literature. It is a curious kind of dialect, because we Italians imagine dialects to be local and we would have looked for a dialect literature rather from New England. But in America dialect is the colloquial speech spoken by everybody in contrast to the cultivated and upper-class English taught in the schools ... O. Henry found his tone with a rare security and timeliness. Of all the writers of his age, it was he who was also best suited to speak in a newspaper to the *whole* nation.[43]

With each letter he received from Chiuminatto, Pavese's admiration for the new language and his recognition of the treasure of information that his Italian American friend provided him continued to grow. In a letter of 31 July 1930 Pavese responds to Chiuminatto after receiving another 'gold mine of slang' from his Midwestern friend in the form of newspaper clippings of the serial novel *The Big House* by Jack Lait: 'My admiration for your wonderful language (about which I wrote "something" also in my essay) has yet increased since the pleasure of your unforgettable conversation and to my eyes you are now the hero, the saint, representative of a new religion.' He then adds the simple, yet revealing line: 'I adore words.'

As a disciple of the newfound 'religion' of slang, Pavese unabashedly writes in his letter of 19 August 1930: 'And, please don't cease to pull on the slang galore. I feed on it, do you know?' After satisfying Pavese's

41 Pavese, *American Literature Essays and Opinions*, 28.
42 Ibid., 40.
43 Ibid., 83 and 89.

request with the usual exhaustive explanations of slang terms, Chiuminatto compliments his friend's drive and, like a trainer, exhorts him to keep sending his lists of words: 'Say, Cesare, if you ever get to be King – give me a Dukedom, at least, will you? And whatever you do, don't reform; just keep asking. I admire the fellow who comes out into the open and fights. Like Carnera! Push-'em-over, Big Boy!'

In addition to keeping Pavese current with the contemporary American literary scene and enriching his linguistic competence, the epistolary exchange with Chiuminatto helped shed light on different aspects of American culture and society, enabling the young Americanist to go beyond the page in his readings of American writers and to find himself in the middle of America and its people. His correspondence with Chiuminatto provided Pavese with the opportunity to measure the real values of a people and to acquire a specialization that comes from a 'fondness that has been lived,' something he felt was lacking at the time in the Italian criticism on North American literature.[44] Nearing the completion of his 'corking' essay on Lewis, Pavese boldly informs his American interlocutor that his ability to delve into the common everyday speech and manner of living of real Americans will distinguish him from his fellow critics of North American literature: 'I'll teach a few fellers that are now overflowing Italy with vacuum-gabble about America, what people must say and how they must say it' (21 June 1930).[45]

Among the topics Pavese and Chiuminatto addressed in their correspondence were the intense football rivalry between the Green Bay Packers and the Chicago Bears, Roosevelt's victory in the 1932 elections, America's reaction to Europe's reluctance to pay its war debts, the assassination of Chicago mayor Anton Cermak at the hands of the 'transplanted' Italian Giuseppe Zangara, and American popular music. On this latter subject, Pavese was especially eager to learn all about the latest

44 In his review of Carlo Linati's volume *Scrittori anglo-americani d'oggi*, Pavese has some reservations with the author precisely because 'non era *informato* in un senso che va oltre la lettera' (he was not informed on meanings that go beyond the literal). See Giuseppe Zaccaria, 'Pavese recensore e la letteratura Americana (con alcuni testi dimenticati),' in *Sotto il gelo dell'acqua c'è l'erba. Omaggio a Cesare Pavese* (Alessandria: Edizioni dell'Orso, 2001), 329–47.

45 In the same letter, Pavese informs Chiuminatto that he had just been awarded his degree upon the defense of his thesis on Whitman. In chapter 5 of his thesis ('L'Epica Nazionale'), Pavese takes Italian critics of North American literature to task for what he deems to be a total neglect of the historical, national, and aristocratic element in the American literary works. See Pavese, 'Interpretazione di Whitman,' 184–5.

jazz and blues hits. In his letter of January 1932, he responds to Chiuminatto's generous offer to assist him in choosing 'American records of the Jazzy kind' and to send along the words of the songs in order for him to gain a better understanding of American literature: 'Now, as for records, I have "Dinah," I have the "Chant of the Jungle," "Lady Play," etc. all by the Revellers. By Whiteman I've "Blue Hawaii" (!!!) and "Just like a Melody." I'll buy the "Saint Louis Blues" just on account of your advice. I think I'll find it by Ted Lewis. Send me the words of all these records, if you can, and – sure – your comments. I'll be tickled. And put down always all novelties in this field, *names* and *comments*. I'll tell the world.'

As Giorgio Rimondi observes, what is interesting about Pavese's request is 'the special attention to the words of the songs, to the literary aspect of the phenomenon, which not only provides him with the opportunity to practice his English but above all proves fundamental for his activity as a writer.'[46] Rimondi goes on to point out the parallels that exist between Pavese's exchange with Chiuminatto concerning American popular music and the Piedmontese author's unfinished collection of short stories *Ciau Masino*.[47] The collection, written during the years of Pavese's correspondence with the Italian American musician, features jazz and blues as a means to explore new and vital modes of expression. Such is the case in the collection's opening episode in which the protagonist Masino, a journalist and aspiring writer who is drawn to America and the blues, seeks someone who will set to music the words to a new song titled 'Blues delle Cicche' (Cigarette-butt blues) and, in doing so, finds himself debating the question of what takes priority: the words or the music.

> io vorrei che, come la musica si è rinnovata ai nostri tempi, si rinnovassero anche le parole. Sa, le parole sono il corpo della canzone, – (sorpresa), – come la musica ne è l'anima, – (approvazione). – Penso a parole che rispondano interamente allo spirito della musica d'oggi: sa un fox non è più un valzer e un blues, (disse proprio *blus*) – non è più una romanza. Veda il jazz – (disse proprio il giaz) ...

46 Giorgio Rimondi, *La lettura sincopata: Jazz e letteratura nel Novecento italiano* (Milan: Bruno Mondadori, 1999), 138.

47 For a further reading of the importance of the Chiuminatto/Paveses epistolary exchange for the Piedmontese author's use of jazz in his writings, see Franco Bergoglio, 'Pavese, Mila, Gramsci: Letteratura, jazz e antifascismo nella Torino degli anni trenta,' *Impegno* 2 (August 2000), at http://www.storia900bivc.it/pagine/index2.html.

– Ah il giazze, il giazze! Ma ne avete già fatte di parole per giazze?

Just as music has undergone a renewal in our times, I would want words to experience a similar renewal. You know, words are the body of the song, – (surprise), – like the music is its spirit, – (approval). – I'm thinking of words that respond entirely to the spirit of today's music: you know a fox-trot is no longer a waltz and blues music, (he pronounced it *blus*) – is no longer a romance. Look at jazz – (he pronounced it giaz) ...

– Ah jazzzz, jazzzz! But have you already written words for jazz?[48]

The above passage recalls Pavese's comments to Chiuminatto in a letter of 17 April 1930 in which he expresses his enthusiasm for jazz as an ingredient of an innovative vitality that permeates the American literary landscape: "Say, Mr chiuminatto, there in America you've got poets as flies in summer. Not only you have your well-known wonderful jazz-minstrels, but, what's more, a lot of other poets whose existence is entirely unsuspected here in Europe.'

With his move from Green Bay to Chicago in April 1930, Chiuminatto found himself in a culturally rich city of booming growth and unquestioned energy. At that time Chicago was also synonymous with the new phenomenon of gangsterism. The Italian roots of a large number of Chicago's most notorious gangsters prompted an exchange of letters between Chiuminatto and Pavese. In a letter of 22 September 1930 Pavese attempts to console Chiuminatto, who had apparently shared with their mutual friend Massimo Mila a dissatisfaction with America. Pavese is curious to know more about Chiuminatto's discontent and, at the same time, advises his friend to take advantage of his Italian American heritage in order to have a better perspective on the two nations. Pavese's observations allow the Italian question between the North and the South to cross borders into the United States:

And you, who are in the tremendous situation of being both an Italian and an American, you must try to comprehend the two nations, try to raise above the petty difficulties. Moreover you must not forget that we Italians are two distinct nations, the North and the South, and that we are the Northern and that the Chicagoans gunmen are the Southern and there is a

48 Cesare Pavese, *Tutti i racconti*, ed. Mariarosa Masoero (Turin: Einaudi, 2002), 326. The translation is mine. Later in the short story collection *Ciau Masino*, Pavese includes the poem 'Il Blues dei Blues' (The Blues Blues); *Tutti i racconti*, 380.

deeper difference of race and history between us and them that nothing can repair.

In his letter of 7 October 1930 Chiuminatto informs Pavese that his indignation did not target the 'thousands of real people, thousands of educated people, thousands of artistic souls right here in Chicago'; instead, he observes, 'I'm all hot and bothered about these damn Sicilian gunmen who have never done a damn thing but ruin the reputation of Italy.' He then gives Pavese a brief lesson of the perception of Italian Americans in America:

> It's all well and good for you to remind me that Italians are distinctly in two classes, the Northern and Southern. But who the hell knows that but us Italians and about 10% of the Americans? The general conception of the Italian in America is based on the Sicilian make-up. Being an Italian in Chicago to-day is not so pleasant; people look at you askance when they know you are Italian, as much as to say, look out! And the general run of America will tell you that they are afraid of Italians, that they would not even rent rooms to an Italian. How do you like that, eh?

In a letter of 27 August 1966 Chiuminatto, in thanking Lorenzo Mondo for the complimentary copy of Pavese's epistolary, recalls his feelings in revisiting the years of their correspondence: 'Through these letters I have vividly relived our relationship as if it were only yesterday. I cannot tell you how many forgotten memories have now returned so fresh.'[49] He then speculates that the epistolary exchange may have ended because Pavese had obtained a level of self-sufficiency and was no longer in need of books or linguistic explanations primarily related to American slang.

In the years following their correspondence, Chiuminatto went on to have a distinguished academic career. After receiving his degree in music education from the Chicago Conservatory in 1939, he briefly taught and directed the College Instrumental Ensemble at the College of St Francis in Joliet, Illinois,[50] before accepting a position of violin professor and orchestra director at Wichita State University in Kansas. Dur-

49 The letter is in the possession of Lorenzo Mondo, who provided me with a photocopy. The translation is mine.

50 In 1 January 1998, the institution became the University of St Francis.

ing the Second World War he was commissioned a lieutenant in Military Intelligence, and was assigned to duty in New York, North Africa, and Italy (Naples and Rome). After the war he returned to Wichita State University and to his position as director of the University Symphony Orchestra, before becoming the first chair of the Department of Music at St Thomas College, serving from 1946 until his unexpected death in 1973.

CORRESPONDENCE

Turin, November 29th, 1929
To Anthony Chiuminatto, Green Bay, Wisconsin

I hope you will yet remember as great a borer as I was with you during your last Turinese year. I got your adress from Mr Mila, our witty friend who is now contributor in a whole row of musical reviews, has got a scream derby and surtout and walks as an equal together with your lovely Mr Della Corte (!). All the day long they are both in search of a concert, to write about.

By the by, I heard – or, better, read – of your own hit in Green Bay. I'll tell the world – as you taught me to say -! From the scraps I got it seemed you came back to your country as an hero and a conqueror. Using another of your teachings, I could say you are now shaking a wicked bow, can't I?

Good luck! I hope we'll soon – we, Maxim,[1] the Misses Franchi,[2] I, and in short all other Italian friends and acquaintances of yours – we'll, I say, hear and see you in some talkie as a fiddler and a sheik – an Al Jolson of the violin.

Do you remember our slang lessons? You see: I took advantages of you the most brazen-facedly, but as for you now the saddest thing is certainly whether I intend to go on.

Put your heart at ease: it was so kind of you to get wasting your time initiating me to the mysteries of your language and nation that I cannot forget it and make myself so bold as to write you all what follows.

I guess you remember yet how fond an admirer and a student of American things I was last year and such I have increased. You also know that here in Italy is almost impossible to find anything American a fellow is seeking for.

One month ago I discovered in Rome a certain 'Library for American Studies in Italy' but also this one is little acquainted with modern poetry – or novel – publications of America and only owns classics or non-literary works.

I succeeded barely in finding something I wanted for my degree's thesis about Walt Whitman. (You don't know, I'll be the first Italian to speak at some extent and critically of him. Look me over, I'll almost reveal him to Italy.)

1 Massimo Mila.

2 The Franchi sisters owned a stationery shop in Turin that served as a meeting place for Chiuminatto and his friends. Thanks to one of the Franchi sisters, Anna, Chiuminatto was named professor of English at the Sunday adult extension school (*Lega d'insegna mento*) located at the Liceo Massimo D'Azeglio, where he taught for three years.

What I am looking for now is some way of study, especially about your modern literature. There is a lot of contemporary poetry and fiction in the Union worthiest of note, but unattainable by us. Not even our book sellers can reach those works. In Italy there is only the Tauchnitz edition to supply them, but this one is too scanty.

I should then like to agree with you about a kind of business. Methinks you told me once you should have accepted such an agreement: each of us should have sent to the other the worthiest novelties of his own literature. But this is a little risky, one does not know enough the tastes of the other and, after all, I should require more wares than you, as it is my very profession to read books. We could then begin envoying each other a hint of the books required and – if it'll be possible and you'll agree – each of us will seek for and send them.

Meanwhile, as the most pressing thing, would you be so kind as to go fetching, whether there is in USA a book – a dictionary, a treatise, something – about modern American language, which can enable me to understand better your contemporary writers? They are full of slang, idioms, I don't know what, and so for an half incomprehensible. I want such a book, as the air I am breathing. Can you fetch it?

Perhaps you don't even assume what usefulness had for me your little lessons of American spoken. Yet I keep those jottings carefully, and scanty as the expressions and words are I could put down, yet as I read modern American authors, I feel more assured, bolder in understanding them, more in touch with their mood of living and thought. And all comes from your lessons of language! Would it not bother you I should like to enclose in my letters a list of words and phrases picked out from contemporary writers and unexplained by our dictionaries and you should send it back to me with your wanted so interesting explanations. But only if you can and like it, I beseech you. You see, I am always the same bore. I beg your pardon. You have certainly other jobs to think about. But if you'll dedicate a little time, you'll do me a big, big gift. Think, 'tis for your own country's sake!

And even more. I make myself bold as to collect the first of these notes, from *Dark Laughter*, a wonderful (and the unique one as yet published by Tauchnitz) novel by Sherwood Anderson, whom I discovered some months ago and whose complete works I'll some day thoroughly read.[3]

This book, if you don't as yet know, make yourself haste to seek for,

3 See appendix for Chiuminatto's explanations to Pavese's queries concerning slang and non-slang phrases in Sherwood Anderson's *Dark Laughter*.

for it is worth the while. Anderson is a true American writer – a poet – not only an imitator of European art, as many ones among your otherwise rank and luscious literature.

I enjoyed also in these days the most sportful biography in the world, the *Gentlemen Marry Brunettes,* which reminded me of our antique Anita Loos' *Blondes,*[4] and the newer reading of *Babbitt*[5] by Sinclair Lewis, a great humorist of yours, but a damned slang-tongued guy for any Italian reader to understand. I became acquainted with Carl Van Vechte[n]'s Nigger Heaven ...

But 'tis too much, to have you abused so. I must drop it out or I'll get your nanny. (These are your lessons which come back.) Don't you feel dejected after such teasing and impudence? And, after all, in such a preposterous English (I beg your pardon-American) as mine?

But be conforted, these are the evils of report, of stardom ...
You have got to be a teacher beyond the Ocean, all the world round. 'Tis a fault of yours, you were too kind with me here in Italy.

Now recollect if you can do something for me, of what I wrote you here (my address is
Via Ponza 3, Torino, Italia) and, as you taught me, slip me the glove, with the best wishes of further success.

Yours sincerely

Green Bay, Wisconsin, December 24th, 1929
To Cesare Pavese, Turin

Dear Mr. Pavese:
I received your letter and that of Mr. Mila just a few days ago, but I am making haste to answer for I shall do so one at a time. I had been waiting for a letter from you, as well as from Max, and I was sure that one would not have kept me waiting long.

I shall begin by sincerely complimenting you on your knowledge and use of English, as well as American slang! You write a wonderful letter and it is my wish that you continue to write me in English; use as much

4 Anita Loos's bestselling novel *Gentlemen Prefer Blondes.*
5 In his rough draft Pavese writes 'Babbit.'

slang as you wish, it will be just that much more experience for you in the using.

As for the proposition you made me, why, I shall be glad to do anything and everything that I can for you. I am sure you know that I am always more than willing to lend you a little help where I know it is going to be of benefit, and with Mr. Pavese I shall be sowing seed on fertile ground! As for the books I am sure there are many here that you would like to read and any suggestion from you I should be glad to send them. By the way, I am sending you to-day a book that I just finished reading myself and which I think is very good. Please consider it a token of my appreciation for all you were to me in Italy – a friend! This last word – friend – needs no adjective to be taken as I mean it.

The book in question is *Sorrell and Son* by Deeping and is by far the most read book of the day. I find it very human – American-like in its development and I so hope it can appeal to you as it does to me.[1] Now, speaking of other books, Mr. Pavese, just let me know which ones you want and I shall take care that you get them, and at the lowest price available. The more recent books are expensive, often reaching the price of five dollars, although you will be able to get books, and good ones, too, for from one-half dollar to two dollars.

I shall not need many books from Italy, Mr. Pavese, at least not just now. If you can, though, I should like to have a copy of that little volume of Arnulfi which is written in the Turinese dialect,[2] and if ever I need other volumes I shall gladly let you know. Since it is your very profession to read books I should be glad to be able to help you find what you want in American literature. If you even wish, from time to time I could send you a list of books explaining more or less on just what subject they treat so that if one should appeal to you I could send it. Just let me know of your desires and consider me at your service!

It was a pleasure for me to be able to explain the list of slang and non-slang phrases that you sent me. I took them exactly as you had them listed and explained them as best I could and as much as I thought necessary to make you understand. I am mailing these phrases, now explained to you to-day and under separate cover and I hope they will reach you. You will note that there are many phrases which are unex-

---

1 Both Chiuminatto and Pavese believe the author of *Sorrell and Son* to be American; instead, Warwick Deeping was English.

2 Chiuminatto is referring to the two-act comedy *Drolarie* by the nineteenth-century Piedmontese poet Fulberto Alarni (Alberto Arnulfi).

plained as yet; the reason is that I wanted to get the more common phrases to you as soon as possible. Too, among these phrases not yet explained there are many that are new to me, so I shall have to seek an explanation myself first. You know that I was away from America for over four years and have not been here long enough yet to become acquainted with the latest in slang phrases. Again, some slang phrases are not of universal use here but are confined to the limits of one state or the other, so I shall need some information. But you shall have them, Mr. Pavese, if it is at all possible.

As for my explanations, I sincerely hope that you will be able to understand them. If there should be any doubt, however, just write me again and ask once more for more explanation and I shall seek a better way of making it clear to you. I want you to be at your ease in reading American writers so that it will always be interesting reading for you; this is why I shall spare no effort to help you to success. Just as soon as I can I shall begin to work at the other phrases you gave me and then send them to you.

No, I have not as yet read *Dark Laughter* but, on your word, I shall give it a thorough reading. Thanks!

Mr. Pavese, I have a young lady friend[3] here who is very much interested in literature of all kinds, and especially in American literature. You will pardon me if I tell you that I let her read your letter and she thought it was wonderful for an Italian student to know English so well and to have such a vast and rich vocabulary! You mentioned *Babbitt* by Sinclair Lewis in your letter and she would like to have you write me EVERY WORD OF YOUR OPINION on this particular American writer. So I do wish, Cesare, that when you answer me, as I know you will, that you will write me anything and everything that you have to say about Sinclair Lewis and his works. She will be anxiously waiting to have me read your opinion to her, for she is convinced that you are very profound in matters of literature; then, too, that is her greatest interest in life! Do it, please, will you?

I am sorry to say that there is not as yet a book of any kind which will explain to you the usage of American slang. The American slang of today may become the Americanisms of tomorrow and in that event, and only in that, will there ever be a book expressly explanatory. If ever I should hear of some book or other of this kind, I shall get it and send it

3 Chiuminatto's friend is Mabel Buckman; see letter of 1 February 1930.

to you; for the present, Mr. Pavese, send me a list of the phrases you do not understand and I'll be this book for you. I hope you don't consider this presumption on my part, since it is merely friendly good-will assisted by a ninety-nine percent knowledge of American slang. You know, slang has arrived at a point where it can easily be coined by any one person and that is why some of it is incomprehensible at times. But all accepted forms of slang are familiar to me!

Once more, Mr. Pavese, be it known that I am at your service always! I think this is sufficient without the usual long line of Italian compliments! Mine are few words, but sincere ones, and too, you know me from contact! Just let me repeat that if you want some book, tell me about it in your next letter and I'll get it off to you as soon as I can. If you have any more phrases that need explaining, send them along too and I'll be glad to work at them for you! I am glad of the chance to be your help-mate! Your Buddy!

I am writing you very little to-day for it is the day before Christmas and there is a lot of excitement here in the house, visitors, telephone calls and what not! And yet I want to get this letter off to you to-day and within a few days I'll write you once more. Say 'hello' to Max for me and tell him that I so much appreciated his letter, even though he did write it in Italian instead of in English. I shall be writing him too before long!

Merry Christmas to you both and the Most Happy and Prosperous of New Years! Until next time then I'm slipping you the glove hoping that you will shake a leg and answer me soon. I am as ever your friend – sincerely

Antonio Chiuminatto

Green Bay, Wisconsin, December 26th, 1929
To Cesare Pavese, Turin

Dear Mr. Pavese:
This concludes the list of phrases that you sent me.[1] You will probably note that there are two or three phrases that I have not explained, but there are reasons, to be sure. I noticed that these two or three phrases

1 Chiuminatto is referring to his list of explanations to slang and non-slang phrases from Anderson's *Dark Laughter*, see appendix for these comments.

which I omitted are of no importance to slang, and by this, I mean that they are phrases used in one instance only – and as such I was unable to find a solution. I hope you will pardon my lack of English, at least, in this case! I shall remember these phrases, though, and if ever I come to know what they mean, be sure that you will hear from me about them. Negro slang is about the hardest to understand, for we hear so little of it and on the other hand we get so much of it in writing! This kind of slang would be as well known to me as the pure American slang were I a resident of the negro States, such as Missouri or Alabama. Even at that, though, I consider myself fairly well versed in it – and am always glad to be of some service to you.

I shall finish my letter here in slang. See if you can translate it.

Say, darby, your letter was a card; you know it? Your scratching is about as bad as mine and that is why I use a machine. Don't let this remark get your nanny, though; I was perfectly able to wad right through your whole letter!

Christmas is over at last and, ye gods, I'm perfectly tickled to death. I called on a few of my friends yesterday afternoon and managed to bum some sigars [*sic*] and some candy. I suppose Max <u>struck</u> you <u>for</u> a present, too, didn't he? But did he get it, that's the question! On Christmas eve I was over town but there was so little doing that around ten-thirty I began to mosey home. (Say, I hope you don't get all balled up now!) On the way home I met a couple of keen mamas and took them home and then I came straight home myself <u>to tune in</u> on the radio a while! Talk about your damn tommyrot!! All Christmas carols which sounded like sleep-songs to me! And so I hit the bed!

I just mailed your other comments and the book[2] so you'll be getting all this in a pile! Well, you see, I'm a fast man when it comes to friends like Mr. Pavese! Ya! I hope it'll be O.K. with you, though; at that you'll be down to brass tacks. By the way, if you run across that book entitled *All is Well on the Western Front* by some Frenchman,[3] try to send me it, will you? Gee! yes, in French.

Well, Mr. Pavese, so long, for this time! Write me again as soon as you can and tell me how you came out with these comments. I hope you get them straight alright! Best wishes to Max and you from your friend

Antonio Chiuminatto

2 Deeping's *Sorrell and Son.*

3 In his letter of 12 January 1930, Pavese notes that Erich Maria Remarque, the author of the 1929 novel *All Quiet on the Western Front,* was German, not French.

[Turin,] January 12th, 1930
To Anthony Chiuminatto, Green Bay, Wisconsin

Dear Mr. Chiuminatto:
I'm befuddled, all in a daze, with your titanic kindness. I'm now seeing the world only through a veil of pink sheets,[1] all bristling with slang-phrases which are meddling together, re-echoing and staring at me from everywhere. I've got now I can no more take a pull out of a bottle together with my gang, without thinking I'm going on the grand sneak. And how flip I get sometimes! And how many keen mamas I'm looking after! And how ... so on. My whole existence has got a slang drift now. You could almost say I'm a slang-slinger. (Ha!)

But I must, for the first thing, give utterance to a whole row of thanks-givings for your long-yearned, hard-hoped, fast-sent and all-surpassing answer to my criminal letter. Criminal and murderous, I say, was that letter, with all its flippancy and hardboiled guyness, but you were so widely christian as to ship your hand to the poor sinner hearkening to him.

I repeat, I'm yet befuddled, all in a daze, with your kindness.

Certainly, all your explanations are quite well, easy, clear, better than any would have dream'd of (I'm studying them by heart), but, I wonder, whence did you get the time to put them down? And, more, being such a work intended for a fellow you remembered scarsely perhaps? There is something of witchcraft in it. I can only stare at such a sight, bruit aloud your praise, go capering about and ... and continue to get the most out of you. I'm sure I'll find no bottom.

Really, I went capering the day before yesterday on receiving your letter and yesterday on receiving the comments.

Forewarned by the former, I was already thinking about something wonderful, darby, whizy, and what not, but the latter, when on my desk here, got me flabbergasted.

All is useful and masterful in your items, and so abundant is the treasure there one is almost dumbfounded, not by lack of clearness but by dint of wealth. I've not to pardon you, as you say, for your shortcomings – certainly you cannot be acquainted with the queerest phrases a writer was contriving, the more so having you got these phrases detached from the context – but rather I must thank and thank again and praise you for your kindness and skillfulness and sound knowledge. Besides, you'll

1 See note 35 of Introduction.

better understand my full satisfaction thinking (the scoundrel!) with what impudent hurry I'm sending you another list.[2]

But we are agreed – you'll explain and send it only when, and if, you'll be able.

Now, proceeding, I'll tell you that reading your letters I got an idea I should like to let you know.

You speak always of slang as of a special language or dialect, which exists by itself and is spoken only on certain occasions or places and so on. Now, I think, slang is not a diversified language from English as, for instance, Piedmontese is from Tuscan, so that a word or a phrase can be told to belong to a class or another.

You say: this word is slang, and this is classic. But is not slang only the bulk of new English words and expressions continually shaped by living people, as for all languages in all times? I mean, there is not a line to be drawn between the English and the slang words, as two different languages usually spoken by different people and only in certain cases used together.

That book you know, *Dark Laughter*, for instance, is written in English, but there are numberless slang-expressions in it and they are not as French words in an Italian book, but they are a natural part of that language. And I said always English, but I should have said American for I think there is not a slang and a classic language, but there are two diversified languages, the English and the American ones. As slang is the living part of all languages, English has become American by it, that is the two languages have developed themselves separately by means of their respective slangs.

My conclusion is then that there are not a slang and a classic language but there is an American language formed by a perfectly fused mixture of both.

Have I succeeded in getting the point before you? Write me something about this also, if you'll have the time.

Now being in a literary turn I pass to the capital *Every word of my opinion on Sinclair Lewis.* Meanwhile you can present my homages to the exceedingly good-minded young lady-friend of yours, first as I like very much young ladies, especially American ones and, second, in order to excuse me if I'll come short of her good opinion which really seems a little flattering and hazarded. However, here I am. I'm sorry to know S.

2 Pavese includes a list of slang expressions and phrases from Sinclair Lewis's *Babbitt.*

Lewis only through *Babbitt.*[3] I've so much to do, I've not yet succeeded in getting at least his two other Tauchnitz volumes *Our Mr Wrenn* and *Arrowsmith.* So I'll speak not about S. Lewis, but about *Babbitt,* which in the main I think is the same thing, being almost impossible that a writer as Lewis, with all his worthes and boundaries, could in a second book have created another world with his accustomed experience of American society.

At the most he could have changed the class of his hero: instead of a real estate man, a politician or a scientist, but methinks the author's world and point of view would always be the same.

Now in *Babbitt,* the first thing which rises one's attention is its lack of plot: not of plot intended as a development of 'interesting' facts – a wooing, a murder, etc. (which things indeed there are) – but also the development of a spiritual adventure such as a research, an experience, a conversion. I don't know. Speaking otherwise, what is lacking in *Babbitt* is a construction, the building of the harmonious whole, the successive passage onwards where a stage presupposes always, inevitably the lower and the upper one. Whatever episode I read in *Babbitt* I can almost always enjoy it without knowing before or further. What of this?

There are so many great books of this kind, beginning from *The Metamorphoses* by Ovid and coming down through the *Decameron* by Boccaccio till for instance *The Earthly Paradise* by W. Morris. But all these books are the aristocratic products of much refined ages when art is absolutely loose from all moral or human cares, and just expresses in its works the poetry which lies in the luxuries of the imagination. The very absence of a progressive plot in them is a hint of this poetry, it is the aristocratic pleasure of the mind fluttering among fine objects, without cares and without end: these gathered fables are all as related by a polite and witty narrator to a selected audience, sometimes (as for the *Decameron* and the *Earthly Paradise*) this narrator and audience are described just in attitudes of the refined life to which are food these nicely and loosely written pages.

But as for *Babbitt* we are in another world. No more of the poetry of nonchalance and dreamyness, without backbone; this book cannot faultlessly lack a construction, for in its bulk it is the expression of a world which with a smile perceives the hideous clumsyness and defor-

3 The name Babbitt appears only with one 't' throughout the rough copy. In making the correction, I have followed the changes made by the original editors.

mity especially moral of the inevitable life. So if the story does not contain the drama – sad or merry, it does not matter now – of this clumsyness, which drama could justify, give a successive significance to the facts of the story, this story is doomed to repeat all troughout always the same thing, always presenting a varied scene of life whose purport is always the same clumsyness or whatever else, and each scene lives entirely loose from another.

For, in *Babbitt*, the only string is an external one, the daily or monthly existence of George F. Babbitt where whatever extraordinary events happen to him, none of them belongs to him save for the fact the author tells us they happen to G.F. Babbitt. We find in the first chapters a certain amount of outlines, which presents us already the whole world and spirit intended to be treated all the book long, and there is no further development, this world is a fixed one, or, if we also change people, places, adventures, its spirit is always the same, without a beginning or an end; these pictures could be continued to the infinite. And this same spirit of the book makes it impossible to avoid monotony, differently, as I said, from what happens in those poems of old, where each particular tale is constructed in itself and the harmonious monotony of the whole is a part of their poetry. Sophisticating, one could say this lack of plot is a part of the plot of *Babbitt* for its hero has certain hampered whims of romance, and his daily life among belied contradictions and awkward boastings would then be a drama of this barrenness and monotony. But G. F. Babbitt does not feel this life as a drama or at least he does not feel it continually with a development of spiritual action which alone could create a construction. There is, true, about the end a continuity and progress of occurrences in Babbitt's rebellion – his love affairs and liking of Seneca Doane and testy and clumsy profession of new principles which ends in nothing or in the childlike repentance of this sad-and-merry puppet, but this does not suffice to create a *real* plot all the book long. Since hundreds of pages long Lewis had only presented us a lot, so to say, of lantern slides, the moving picture begins only towards the end, too late to build the novel, so that also this adventure of Babbitt's rebellion restricts itself to the common size of one of the numberless pictures scattered all throughout the book.

Settled this point about the frame, it remains however to say what then is good in this book so widely read and so indeniably amusing.

I think *Babbitt* can be well understood only if regarded as a suite of different pieces, each of them pent up in itself, nowhere attaining a climax, or at least each of them beginning, proceeding and concluding by itself alone: too light work to be called a novel and yet so full, so rich, so complete in its way to create by dint of loose short stories, of sketch-dialogues, of draughts, of jokes, etc. a great mythus (as we say today in Italy) of a mankind seen under the point of view of a grotesque matter-of-factness full of the funniest and saddiest inward contrasts between the spoken boastful word and the inmost spirit. But there is no hypocrisy – and here lies the originality of S. Lewis. Almost all these persons of *Babbitt* are grotesque ones, not villains. They are braggart, petty, coarse and silly, ludicrously in earnest, but outwardly they appear and believe themselves so good-minded, so nice and capital 'their city – a city built for giants.' And at the bottom, they, G. Babbitt and Paul Riesling at least are so despairingly human and true – their outbursts! And all this world is (as I said) seen only with a curious and amused eye, it has no climax. Since the first page the author has looked at the life and copied thence a piece, careless of developments. In another page he has drawn another picture quite indifferent what the first one were. You could shift the places of all these episodes without changing the purport of the book. It looks like a book of poetry, a collection of poems written in different cases of the life and huddled together only in order to make a volume.

But certainly this is no capital fault. We have here huddled together the bulk of numberless little sketches as of a journalist of genius, daily accustomed to put down a column of satirical prose on his contemporaries. Of a journalist Lewis has the great worthes of freshness, spontaneousness and seizing skill, and the little inevitable defects of loose style, minuteness and flippancy sometimes.

Similarly, the protagonist, Babbitt, has the worth of being wholly created since the first chapter already and the defect of returning in every successive one always the same, without a development, a movement. But he is delightful in this sameness. It would now be too long – and this 'opinion' has already the size of an essay – to follow Babbitt in all his doings but certainly, he and all the people of the book are real personages, living in their grotesque world around with so much fitness as to look like a common man living in common life.

I must then add here that I like *Babbitt* also for another reason but this not an aesthetic one. It is the most complete picture of contemporary America in its whole character: throughout manners, language, culture, doings, the whole life in short. And this refers itself if not to the piece of art to the powerful mind of Lewis himself, certainly one of your greatest living writers.

It's done. I hope I should not have mistaken a word for another, smartly succeeding so in getting my ideas all balled up. You'll kindly give me a sincere hint of my lecture here in your next letter. But I should also like, were it possible, to have something written down by the curious young lady-friend of yours, about American literature or whatever else there is of common interest. Would she be interested in it, I should gladly inform her about our modern Italian writers and culture. As for me I would have her speaking about Edgar Lee Masters or Vachel Lindsay whose works also (*Spoon River Anthology* by the former, and methinks *The Congo – The Chinese Nightingale – The Golden Whales of California* by the latter) I should pray you to look for, whether there is a cheap edition of them.

But there are other troubles for you. Would you be so kind as to go fetch them, I should pray you to send me a copy of Waldo Frank's *City Block* and something of Ernest Hemingway (*The Sun Also Rises – Men Without Women – Farewell to the Arms*) or whatever else is attainable of him. Especially about the latter there is much talk now here, but no edition of its are seen.

And still there are scores of modern American books I should like, someone really I need: by J. Dos Passos, by E. Cummings, by W. Carlos Williams, by Countee Cullen, by Eugene O'Neill, by Robinson Jeffers, by Carl Sandburg, by Sherwood Anderson, etc. They are numberless. To buy them by means of an Italian bookseller, there is the danger of finding himself gratified with a cheap edition of five dollars. You see how your christian help is here necessary for me. We'll digest those books little by little, in future letters. Each time one or two among them, and you'll seek for and mail them, together with your bill. Now let us begin with Frank and Hemingway.

Do you know? I found an American library in Rome very rich with American works such as historical and critical ones. Some classics also, such as Thoreau and Howells. I'm borrowing two volumes a fortnight by it. But as for modern, living productions, there is nothing. There is only your help there yonder.

Accordingly, I send you now the *Drolarie* by Arnulfi, you wrote about, and *À l'ouest rien de nouveau* which you are wrong in believing a French book. It is by a German author, as you'll see perusing it, for it is worth while. As I don't know whether you are conversant with German language, I don't send you the German text, nor the Italian translation which does not exist by way of a legal prohibition. It seems that this book has the wrong to describe the war how it is really, an atrocious thing, and naturally we Italian babies are defended to know it by means of a direct translation. We could become too moody and refuse the next war. Mr Chiuminatto, we also wonder how Fascism will fan out.

But I must leave off. I wind up my yarn with a final thanksgiving for the book you kindly sent me. I'm waiting for it, and I assure you that hardly I'll have received it, by the by, I'll read it notwithstanding my many scholarly occupations and I'll write you something about it.

And still I beseech you to undergo the expounding of my shameful Babbitt-list only when you'll have nothing else, really nothing else to do. You're so kind I should feel sorry to bother you again.

Now I'll slip you the accustomed glove and am

Yours sincerely

[Turin,] January 22nd, 1930
To Antonio Chiuminatto, Green Bay, Wisconsin

Dear Mr. Chiuminatto:
Your gift of such a book as *Sorrel and Son*, caused me and Max to think of an answer. Here it is, in this same package. When I perceived the wonderful plot of *Sorrel and Son*, I bethought of an Italian book, – moreover, a Piedmontese one – written by a friend of ours,[1] which is dealing with almost the same situation of a father trying to rear his son.

As you'll see, this book was issued only last year and really it is one of the worthiest contemporary books in Italy. I cannot speak of so wide a diffusion of it here, as of *Sorrel and Son* in America, for its very nature defends such a diffusion. Against Deeping's which is a book of universal appeal for its – in a good sense – triviality of experience, its elemental simplicity, being the expression of a life among common wants and deeds, a life which is what it is, by itself, without a weight of tradition or culture, save what is common to all middle men; against such a book, we have here in these *Sanss-Sôssì*, a world of extreme complication, breeded in a literary mood, old of ages by historical experiences and, more, bounded to a certain liking towards a definite region of the Country –

1 The novel, *I Sanssôssì* (1929), was written by Augusto Monti, the celebrated educator and Pavese's former professor at the Liceo Massimo D'Azeglio in Turin.

Turin and the Monferrato, the dialect-title – which thing can but keep aloof most Italian readers.

But the miracle of the book is that with such a dangerous fore-ground it has succeeded in shaping a human world where such foreground becomes poetry. But you'll see by yourself, for you also are a Piedmontese almost, and a scholar, a learned one, and you can well understand such a poetry as the *Sanss-Sôssì*'s.

Look only at this: these two books are the same fable related the former in America and the latter in Europe. Never the two continents reflected and diversified themselves better than in these two books.

We are sure that you, who were so much in Turin will like this fond description of the city since last century, of his hills and country such as you'll find here.

And we close this note again renewing our thanks, I for the book received, and Max for that he will.

A 'hello' by your friends

Green Bay, Wis., February 1st, 1930
To Cesare Pavese, Turin

My Dear Cesare:
Your letter of January 16th[1] just arrived today, and it is with pleasure that I am the receiver of it. I knew from your very first letter that I was about to enjoy some wonderful talks with you and now I do hope that you will continue to write me as often as you can, while I shall promise to answer very promptly and occasionally write you myself of my own free will.

I read and re-read your letter and then I read it to the young lady of whom you already know. She was considerably enthused with it and surely had very good reasons to be so. Above all did she enjoy your comments on Sinclair Lewis's *Babbitt*. She thinks, though, that it is too bad that you should be judging American society from Lewis's depicting of it, for she is very much convinced that Lewis always did and always will deal with the extremes in things.

Just before I mail this letter to you I shall call on her again, for she

1 The rough draft of this letter is dated January 12.

may have a little letter of her own to inclose with mine. If she does write you, too, I know you will enjoy her comments for she is very educated and is one of the most refined little bodies I ever met. She will talk to you about Lewis, I am quite sure. If she should not write you with my letter, you will be hearing from her later on, maybe in my next letter.

Miss Mabel Buckman, for that is her name, thinks very much of you as a scholar and especially so in English, and you may be sure, Cesare, that this is not an idle boost. You certainly do write a wonderful letter; there is life and spirit purely American and you must be complimented on your ability to think thusly in English and still be so spontaneous about it. Slip me the glove, Cesare, that's good work!

We were both surprised this morning to note what wonderful use of slang you have, and how so very appropriate you make it. I wish now that you had always been a pupil of mine; I really should like to have that credit. Ye gods, I'll get some of it, Cesare!

On the 30th of January I gave my second concert in the city of De Pere, about six miles from here. It was a success from beginning to end and I had a most favorable criticism in the papers. As soon as I can I shall write all about it to Max and I shall send him the clipping from the paper; you will have your chance to read about it then. I do not want to take up any of your time here. Suffice it to say that I am getting famous! Ya!

I shall refer myself now to the paragraph of your letter where you spoke of slang, as not being separated from what I shall call real American. Well, you are right in what you say, Mr. Pavese, save that what I wanted to say before was that very many forms of slang are not of good use, that is, they are insulting forms of speech. When I speak of classic English I mean that kind of English which was current years and years ago and which still remains to-day, even though it may have been even slang at that time. When I speak of slang now, though, I mean that form of English which is current and yet new to us, something that is produced in our times. Oh, I agree with you that real American and American slang now go hand-in-hand, but we are still in the period where we distinguish slang from what used to be our American language. Get me? I merely called one form 'classic' and another 'slang' so that you would not think that the former were something relatively new or the latter a part of our one-time English.

I have some good news for you! I just came back from downtown and bought two books for you which I am sure you will like. One is Sherwood Anderson's *A Storyteller's Story* which is an autobiography of the author, and the other is one that you wanted, Ernest Hemingway's *A Farewell to Arms*, which is one of the most popular novels of to-day. What I want you to do is this! Read *A Storyteller's Story* and then please give it to Maxim Mila as my remembrance of him, for I promised to send him a remembrance, too, as I did for you. Since this is a very good book and by an author, too, who appeals to you, I am but killing two birds with a single stone! I know that you and Max are very good friends and that this arrangement of mine will not offend either of you. Were I to think so I should not have done it as I am.

Farewell to Arms is the one you wanted. The price is the lowest I could get, that is, two dollars and a half ($2.50). Just give me two dollars for it, Mr. Pavese, and I shall be just as happy to have you get it! I am so glad that you are sending me *Drolarie* by Arnulfi and *À l'Ouest rien de nouveau* which I should very much like to read. When I see your bill on these then I shall know just about how we stand on our current accounts!

Within a few more days I shall have something about *City Block* by Waldo Frank. I could have had the book to-day but the price was too high and so I asked the clerk at the book-shop to try to find out if I could not get a cheaper edition, which she will do for me within a few days. You see, Mr. Pavese, these are recent books and so the prices are still a trifle high. But you shall have them if I must trouble every bookstore in America on the hunt for low prices. Now I had to buy *Farewell to Arms* for two dollars and a half because that is the only edition at a standard price! Too, this book is of very recent publication that accounts for the price.

As soon as I can get the edition I want of Waldo Frank you shall have it and it wont take long. Too, I shall bear in mind the other authors you mentioned and little by little, as you desire, I shall get them to you. And now, too, just to be business-like, which means being honest as well, I am inclosing the original bill of the volume *Farewell to Arms*. You will note that there is a charge of one dollar ($1.00) for the Anderson volume, but this is my contribution to Maxim for his courtesy to me when I left Italy. All you will need worry about is the two dollars and a half! Ha! (Remember, too, that I said I only wanted two dollars ($2.00) for it). It will make reading cheaper for you and it means a lot of pleasure to me to be able to do it. What is fifty cents now and then! Nothing—and it means so much more to you!

Mr. Pavese, rest assured that just as soon as I can you shall have another complete list of the slang phrases you sent me. I shall give you the best of my efforts, for I know they are appreciated and do go to a great advantage. If you have any more send them along – they shall be welcomed as the flowers in May! At the most there may be some new phrases which will not be fully explained, but as you can easily realize, I am working without the text. As it is, though, I shall give you examples so that you will be able to get the idea in one way or in another! Slang is very elastic at times, you know! But it's great, isn't it? Ya, we Americans are darn proud of it! We give every man his dues with a few words – but O me, O my, what words!

Tell Maxim that I got his letter and shall soon be answering it. I shall get your books off to you this evening yet, if I can, so that just about the time you get this letter you will be getting the books, too. I believe in snappy service –that's the boy all over! And remember that I am at your disposal anytime and all the time, Mr. Pavese, and with pleasure. I merely hope that this friendship will someday blossom forth in America!

I am promising to write you soon again and am hoping, too, that you will write me just as soon. With all best regards for this time to yourself and to Max, believe me your sincere friend as B/4

Antonio Chiuminatto

Green Bay, Wis., February 11th, 1930
To Cesare Pavese, Turin

Dear Mr. Pavese:
I want to thank you immensely for the lovely volume you sent me and which I received just yesterday morning, *I Sanssôssì.* When I sent you and Max those books I didn't mean that I expected you to reciprocate, much more so since I was doing it for the volumes of Victor Hugo which you both so kindly gave me on my departure from Italy. Just as soon as I have read it I shall let you know what I think of it, though I already know I am going to like it if it is all about Turin and the neighborhood.

As for *Sorrell & Son* by Deeping, I should like to have your full opinion on it later. I like the plot itself for I find that there is real achievement in it, in spite of the childish American spirit which you seem to find in it! If sincerity is childishness, then I am in favor of it – give it to me always! Deeping, too, is a powerful writer and possibly more American than Sinclair Lewis! Well, I'll wait to hear from you now.

Last night I finished your comments on *Babbitt*![1] I was just wondering now whether or not I should keep these comments to see if I have them all when your list arrives. Upon second thought, though, I decided that I had better send them to you and then when your list does arrive I can take care of it if I have omitted some.

I started my comments, that is, these that I am sending you now, from Chapter Sixteen (XVI) of the American edition of *Babbitt* and hope that you will be able to follow from your own edition. I started from this chapter because it was in the neighborhood of where you left off on the list you sent me. Now, as I read along I commented on all that I thought you might not understand, for I want you to get as much out of Sinclair Lewis as is possible, and the spirit of his work, in slang, is not easy for a foreign student to understand.

You may find some slang expressions which I did not comment, but there is a reason. Some of his slang is not current, but rather limited to the occasion and therefore coined! In this case I have either omitted it all together or I have but given you the meaning of the period in which it was found. I feel that you should learn our current slang first, and only after that take on the excessive baggage! What I mean by 'excessive baggage' is such slang as you found in that speech by Mr. Monday, the evangelist and reformed boxer!! There is no need for you, Mr. Pavese, to get into this kind of slang – for even Lewis himself has made it a personal thing – with Mr. Monday! Whereas his slang in his other characters is general! Get me?

Slang exclamations are probably the hardest to explain and just because there are so many of them that are synonymous; oftentimes, too, they but express a certain mood or feeling but really do not mean a[n]ything in themselves, something like the Italian exclamation of 'Oilà' which means much and yet means nothing! I do want you to get as much out of Babbitt as possible; I want you to understand him better, as you told me, and that is why I have used the tactics that I have. Now, I think I have given you all that will be necessary to understand that book, but if not, why, just write me again with a list and I shall take care that you are given prompt attention.

I received a letter from Miss Anna Franchi yesterday, in which she told me that she had borrowed your comments, the ones I sent you the very first time. She asked me to make carbon copies so that she could have a

1 See appendix for these comments.

copy too. I don't mind doing this, at all, for her but since I have already finished your comments I do not want to make another copy – it is long work! I answered her immediately and told her that I would be glad to do so henceforward, but I very kindly asked her not to trouble you for these comments, since I considered them very personal – only between Mr. Pavese and myself. I said they were an inter-nos with some comments which might not over-appeal to some young ladies and so asked her to refrain from asking you for them.

Besides, I told her that I had explained things as I would to Mr. Pavese only, and not as I would most probably to someone else. I told her, too, that the next time I comment on slang I would make a carbon copy for her – and that I'd be less personal in my commenting and more pedantic.

So if she should ask you for these comments, Mr. Pavese, do just as you see fit and proper. If you care to let her have them, well and good, and if not, why, just say no. I have already asked her not to ask you for them – and trust that she will not. When I told her that I was doing some slang commenting for you, I little dreamed that she would ask you for the comments, but once more I learn how the women are!! At any rate use your own judgment!

By the time you get this letter I hope you will have received the books I sent you and Max. I just telephoned the book-shop but they have heard nothing as yet about your *City Block* by Waldo Frank. I shall wait a few days yet and then I'll do some investigating of my own – I hate to wait! I believe in speed and service in everything – productiveness – what say, Mr. Pavese? I just discovered a publishing house where I can get volumes at publishers' cost – so I hope that the books you want can be found at this publishing office. The lower price may not be very great, but it will always be enough to cover the postage in sending to you over there!

Say, Mr. Pavese, I have a wonderful proposition to make you – if you care to accept! During the summer months, the vacation months, from June to September, our government public circulation libraries give every one a chance to take out at least six volumes for this period of the vacation – just as they would for a 14-day period. Now if you want to, why, I could send you all summer to read them and still get them back to me on time – and in good condition! I'd suggest your getting some of the good books that are expensive – it will give you a chance to look them over and then you can dedicate your time later on to buying them.

One of these days, too, I am going to speak to the Director of our library here and I am going to ask him if he will not issue a card for Mr.

Pavese, valid for the period of a month before applying any fines. In this way I can send you books and you can then select those that you want to buy from those that you but care to read. Now I don't know whether or not I shall be able to do this, but I'll try. The fine on any loaned book is one cent (1¢) al giorno dopo la scadenza del privilegio, che generalmente è di 14 giorni. In short, Mr. Pavese, I shall try to do anything and everything to make it American-like – all around ease – in your reading.

Don't forget to say something to me about that summer vacation proposition! That's a darby – and you could keep six books, at least, for three months, and after that send them back to me! Paying a fine on some books is much better than buying the book and certainly is cheaper, too! In buying books for you, remember, remember that I am getting the lowest price possible – so just keep your conscience calm! I never select a book unless I know I have the 'best' at the 'lowest'!

Well, Mr. Pavese; say hello to Max for me and to the others who might still remember of me! Some day if we meet in Italy again or in America, we'll have a grand and glorious old time – and O me, O my – how the slang will be slung! I'm slipping you the glove as always did your little pal.

Antonio

[Turin,] February 22nd, 1930
To Antonio Chiuminatto, Green Bay, Wisconsin

Dear Mr. Tony
You'll excuse me if I did not answer immediately to your letter of February 1st but when I received it I was lying up with flu and only now I begin to walk and go out. Notwithstanding I was very pleased with your kindness and began at once to read Anderson[1] whom on the first occasion I'll hand down to our Mila. A great book! You had a lucky hunch to send it as a 'two-birds': I read it with the greatest pleasure and I'm now convinced Anderson really is your best living writer, one of the great poets not only in America, but in the whole world.

But, to the point now: I must chide you earnestly for your never-ending praises about my English. You old cuss! You must stop writing I'm a

1 *A Storyteller's Story.*

wonderful slang-fellow and American stylist, and what not: you must stop, otherwise I'll undertake here – Italy a slang institute for young immigrants with what results for your own country you'll know by and by. Out of fun, I think you are overrating a little when you put down I'm already thinking in English. I'll tell you what: two months ago I had to write a letter to an English young lady, an acquaintance of mine, and among the rest, I asked of her to send me back my letter corrected, that is with the greatest blunders pointed out in a list.

Ye Gods! After the inevitable lecture about Botticelli and Frate Angelico all English misses that have been in Italy are always bound to do, I perceived a two-page list of phrases I had mistaken or misused. My letter had been three pages long.

You know, it is these hits that cause me to think a little about myself. And so you must absolutely stop your too elated praise, otherwise, you, if I must believe you thoroughly, have to send me back my letters signed by the whole body of a special jury of the best citizens of Green Bay, Wis.

But undoubtedly you have other to look after and so let us on.

I give again my thanks to Miss Mabel Buckman, for the opinion you report of her about my comments. Say her I am infinitely pleased to have already in my craft such a charming list over which I only regret to know so little and repeat am always waiting for a word of hers. I'm wondering what literature is her concern since you speak only always of Lewis as related to her. Does she interest herself of modern national literature the same as of arts and other cultural things out of simple fashionable interest? Or is she a deeper scholar of spiritual concerns who seeks something more in literature? In which case she'll certainly not be devoid of European knowledge, for nothing is more original and promising than your own character, provided it is compared with our preceding and successive ones.

Moreover should she have studied Greek and Latin we would be both of a unique nation, for this knowledge unifies all, it is the great ground of all world entire[.] I should like to know these things about her. Won't she be so kind then?

As for us, Mr. Ch.[iuminatto], I'm reading about your success and send you a cheer up. You are on a good beginning and it seems my prophecies go effecting themselves. When I meet Max I'll let him know and I'm sure he'll only be sorry that he was not in De Pere to hear, and review your exhibition. He has become a damned newspaper man and has only now more concerts to advertise and musical scores to write about. But you know this all, I think you are associated with *La Rassegna Musicale* and stumble now and then on the glorious M.M. which has cause us to call him 'duemila.'[2] So, be sure, hardly I'll be able, Max will have the book and the tidings and he also will be exceedingly glad, I'm sure.

About books, I hope now you'll have received Arnulfi and Remarque which I mailed together with the letter of Jan. 16th.[3] I bethought only after the expedition their package was not so steady, but as the post-office accepted them as they were. I hope you got them not in bad state at least. However if you have not yet spoken of them in some letter which is coming tell me something about in your next.

As for the *Sanssôssì* I mailed on Jan. 23rd va sans dire it is a gift. Max and I send you as a token of our gratefulness for your troubles there in America on our behalf.

So, on your debit, there is only to enter about a dollar which makes the amount of the books I sent together. I don't know why you would be so kind as to decrease my own debt from two dollars and a half to only two ones.

We must not begin thus, otherwise, we'll never be business-men as you intend. The more, so as you have already to waste not a little money about the stamps I reckoned your last package fifty and seven cents, more than a half-dollar. A half here and a half of deduction from the book, it is already a dollar you are losing. And so on.

No, Mr. Chium[inatto] we must be more exact. Now to cut it and make you contented, I'll send you only the dollar of difference between my debt as you state it ($2.00) and the dollar on your charge and I thank you (for the prices you can see the back of the books), but in the future we'll be more business-like. Otherwise you must think, I'll be obliged to stop my ordinations lest you may be losing in the bargain. It's very well to enclose the bills in our letters, but we must also pay some attention to them otherwise it is useless.

Now with this my letter our accounts about Arnulfi Remarque and Hemingway are all settled. When I'll have received Waldo Frank's book's bill and others' I'll explain you at once, we will start another current account that I'll settle as ready as I can.

2 By signing his articles for the musical journal *La Rassegna Musicale* with his initials M.M., Massimo Mila earned the nickname of 'duemila.'

3 The rough draft of this letter is dated January 12.

The new book I expect by your kindness are the following by James Branch Cabell *Jurgen* and *Manhattan Transfer* by J. Dos Passos. These and Frank's I take the liberty of solicitating you to send. I want them.

With more leisure you can look after the already said ones by Edgar Lee Masters (Whose *Spoon River Anthology* is a Macmillan edition) and by Vachel Lindsay (*Collected Poems* Macmillan Ed. 1923). Add to the two, one of Carl Sandburg – *Chicago Poems, Smoke and Steel, Slabs of the Sunburnt West* – whatever you find but one among them, at least, certainly.

As these last ones are all books of poetry, they'll be somewhat high-priced, but once in a while I intend to waste myself and so don't stick to the half-dollar edition for you won't certainly find it.

Afterwards we'll economize. Thank you.

Mr. Chiumin[atto] I beg your pardon again for my exaggerated list of slang words I sent you last time and am now waiting patiently for the comments. But I repeat you must not hurry.

Mr. Ch[iuminatto] I also hope that our friendship will some day blossom forth. America!

If I'll get what I am after ... you'll see! Now I've only to study, study as I can, your language and your things.

And I assure you I'm not sleeping. As you know I'll get my degree this fall and I have just choiced to present an essay about an American literature topic – the poetry of W. Whitman which I've been long perusing and out of modesty I think I know better now than anybody else in Italy: I've hunted since two years all what is attainable here about him. Now I'm writing my essay and am quite satisfied the way the work goes on. Perhaps sometimes I'll want about this a favour, not a least, by an American scholar, and I'll bethink of Miss Mabel then ... But now 'Bottle it!' as they say in *Nigger Heaven*[4] and let us go to bed.

Remember: Cabell, Frank and Dos Passos. Thank you a thousand times. Good-bye.

Your Buddy
Ces

4 A reference to Carl Van Vechten's novel.

[Green Bay, Wisconsin,] February 24th, 1930
To Cesare Pavese, Turin

Dear Pavese:
I am sending you these comments from *Arrowsmith* of Sinclair Lewis, which at present I am reading for you.[1] These comments take you to the end of chapter Nine (9). If you are now reading this yourself, so much the better, and if not, I imagine you will read it soon, in which you are already assisted.

I have commented on anything and everything which I thought you might not understand. If there is anything which I have left out and which you do not understand, write me about it and I shall explain. Some phrases have been left aside because I deemed it unnecessary to burden you with them. As I go along in my reading now, I shall comment for you, and at the end of every ten chapters or so I shall forward the comments to you. I am very much interested in following your line of reading, so that I can be of better help to you.

Please do not mention these comments to Miss Franchi! I have done them for you and for you ONLY! Now if you do not say anything about them – all will be well.

I am wondering just what your opinion of *Arrowsmith* will be? I liked *Babbitt* much better – whereas in *Arrowsmith* Lewis appears to be very much exaggerated in his depictings and seems to have a special liking for the sordid things which he will a[l]ways put into first place and evidence. There is no plot again as in *Babbitt*; only sketches from here and there, though possibly more connected up than in *Babbitt.* He has selected a weak spot of the medical profession in this book – Mr. Arrowsmith – and seems to want us to accept him as the guiding light of the medical profession in general – which I cannot agree with now or ever! It is the story of one who starts going down, down and just keeps on going down, too. This is no criterion – no matter what Lewis might have to say in defense of his book. He tries to make the medical profession a ridiculous one – one in which men or [*sic*] not men but only business men and exploiters of human weakness – which is not the general truth, in spite of Mr. Lewis's apparent sincerity.

Let's hear from you now —— As ever – just —— *Antonio.*

---

1 See appendix for these comments.

[Turin,] March 1st, 1930
To Antonio Chiuminatto, Green Bay, Wisconsin

Dear Mr Chiuminatto:
I was just reading the *Spoon River Anthology* which I want you no more to trouble about as I found it here on loan from the Y.M.C.A. library, when I received the wonderful bunch about *Babbitt* you mailed me on February 11th. Ye Gods and Goddesses, it's too much and they say French people got the standard in kindness all over the world. There is a fellow somewhere about the river Fox[1] who will someday send me his shirt last I should want one. Say, Mr Chiuminatto, it's too awfully nice of you to behave so. You'll lose your chances to hustle in the world and conquer the place you deserve, if you go on so wasting all your time in typing me slang-comments. I feel lost in your graciousness. You cause me to dislike all acquaintances of mine, as I find out none of them has the one per cent of your kindness. I peruse and devour the whole of your sheets with the greatest eagerness, trying to make the best out of them and also to feel worth of the stuff where I don't always succeed, but, honestly, Mr Chiuminatto, don't take it too much as a duty wasting so much of your time. When I begged of you the boon of some explanation I did not mean to overcharge you so. Methinks now day and night you sit typing comments for me.

Not only you receive my brazen-faced lists as 'flowers in May,' but now you start also an office of your own to pick out the raw material. You know, I understand you believe in 'productiveness'; but beware of the nervous depletion which will certainly overcome you. That day, I'll mail down the prescription of the hypos I'm myself already – giovinezza, primavera di bellezza[2] – practicing.

I guess, it's useless now I proceed to praise you for the carefulness and clearness of your new list. I should only repeat what I've already written a month ago on replying your first letter. With such a teacher, I cannot fail a 'glorioso parto.' Besides, the best compliment I can pay you is to profit from your lessons. You bet I mean to be a go-getter, but to succeed!

As for your own opinion about *Babbitt*, you already know I think the same and, moreover, now I've received all your useful explanations, I

1 Reference to the Fox River that runs to Chiuminatto's hometown of Green Bay.
2 Reference to the anthem of the Fascist party, 'Giovinezza.'

stick only the more into it. Those personae are really capital fellows and it is an endless carnival of fun to follow them throughout Lewis' slang-stunts of style. I must thank you also for this, that your two letters have renewed and increased my own delight in this wonderful book. Now, I'll cast aside my studies and buy at Casanova's Lewis' two other works *Our Mr Wrenn* and *Arrowsmith*. It's too like a merry-go-round the review their author wields on American 'sassiety.' I wont procrastinate and so you wait for another task to fulfil. I hope, however, to be now on a firmer ground, thanks to your all surpassing help.

As for the *Sanssôssì* have it and keep still. You have such things on your conscience, you could not have them wiped out even should we mail you the whole peninsular boot.

What you say of *Sorrel and Son* is quite true and I don't know what you're complaining about the 'childish American spirit I seem to find in it.'[3] What I said about its simplicity and triviality was, as I warned you, in a good sense, that is, the description of what I thought were the nature of the world the book performed. I certainly blundered in my English as I meant that its characters were common people, stripped of all the classical learning which underlies the pages of the *Sanssôssì*. I simply marked a difference between the books without giving a judgement. Now, if you like, I can tell you that surely Deeping is a powerful writer and to prove it would suffice the XXVII–XXVIII chapters, the love-affair of Kit and Mary, 'the face like a flower' a wonderful episode, and the pages on the death of Sorrel, surely the best of all. To say nothing, you know, of the plot taken as a whole, a true story, all made up of original and alive characters scattered, in your saxon way, without savings, to fill a real world. But about Deeping's being more American-like than Lewis I should disagree on account also of the author's choice of England as his background. So little he felt a true want of American things!

We are agreed that it's not a novel background which brings the spirit of its nation in the style, and it would suffice the sheer Frenchness of certain exotical novels by Pierre Loti to prove it, but here in the case of *Sorrel and Son* there is something else. Not only the places, but also the characters are English people, and not only the accessory ones, but the true protagonists with their English sense, as for Sorrel, of a living continuity in his own son, notwithstanding death: and as for the son, with the sense of duty and manly conduct of life, the true self-

3 There still remains the misunderstanding that the English author Deeping is American.

denying and matter-of-fact spirit which has made the greatness of the British empire.

What there is American-like in it is perhaps only that matter-of-factness in the exercise of one's duty and in all other tricks of life and above all, the complete absence of any traditions. This last characteristic, though, methinks has become a little a conventional one in American concerns: I'm discovering that, if ever there was a nation yearning and struggling for a past, a tradition, an ancestry, in short, an aristocracy, that's yours. All your writers are now concerned with this problem, how to create a national background and spirit – be they aware of it or not. All your Mid-Western writers for instance – Anderson and Lee Masters, etc., – describing country- and little-town-life, to say nothing of all nineteenth century writers, like Hawthorne, Whitman and Twain, who, either by opposing America to Europe, or reviving colonial life with the passion of the true folklorist, have created the myth of your new nation and history.

In this sense *Sorrel and Son* has a certain romantic glamour on it which blurs its true poetry of life. It yields to a kind of easiness, to a delusion of picturesqueness which just shows itself in its research of what is more common in the foreign landscape: the inn- and college-life, a certain stiffness and tautness of the characters, Kid, the earnest one, and Buck, the villain.

But, after all is said, I repeat *Sorrel and Son* is a good book, an unforgivable plot with some very seizing pages.

Say, now, Mr Chiuminatto, have you not yet received Arnulfi and Remarque that you don't speak about in your letter? Nevertheless you have already Monti which I mailed just ten days later. How come? Would they be lost? Say me about, for as I wrote you the guilt would be mine, and I would then repair.

I've read your innuendoes on Miss Franchi but till now I did not receive any request of the comments and accordingly hope I will never on account of the Italian word which explains the phrase 'that's what gets me.' As for the future you will act as you'll like and all will be for the better. I think after all Miss Franchi was a good friend of yours here in Italy.

And now to the great novelty of your letter, the corking proposition you make me. I think, here also, it's useless to indulge in eulogistic prose about your well-known kindness. You really are keeping an eye skinned on all that can avail me and I've only to thank you for such earnestness of purpose. You bet I care to accept! I'll do more: I'll here at once unite a list of authors and books among which you can find out six the libraries possess. You understand, I put down many titles in order you can find out at least six. I'll agree with whatever condition you'll put on me: I know too well your skill and understanding, for me to advise you. As for the card you intend to ask of the Director, I also think it's difficult to obtain. You try, however. Meanwhile we'll open another current account.

I maintain here the ordination of the three books I wrote about lately, and this as I want them readily – you remember: Cabell, Frank and Dos Passos – but stop the purchase of those of poetry Lee Masters, Lindsay and Sandbur[g].

As for Lee Masters, you know, I found it here – and Lindsay and Sandbur[g] I enter in the list you'll look for in the public circulation libraries.

Other books, you can keep in mind to make up the six allowed to loan, are:

The Man against the Sky by Edward Arlington Robinson
Tulips and Chimneys, [*XLI*] *Poems* by E. E. Cummings (this you can also buy and send me, at once, if it's not too dear).
Blue Voyage by Conrad Aiken
Roan Stallion by Robinson Jeffers
Winesburg Ohio, A New Testament and Mid-American Chants by + Sherwood Anderson
The Sun also Rises and *Men without Women* by E. Hemingway
+ *The Great American Novel* by William Carlos Williams
+ whatever work by E. O'Neill
Caroling Dusk by Countee Cullen
whatever work by Ben Hecht and by Pr. McAlmon
The Making of Americans and *Tender Buttons* by Gertr. Stein
The apple of the eye and *The grandmothers* by Glenway Wescott
Gatsby the magnificent by Scott Fitzgerald
+ *The case of Mr Crump* by Ludwig Lewisohn
(the + denotes that this book has the preference)

And so, Mr Chiuminatto, you have your choice. Perhaps before June when the loan will begin I'll want hurriedly from your kindness some of these books and then I'll write you to look for and buy them.

Methinks the many books of poetry which are here noted will not be likely for a circulation library to possess: you can however reply me about, and we'll decide something further.

And now, I have taken advantages of you in all possible manners. I skulk away and on the bargain sting you in the rear: here's a list of some words from *Babbitt* I yet am puzzled about and some others gleaned from Van Ve[ch]ten, O. Henry and Anderson.[4]

Ah, Mr Chiuminatto, if it lasts so, you'll have translated the whole body of American literature! I guess you are muttering: Damned fool! I'm too late onto his intentions now. He has made a shipping-clerk of me and, what's the worst, he teases me with the very words I taught him. Blow him! Don't you, Mr Chiuminatto?

But, think it out: ain't you enticing people with your unearthly serviceableness?

Always chums

Green Bay, Wisconsin, March 15th, 1930
To Cesare Pavese, Turin

Dear Mr. Pavese:
I need 'big' sheets of paper when I write to you, so please excuse the lack of elegance! I have the biggest I can get into the machine – and I mean to type it full too!

Ya, Oh, ya, I knew you'd start to chide me for a few of my good ideas, and naturally you would have to pick on the one about the price of your book! Well, I won't argue, Mr. Pavese, I'll stick to the broom-handle and sweep the right way, then. You get the bills for the books, get me? And you pay for them when you can, but you pay for them, right down to the last red Indian penny! I want to be the best of friends with you, so don't forget that I'll be pulling with you and not against you.

Now I'll comment your letters, paragraph by paragraph, so that nothing escapes my eye! Here's your letter of February 23rd.[1] You say that some young English lady criticized your letters! Well, she should have done so, if you were foolish enough to trust in a woman, mere woman, that they are pedantic and most unobserving. Just because you told her

---

4 The list of words was evidently included in the final copy of this letter.

1 The rough copy of this letter bears the date of February 22.

to find the errors, she got her lantern out and looked for them, and when a woman gets her lantern out to look for something she always finds it. She failed to note how elastic is your thought in the expression and all she found was some little grammatical error. Oh, I'll admit that there are times in your letters when a grammatical error does creep in, but it's wonderful to note, too, that it certainly does not cramp your style any! Take my word for it then that you write a lovely letter, such as many a boy and girl from our High Schools would like to be able to write! They can't do it as you do because they know too much English and have nothing to use it on! Don't worry about the hits – especially if they but come from women! Ye Gods! Frailty, thy name is woman! (With courtesy of Shakespeare.)

I want to thank you for the dollar bill ($1.00) that you inclosed with this letter. You need not be in such a hurry to get the money to me – I am quite sure that you will not turn out to be a piker![2] According to your wish – and mine - this will close our debit and credit on Arnulfi and Remarque with *Farewell to Arms.* Henceforward I shall strictly bear in mind the pact whereby we are to exchange books! You get no more reductions, old socks, so put that in your pipe and smoke it! Now we're good friends, I suppose! You tell the world, I haven't the heart!

With this letter I immediately ordered the following books for you, accordingly: –

Jurgen – James B. Cabell.
Manhattan Transfer – J. Dos Passos.
Chicago Poems – Vachel Lindsay, I mean, Carl Sandburg.
Spoon River Anthology – Lee Masters.

With these will also be *City Block* of Waldo Frank.

I have it now from your letter of March 1st that you already have the *Spoon River Anthology.* Well, when I get it I shall keep it myself or sell it to Miss Buckman, since she wants it, too. Besides I am always glad to have a book selected by you. As for the others I shall send them to you when I get them and I am expecting their arrival any day now.

As for the summer vacation proposition, I shall call on the Director of our Government Library early next week. I already have an appointment with him and I shall explain things so that you get the books. If he does not see my point I shall take the books out on my own card and

2 The slang expression is underlined in pencil, presumably by Pavese. The term 'piker' is included among the list of words and phrases from *Babbitt* that Chiuminatto sent Pavese.

send them to you, hoping that you will send them back on time, so that I shall not have any trouble with the library. Just leave everything to me, Mr. Pavese, and know that I shall do all I can for your betterment and interest. I have all the dope from you now – so here's hoping!

Last week I saw the film *Men Without Women* from the story by Ernest Hemingway – and it was wonderful – a psychological story of men trapped in a submarine! Very gripping – or shall I say, thrilling! I imagine you are going to like the book, so I'll try to get it on the library list.

I liked your dissertation on *Sorrel and Son* immensely, only that I was sorry to think that you thought I was razzing[3] you in my last letter. No, I see your point of view and it's perfectly clear alright with me! If I can get such nice, lengthy and wholesome criticisms by giving rise to argument, then I'm going to do it after I read any and all books in which you are interested.

I just received a letter from Miss Franchi whereby it is agreed that she will not ask you for your comments – so I shall continue to explain things to you as best is fit between us, slang, Italian and 'dirty' English or Italian, as the case behooves! Anything, in short, to be most explanatory!

As for the slang phrases you sent me, well, I'll fix them up as soon as I can. I notice that there are some phrases that make it almost imperative that I have the book, for standing alone, as they do, it is almost impossible to give them a proper interpretation. I mean, those of Van Vechten and Anderson. If I knew beforehand just what books you would read I could get them here and read them myself, contemporaneously commenting for you, as I did with *Arrowsmith* and as I shall do with *Our Mr. Wrenn*, when I can get it. Some damn fool is reading it from the library and I can't get my hands on the book at all, as yet!

I am reading *Elmer Gantry* of Sinclair Lewis just now, but I am not commenting it. If you plan to read this one too, or his, *Main Street*, or any other of his volumes, let me know and I'll gladly comment them for you. It is no extra work for me to read and comment – they go hand-in-hand, you know.

At this point I have come back from the library with *Our Mr Wrenn* and shall proceed to read it and comment it to you. So just hold off your

3 The slang expression is also underlined in pencil, presumably by Pavese since he asked Chiuminatto for an explanation of the phrase in his letter of 5 April. Chiuminatto provides the explanation in his letter of 28 April.

reading of it until I send you my comments, if you will, within the next two weeks. (No, Mr. Pavese, I do not write day and night; I merely take an evening off now and then and read and comment from 7 PM to a little after midnight during which time I can cover a lot of territory!).

May I ask of you – a favor? See if you have some snapshot, photograph, or the likes of yourself, and send me it with your friendly autograph, will you? I should so much like a picture of my old pals. Ask Mila to do it too – and I shall reciprocate with the same! Get it? Then, —— after it!

I went to the library just a while ago to look up *Babbitt* for you! Here it is: – Chapter XXXIV.

Flivver – automobile mal-andata – di poco valore.
Frog-Face – Faccia da Rana – che si dà ai brutti.
Flathead — Testa Piatta – che si dà ai cretini.
Farinaceous — Farinaceo — individuo a tanti pezzettini psicologici.
Freezone – la Zona Libera – dove si lascia l'automobile senza pagare. Sono le zone fissate dalle autorità.
Flapdoodle – Capriccioso –
Fog-Horn — La Trombetta che si suona nel porto durante la fitta nebbia. Avvertimento alle navi, e che si dà agli individui che hanno una brutta voce e che sono poi dei chiacchieroni.
Qui si scherzavano di Babbitt – dando a quell'F ogni significato possibile ridicolo.
Tutt'altro spiegherò a fogli appositi; è meglio, così li può tenere tutti insieme.

Let's get back to solid English!
Well – well, I guess I have nothing else to say for now, Mr. Pavese. Just keep writing me and ***keep me posted***[4] as to what you are going to read, and in this way I may be able to prepare the comments for you. Remember that within a month you will have *Our Mr Wrenn* – so don't rush!

As for all the other volumes – and the library proposition – well, I'll take care of that nicely if there is any way of doing it.

Say hello to Max – and accept a hearty hand-shake from yours truly!

Your American Buddy –

Antonio Chiuminatto

4 The slang expression is underlined in pencil with the words 'avvertito' and 'advertised' written between the lines, presumably by Pavese.

Green Bay, Wisconsin, March 18th, 1930
To Cesare Pavese, Turin

My Dear Cesare:
Good news – ye gods – good news!!!!! I have your books for you from the library. I have just returned home from my interview with the Directoress and she has considered the grand and glorious name of Prof. Antonio Chiuminatto, with regards to his friends.

Right here beside me now I have the following books: –

Sun also Rises – Ernest Hemingway.

The Grandmothers – Glenway Wescott.

Roan Stallion, Tamar and other Poems – Robinson Jeffers.

Now listen to me! I could have had many of the other volumes you asked for – but I felt it useless to send them to you all at once, under the conditions that were made me.

These are the conditions granted me by the Government Directoress of the Green Bay Public Library, which conditions I have agreed to and which I trust you, too, will agree with, Mr. Pavese. Then we can sail along O so nicely!!!

You will be allowed to keep the book or books of the Green Bay Public Library for TWO MONTHS (2 Mos.) from the date of the loan. Ordinarily they are allowed to be kept for only 14 days – but this is the especial condition granted to Antonio Chiuminatto for his pal Mr. Pavese, since he is so interested in our works. Ya! Any book that is torn, or in any way, damaged when returned, must be REPLACED with a NEW one by me. Every book that is overdue will be taxed with a 2¢ fine for each and every day, beginning with the date of expiration.

These three books which I am sending you date from to-day, March 18, 1930 and must be back in the Green Bay Public Library on, or before, May 18th, 1930. After that there will be a fine of 2¢ a day for each book.

Now don't let all this worry you, Mr. Pavese. NOT AT ALL! I have thought it out like this – it will take two weeks for the books to reach you and two more weeks, more or less, to get back here to me. You will still have ONE MONTH in which to read them. I have sent you three books for I think you can easily read the volumes in a month. If not let me know and I shall only send you, next time, as many volumes as you think you can read in the time allotted you.

Let me know how you feel about this proposition and next time I may be able to get them for you on a THREE MONTHS' Loan! I have arranged it so that you will be able to have AS MANY BOOKS AS YOU LIKE for the summer vacation! Get that? AS MANY AS YOU LIKE, so send the list along!

Tomorrow morning your books will go to the post office – and I hope you will be pleased – and satisfied. Read them at leisure – and try to get them back to me on May 18th, or as soon after as possible, so that we don't leave a bad impression from the start with the Library Officials. Get me? Even if we do have to pay a fine – it will be little – or far better than buying the books – and cheaper, too!

Good luck – Cesare, old socks – and remember that I am always at your service – even with our Mr Wrenn. – Say hello to all for me; slip me the glove! Your Buddy

Antonio Chiuminatto

Green Bay, Wisconsin, Tuesday Morning, March 19th, 1930
To Cesare Pavese, Turin

Dear Cesare:
This morning the book store telephoned to me to tell me that your books had arrived. So I opened this letter once more to add this post-script.

Here are the volumes which I shall immediately send on their way to you: –

Jurgen – James Cabell – $2.50
Manhattan Transfer – Dos Passos – $2.50
Chicago Poems – Sandburg – $2.00
TOTAL – $7.00

I was told that for the present your book of *City Block* by Waldo Frank is impossible to get. It was only recently published in a limited number of copies which were all sold. The book now awaits a second printing. I shall search for it myself, Mr. Pavese, and in a short time I hope to have it for you in spite of the difficulty.

I tried to cancel the order for some of the books you asked me to get, and they may be cancelled, but in the event that they come to Green Bay just the same, I shall send them to you – for canceling an order here is forbidden by law! So think twice now before you order – because little Tony is snappy – right on the job, you know!

Your account now opens with SEVEN DOLLARS ($7.00) for the volumes listed above. Kindly note that I am not favoring you with any reduction; you pay just what I pay! Just as soon as I get the bill I'll send it to you, as agreed.

As for the receipt of these books you will be getting them all at once, those from the Public Library and those of your own. It would be best to read those of the Library first, for they are on limited time of reading, while the others are yours for keeps and can be read at leisure.

With pleasure in your service, I am as ever – your Buddy.

Antonio Chiuminatto

[Turin,] April 5th, 1930
To Antonio Chiuminatto, Green Bay, Wisconsin

Dear Tony:
Well, we have now got a fair bond of a friendship, a little bothersome perhaps on your part on account of the way I'm overworking you, but, out of this, I hope we get some usefulness from it. As, for instance, to receive letters with such strange stamps which cause janitors to stare a bit of a time. It's grand to be addressed as Mr So and So from the Bezuzus[1] country of Green Bay Wis.! I beg your pardon, young man, but I must at once return on the subject of business. Don't think to get off so easily: you've stuck to a Piedmontese, 'genus acre virum'[2] as the up-to-date Vergilius, father of Dante, Pa.[vese] etc., says somewhere and you'll see. Just about post-stamps I've got to speak.

I noticed what a waste of 'Golden-Gates' and 'Liberty's statues' you are practising in your mailings of books and as I know that also a cent is a part of a dollar, I pray you to enclose hence-forward with the bookseller's bill the shipping clerk's. Get me? See! Yes, 'unto the last red Indian penny,' that's my gentlemanly retaliation for your reprimand. So, stick to the broom-handle and smoke it.

---

1 Pavese includes this term in his list of slang expressions and phrases from *Babbitt* that he sent to Chiuminatto on 12 January. On 11 February Chiuminatto returns the list with his comments, including an explanation of 'Bezuzus': 'Un nome qualsiasi come si direbbe Tizio Caio.'

2 *Georgics*, book II.

And there's also another complication: giving vent to your righteous indignation you gave forth certain phrases you've now got to explain me on the bargain. What the devil were you meaning in such nonsensical words as 'I'll be pulling with you and not against you' and 'You tell the world, *I haven't the heart!*' and 'to raz someone'? You see. I also am 'right on the job.'

But to stop kidding, I want to thank you infinitely for your troubles which never seem to come to an end, but always voluntarily to breed and multiplicate. I'm almost terrified with the awful kindness I've started. I got your three letters about *Arrowsmith*, began the book and your comments are the accustomed darby!

Now, I put Lewis' book aside to hurry on the library's ones which I got safely and be sure, I'll leisurely wade through. I began with *The Grandmothers*[3] and want once more to proclamate there is no other living country in the world which be able to boast such a contemporary literature.

You are the peach of the world! Not only in wealth and material life but really in liveliness and strength of art which means thought and politics and religion and everything. You've got to predominate in this century all over the civilized world as before did Greece, and Italy and France. I'm sure of it. What in their little sphere have American Movies done in old Europe – and I've always abused those who mantained it was their financial organization and advertisements which brought them up: I say it is, not even their artistic value, but their surpassing strength of vital energy don't mind whether pessimistic or joyful – what, I say, have done Movies will do the whole of your art and thought. Each of your worthy writers finds out a new field of existence, a new world, and writes about it with such a downrightness and immediateness of spirit it's useless for us to match. Don't think I'm here coaxing you for some hidden purpose, or for the bad taste of a rhapsodical style: I'm in my earnestest when stating that a good modern European book is, generally speaking, only interesting and vital for the nation which produced it, whereas a good American one speaks to a larger crowd springing, as it does, from deeper wants and really saying new things not only queer ones, as we at our best are to-day doing.

I beg your pardon for this lot of spiel but you know, I'm so stuffed with American readings, I must sometimes give a little vent. Otherwise I'll be choking.

---

3 By Glenway Westcott.

I see *The Grandmothers* is another book about your history, one of your national books, which demonstrate a thing not yet generally known here in Europe: that you, as a nation, have already a tradition and a pride, a great thing which fills your last want. Now you can really go and conquer the earth.

To which let us come down.

Did you never fall in with the works of Mr Artemus Ward,[4] ob. About sixty years ago? If you didn't, you drop this sheet at once and stir about, till you find out and read them. It's a capital fellow, a wonderfully American one, something of an Anita Loos in checkered trousers and Yankee spelling. It's a terrible knocker of great things and as for little ones he has a charming naive philolosophy of his 'than which there is no whicher.' You must read the way he gets along with the 'show biznis,' his war-correspondance from 'B.[aldinsville] Injianny'[5] and his letters to the English Punch.[6] A half page of his to sample the stuff.[7]

Ain't it really corking? And you can go on, he is always the same feller. I want to write something about these humorists: from A. Ward to A. Loos they are an exceedingly interesting gang. Many things in your two-reel films – Mack Sennet, Christie,[8] etc. – can be understood only by means of these 'harbingers.'

Now, to pull on you the accustomed something, I should pray you look after the publisher's imprint and the date of the first edition of *Cradle of the Deep* by Joan Lowell, which work I read here in a translation and should like to know about in order to quote it right in an essay of mine. Get me? The imprint and the date, not the book: I know it already.

As for the works you intend to send me in your next mailing on May, you can keep an eye to the list you have already and besides I jot here someone more:

Claude Mckay – Amy Lowell – Ezra Pound – Countee Cullen. Whatever work of these authors and, note it, also of the preceding list's, will do. I say this for I remember having written there about some one: what-

4 Pseudonym of humorist Charles Farrar Browne.

5 Indiana.

6 Artemus Ward was a contributor to the English magazine *Punch.*

7 Pavese left a page blank in this letter, evidently meaning to fill it with a passage from Artemus Ward.

8 Christie Film Company was an American pioneer motion picture company founded in 1916 in Hollywood, California, by Al Christie and Charles Christie, two brothers from London, Ontario, Canada. Christie studios emphasized situational comedy.

ever work, and about some other: only certain books. Of both lists you can send me whatever book you find under whatever name. For instance, by Dos Passos, W. Carlos Williams, and W. Frank there is a lot of works I don't know about: you select and mail: I'll accept everything.

I wonder what has happened to the second package of books you mailed the same day with the library's I got already. However, hardly I'll have it, I'll write you something about.

As for the photos, Maxim told me he will send you his, here you have mine. It's the only snapshot I got among my papers and so I send it. You photographers are damned slow people and I'll get a new good one only next week. I've waited already too much and so I send this. Hardly I'll have the new one, I'll write and enclose it. Now, look at ...[9] But, you know, I'm a lovelier young fellow. Don't worry about and don't advertise me too much. Naturally I'm waiting for yours, at least, in your soup-and-fish, spiffy young man. Always yours.

[Turin,] April 17th, 1930
To Antonio Chiuminatto, Green Bay, Wisconsin

Dear Tony:
I have at last succeeded! Photographers are worse than tailors. Here's my close-up, all for you.

On this same day I'll try to pack back the Kellog's[1] books. You see, in fifteen days I've got through.

Am I not right on the job? In order you don't think I've only turned over their leaves, I'll give you a snappy critical sketch on each. Don't shudder: it's like the dentist.

Best of all is surely *Roan Stallion.*[2] Say, Mr Chiuminatto, there in America you've got poets as flies in summer. Not only you have your well-known wonderful jazz-minstrels, but, what's more, a lot of other poets whose existence is entirely unsuspected here in Europe. There are a few

9 There is a blank in the rough draft.

1 The library in Green Bay.
2 By Robinson Jeffers.

wits here acquainted with and they seem to like the secret. This Mr Robinson Jeffers threatens to become another Whitman of yours, with his eagle's glance from California, as the other fellow for Long Island. His idyllls of the coast-range (*Roan Stallion, Tamar, Fauna,* etc.) are all things that let people staring around. Their simple background of not affected rough life (especially in *Roan Stallion*) which in a blink soars in the highest lyrical heaven involving a whole vision of history and America is something worth reading. I'm too warm with it already to give a sure criticism about, but I'll keep an eye on this writer and come back to him.

Meanwhile, what's wonderful, he also is a Midwesterner almost, by birth. You are filling the American Literature with Midwestern geniuses: Lee Masters from Kansas, Dreiser from Indiana, Lewis from Minnesota, Anderson from Ohio, Hemingway and Sandburg from Illinois, Wescott from Wisconsin: you've got to be new New England. Smart fellow also that E. Hemingway. I keep yet untouched the *Farewell,* which I never find time to read, but as for *The Sun also rises* I went through and found it an extraordinary piece of description of our own generation. The freshness of it, almost its candidness in the utterance of the riskier and more complicated things of our mentality is unmatched.

And as for Westcott I must repeat that it would be of unvaluable opportunity here in Italy where everybody keeps the wrong ideas about you American people. It would show the deep roots and earnestness of your nationality and teach someone to regard, with another consideration that the wealth's, your rising importance. There are the stories of Great-Aunt Mary and Uncle Evan especially which beat everything. You must read this book.

Say, Mr Chiuminatto, apropos of Hemingway would you kindly explain me if *Sun also rises* means 'anche il sole si leva' or 'il sole si leva anche'? It's a difficult stuff this of adverbs in English.

I'm yet wondering what happened to your Cabel[l]-Dos Passos- and-Sandburg package: you say you mailed it on the same day with the other books wrote about, but as yet I rec'd only the aforesaid ones. Would the whole have shipwrecked? This reminds me that you have not yet spoken about the Arnulfi-Remarque mailing. I hope they have not gone to the Devil as I fear mine have. However write me.

Now, thank you, and keep smiling contemplating yours

Turin, April 22nd, 1930
To Antonio Chiuminatto, Green Bay, Wisconsin

Dear Mr Prof:
At least I got your money and here it is in plunks.[1] I wrote you, only a litte ago, two letters, I've now nothing more to say. No: perhaps I'll undertake really for a 'real' publisher a translation of Lewis or Anderson to make them more known here in Italy. You see your lessons begin to bear fruit.

By-the-by, if you have time, apply to the Post Office, to ferret out something about the lost books of Sandburg etc. Naturally, should you have got them registered, you could somehow complain and get some compensation.

But I know what damnation it is to go about in offices so I would not have you worried too much.

Do what you think better and least troublesome. I already gave in. Notwithstanding this mishap, we can yet be satisfied that the ill-luck were not for your other mailing: do you think what a fine we should have had to pay, before we could get the books again?

When you'll have received my package which is now starting and I hope will arrive in due time, you can begin thinking about the next loan. You have already the list. Good-bye you fiddler

C. Pavese

Chicago, Illinois, April 28th, 1930
To Cesare Pavese, Turin

Dear Cesare:
It was with immense pleasure that I received your letter here in Chicago this morning. It was forwarded to me from Green Bay. Just now, then, I am taking time off to answer you and say what I had wanted to say long ago but for which I could find no time.

As you will know I am here in Chicago and have been now for over

1 In his letter of 16 May Chiuminatto corrects Pavese's use of the slang expression 'plunks.'

two weeks. I am kept busy, yes, very busy, making acquaintances for I want to locate here permanently. As it is I am trying to get a teacher's position in one of the many conservatories and from this line of work go back up the hill to my aspirations. Since I am a perfect stranger in this second city of the United States it takes me a lot of time to get around and keeps me overly busy. This is why I have not been able to dedicate my time to you of late as I should have liked to do. I know you will excuse me and understand; as soon as I get a footing again I'll be at your service with heart and hand!

Thank you so much for the snap of yourself! It always makes me feel so much more in contact with one, while writing, if I have a snap or photo of them at hand. I'll tell the whole cock-eyed world you're still the same Pavese! Say, we could have a nifty[1] time if you were here with me in Chicago.

I am glad you got the books and hope that you will be able to read them all before the time comes for their return. As for the other books, the ones you bought, well, since I knew that you would be busy reading the library books I just held those over and read Carl Sandburg myself. Great! You'll like him alright!

Mrs. Allegro left for New York day before yesterday. She is sailing on the Augustus which leaves from here on May. 3rd. She has your three books in her trunk and will give them to Max Mila, who she knows, who will then see to it that you get them. (*Chicago Poems, Manhattan Transfer* and *Jurgen.*) Up until Mrs. Allegro left Miss Mabel Buckman was reading *Jurgen* so that she will be able to talk to you about it later on if you care to do so. She will be in Turin around the 15th of May, just about the time you will be sending back those library books, so you see, you will not want from reading matter. I don't know whether or not my mother finally got the statement (bill) from the booksellers, but I do know that the price of the three books was $7.00. *Chicago Poems* was $2.00 and the other two were $2.50 each.

Just as soon as I can get around to it, Cesare, I shall try to have books forwarded to you from the Central Chicago Library. It may be harder to do here since no one knows me and in that way I cannot give what would be an accepted guarantee. At any rate, though, I shall try, and if not possible I shall instruct my brother at home which books to forward you from the Green Bay Library. Get me? Good idea, eh?

---

1 The term is underlined in pencil, presumably by Pavese. The words 'smart' and 'stylish' are inserted in pencil under the word 'nifty.'

I was about to finish your comments on *Our Mr Wrenn* when I left home. I only had about sixty more pages to comment. As it is I shall probably go home for Decoration Day, May 30th, since the next day is my birthday, too, and then I shall take my comments with me to Chicago and get the book here to work on for you; I realize what benefit these things are to you and I'm out to give you every ounce of my good will and friendship. And if it should kill you, well – let me know in advance what flowers you prefer!

I cannot send this letter without reciprocating the favor of your snap. Hence I am inclosing one of myself – very natural, too, for a change, and which was taken by Mrs. Allegro out on the sidewalk in front of our home in Green Bay. Please accept it with all the warmth of friendship that I myself experienced when I received yours this morning!

You'll get the soup-and-fish later on – that is, when I can get it first.

Say hello to Max and tell him that I got the *Rassegna Musicale* and that I shall tell him about his articles.

I'm sorry to have to stop writing, Cesare, but I must. I have some special practicing to do and then must make a visit, too. It will not be long now, I hope, before I can quietly take upon myself your duties.

Here is explaining the phrases you asked about: –

To pull with someone – lavorare d'accordo mutuo. La frase viene dall'idea di due cavalli che tirano lo stesso carretto, tirano insieme insomma lo stesso peso.

We are pulling together – lavoriamo insieme – ognuno faccendo la sua parte.

I haven't the heart. – Non ho il coraggio. Si dice così parlando di sorprese brutte e si può anche dire in senso ironico. Uso variato.

Quando [s]i chiede ad uno di raccontare un fatto brutto, straziante, dirà forse, e bene – No, I don't want to, I haven't the heart!

Now, since Mr. Pavese hasn't the heart to tell the world how good he is in English, I'll do it. (qui si dice della sua umiltà.)

To razz someone – leggergli la vita.

I'd like to say more to you but just must lay off! I'll write again as soon as I can.

I'm always remembering you, though, and am greeting you with my friendship hunc et semper – as

Antonio Chiuminatto

My New Address
Antonio Chiminatto
4421 North Lincoln Street
Apt. 3-A
Chicago, Ill. (inois)
(USA)

Chicago, Illinois, May 7th, 1930
To Cesare Pavese, Turin

Dear Cesare:
I have just come back from the Chicago Public Library where I was on business for you. I'll tell you about it now as I go along.

First of all here is all the information I got from the volume of *The Cradle of the Deep* by Joan Lowell.

Copyright, 1929, by Simon & Schuster, Inc. (Publishers).

37 West 57th Street, New York City.

Printed in the U.S.A. by Vail-Ballou Press, Binghamton.

Bound by H. Wolff Est., New York City.

Designed by Ander Braun.

First Edition, 75,000 copies – March 1929.

Second Edition, 25,000 copies – March 1929

I hope this serves your purpose now!

I also had an interview with Mr. Levin, the Chicago Librarian, with regards to sending you books as I did from Green Bay. He tells me that I cannot send you books for a three-months' period since I am not a resident of Chicago a year yet. He is willing, though, to let me send you books for the Vacation Period, which is from June 1st to October 1st, and in which period I can send you any TEN BOOKS you want! If these books come back before the expiration of the period then I may send you another TEN BOOKS. Not so bad, eh? This is the cat's whiskers, alright!

I have already notified my brother in Green Bay that you are returning the books I already sent you. Not only this, but I have instructed him to send you THREE more books from the list you gave me. So now, just as soon as your books get here he will take care of everything for me. Rest assured that you will keep getting the books you want in one way or another. I can always instruct the librarian at Green Bay by letter as to the books you need, and my brother can at least pack them and get them off to you.

If you have a list ready of TEN BOOKS you WANT, let me know as soon after the first of June as possible, so that I can get them from here in Chicago and send them to you. They will be allowed to be kept until the first of October, that is, they must be back in the Chicago Library on or before that date. Mr. Levin also told me that they have an excellent American Library in Paris, France, from which you could draw books. As it is I think it is better for you to trust in me – you'll get service just as well, either from Green Bay or from Chicago.

The Chicago Library is really wonderful, Cesare. It is a huge building in itself and very artistic and in some ways reminds me of the Madaleine in Paris. They have nearly 2,000,000 volumes not to say anything of the increase in current books each month. You ought to be here!

Within a few days now you will have the volumes that you are worrying about. I feel sorry for you, but I know how glad you will be when you find out that they did not go lost, but were merely held over for convenience's sake. Mrs. Allegro will be in Turin around the 15th of this month at which time you will have your dear friends Sandburg of this city, Dos Passos and the other volume of Jurgen!

Say, I wrote you about a century ago already that I had received your LOVELY photograph. A Million thanks, Cesare! Gosh, it surely is good to have your face around again! I'll send you one of mine just as soon as I get around to have it taken – ya, with the soup-and-fish!

Explanation: – Sun also rises. It all depends on the use of emphasis. If I say, Sun also RISES, then I mean – Il sole si leva anche. If I should say, though – Sun ALSO rises, then I mean – Pure il sole si leva. I think, though, that the author intended that 'also' as a neutral – Il sole, pure, si leva! L'intendimento comune è – Il sole si leva anche! Volendo dire che non solo il sole tramonta, ma pure si leva di nuovo.

Here's making a correction on your English, if I may. The verb – to explain (spiegare) is always followed by the preposition 'to' where the dative case is used. Examples:–

Explain this to me. (This – accusative case – me – dative case.)

In general, the accusative case, if used, should immediately follow the verb, and in its turn is followed by the dative case with 'to.'

I explained this lesson to him!

Will you please explain this thing to me?

I notice that you very frequently misuse this verb, hence the correction.

This is all for this time. If you have any explanations that you want from your readings, just let me know, as usual. With all best wishes to you and Max, I am as ever, your Buddy in America,

Antonio Chiuminatto

Chicago, Illinois, May 16th, 1930
To Cesare Pavese, Turin

Dear Cesare:
I received your registered letter of April 22nd, and also the 'jack,' or as you called them, the plunks! 'Jack' is our slang for money, in general!

It was nice of you to be so prompt, though it was not necessary, insofar as you have not as yet received the books. I know you are worrying about them, and rightly, too, but to-day or tomorrow you will have them from Mrs. Allegro who is now in Italy. I am sorry that my plan of keeping the books here caused you to run around to offices; as it is there is nothing to worry about. You will soon have your Dos Passos, Sandburg and Cabell, for which you have already paid me in advance!

Still speaking of books I have done everything possible to get a copy of *City Black*[1] by Waldo Frank, and now only one way remains open to me. I just received an answer to my inquiry with the General Publishers of New York, who, for your information, answer me as follows:–

'We are in receipt of your letter dated April 4th with regard to the copy of *City Black* by Waldo Frank, which you have just ordered from us.

We regret to state, however, that his is a book which we do not supply, on account of the character of the same, but you can obtain it from Mr. Waldo Frank, the author, whose address is Darien, Conne[c]ticut.'

I shall now write Mr. Frank and ask him to send me an autographed copy of his volume, which I shall send to you with the relative price. Under these conditions you may not even be able to get that book! It is

1 Chiuminatto mistakes 'Black' for 'Block' in the title, which Pavese corrects in his letter of 10 June.

evident that he treats of the City Negroes,[2] if I am not mistaken from the title, and his way of doing it has been censored by the government. You'll get the book, though. If I have to turn Hell upside down! I'm a go-getter and that's all there is to it!

I've been waiting for word from my brother in Green Bay. I gave him a list of books you wanted and he was to have sent them to you in these days. I'll let you know something definite just as soon as he writes me. In the meantime I'll get a list of the year's best clàssic sellers and then send you TEN of them for the summer months from the Chicago Library. YOU'LL have all you can take care of, don't worry!

I am inclosing herewith, Cesare, little bits of humor from the *Chicago Daily News,* which may interest you. If you like them let me know and I shall send you these bits regularly. One of these fine days I shall also send you a complete Sunday Edition of the Chicago Paper, so that you may use your judgments on our ways of handling news. I am sending you the 'Maybe I'M Wrong' because of its word-tricks and keen humor. You'll find slang galore (a beaucoup) in these little bits, which is the reason I am sending them to you. I'll comment these to you, where I think it will be needed. NO. 1 of 'Maybe I'm Wrong' –

To be sitting on top of the world – Aver di tutto e come si vuole.
Tightwad – un avaro (stingy – agg. – avaro, tirato).
To talk back – Rispòndere male – come fanno i bambini quando li rimproveriamo.
Cad – Mascalzone.
Ministers – I preti protestanti.
Lovelorn – quelli ammalati d'amore!
Matches – L'addattamento di una persona ad un'altra, come le coppie che si vogliono bene.
tight – avaro.
crap-shooter – giuocatore di dadi.
Bones – (slang) i dadi! (dacché son fatti di osso).
Heart balm (balsamo per il cuore) si dice del[l'] aggiustamento finanziario per rottura di promessa di matrimonio. Quando si va con una signorina per dei mesi e che poi se la pianta, se l'uomo ne ha dei soldi

2 Chiuminatto's misreading of the title leads him to this erroneous conclusion. He may also be confusing this book with another of Frank's works, *Holiday,* which is a novel about the struggle in the South between the white race and the black.

lei incomincia procedura per rottura di promessa e chiede una certa somma quale 'heart balm.'
Necking – feste in automobile fra i giovani allo scuro!!
dumb – cretino.
sink – lavandino.
to be on one's last legs – Essere quasi alla fine, o di vita, o di mezzi finanziarii, ecc.

Ora vi è *The Modern Dictionary* che è niente male! You will find witty and sarcastic definitions for some of our slang and classic words! It's all for a laugh! Then there are three comic strips, one – Mutt & Jeff – which is very good!

Mr. Pavese, I was mighty glad to hear that you will undertake a translation of some American writer. May I make a suggestion merely by way of wanting to help you. You go ahead and translate, and when you have finished, send me your translation which I will most carefully look over, NOT OVERLOOK, to see that you have nicely straightened yourself out on slang, etc. Two heads are better than one, even though mine may be a cabbage-head! Two or three times like this and you will be a PERFECT translator! I'm sure I can help you and if you care to, I shall be only too glad to take a hand without taking any credit!! The publishers ought to be proud of you!

Until next time now – I am your Buddy as ever –

Antonio Chiuminatto

[Turin,] May 17th [1930]
To Antonio Chiuminatto, Chicago

Dear Buddy:
I got somewhere – besides your tiny photograph for which I thank you – that the last of May is your birthday and so I hurried, as fast as I could, to have you honored and thankgiven as you deserve. No, I blundered: not as you deserve, for it's impossible to overtake you in kindness, but as it is granted to me, poor fellow that I am.

So, you'll receive, in a few days since, there in Chicago, a little present I dare to make you, to sweeten – posthumosly (it's my habit) – your birthday. It is some liquor-center chocolates (Perugina!) you wrote me once you are so fond of.[1] Please, accept it as a token of my friendship and good will, and don't worry about the trouble, as it is your hypocrite habit, or, if you really will worry about something, let it be about the pettiness of the gift and you'll be right.

Would the chocolates arrive in Chicago someway marred (the shop-clerk assures me they become dried within, in a spell of time) you could then think that you are in Prohibition land and that the Gods are overlooking it. But the ditto clerk swore me the sweets had arrived the day before from the ... factory.

You have certainly rec'd now my two silly letters about the 'lost' books, and you'll, I hope, excuse me for my flurry.

By the way, if you intend to go on with your mailings of library books (and I'll be tickeled to death if you will), put, for the moment, any other name apart and send me only Lewis's books except B... A... W...[2] which I got here. Will you? The reason is I want to know him perfectly in order to write about him, an essay asked for by a certain literary review of Rome. You hear: I'm hustling (and boosting accordingly). The essay would be presented in the summer, so, if you can, give me a lift.

Say, I'm yet waiting for your ritzy photo. And I've yet a grand news, I'll write about hardly I'll be sure of it and best wishes

---

Chicago, Illinois, May 27th, 1930
To Cesare Pavese, Turin

Dear Cesare:

Let me tell you a little story that will sound nice to your ears! I have here at home now TEN VOLUMES to send you from the Chicago Library. Ya, damn it! I went to the library this morning at ten minutes of ten and I have just returned home at six-thirty P.M. which means late afternoon! Well, I was mighty glad to do it for you, Cesare, so know that I am not lecturing you! I went through the index-files on all the authors you mentioned and selected their finest works and latest ones, too! I could not

1 In his comments on *Babbitt*, Chiuminatto mentioned how much he liked Perugina liquor-centered chocolates as he explained the meaning of 'nut center chocolates.'

2 It appears that Pavese intended to include here the titles of books by Sinclair Lewis that he had already read, *Babbitt, Arrowsmith, Our Mr Wrenn,* and perhaps some others.

take out some books because they are in a 1929 edition and the library does not allow them out of sight for more than 14 days. You may only take out books on a long permission when they have been in the library over 18 months! Next time I'll be able to get the ones I couldn't get this time; some were already out on loan and could not be had!

The conditions are these: You may keep the books all summer; they must be back in the Chicago Library on or before OCTOBER 1st, 1930! For every book kept overtime, there will be a fine of 3 cents a day! All books damaged in any way must be replaced with a NEW one!

Here are the books that you will get:

POETRY — Legends —— By — Amy Lowell (Ed. 1921)
Lee (Dramatic Poem) By — Edgar Lee Masters (1926)
Collected Poems — By – Edwin A. Robinson (1921 ed. of 600 Pages, with 'The Man against the Sky'

PROSE —
Costumes by Eros — Conrad Aiken (1928)
Horses And Men — Sherwood Anderson (1928)
A New Testament — (1927)
The Enormous Room — Edward Cummings (1922)
Cities And Men — Ludwig Lewisohn (1927)
Men Without Women — Ernest Hemingway (1927)
Broken Necks — Ben Hecht (1926)

Now if you get these books soon, don't rush; you have all SUMMER to read them. Be sure that they are but here on the First of October, 1930. You will find that this is a collection of gems – and that another collection is awaiting you at the return of these.

Your books of the Kellogg Library were received this week and were returned by my brother in Green Bay. He does not mention whether or not a fine was due, since they were to be in the library on the 19th of May, but even if there was a fine, it could not have been very much.

As for the shipping of these ten books, Cesare, I may have to send them to you in two packages, in order not to be overweight! At any event with things running normally you ought to have the books shortly after you get this letter. In one package or two, you will get all ten of them. I shall have them registered against lost or damage and shall kindly ask you to do the same in returning.

May you have an enjoyable SUMMER VACATION with these volumes, which is my pleasure and enjoyment in being able to send you. Just think of me once in a while and write!

Did Mrs. Allegro give you your books of Dos Passos, etc? That is, through Max to whom she was to forward them? Well, I suppose you are considerably at rest now mentally, since you know what happened to those three volumes! Ha!

GOOD LUCK, Cesare – and with all best regards and best wishes to you and my friends – I am as ever your Buddy –

Antonio Chiuminatto

Chicago, Illinois, June 5th, 1930
To Cesare Pavese, Turin

Dear Cesare:
It's my twenty-sixth birthday; yes! Do I ever feel old. Oh boy! All I need is a hickory cane, with a bend in it, and I'll feel right at home!

I want to thank you for the liquor-center chocolates, although they have not as yet advised me of their arrival from the customs house! They will inform me when they arrive as I must pay the tax on them – but, O gee, O gosh – I'm glad to do that for I'd give my kingdom just now for one sip of Chartreuse! I'll let you know in my next letter how this affair is panning out!

My hurry and scurry[1] in things always get me in wrong, damn it! Just two days after I sent you the TEN VOLUMES from the library I get your letter asking for books of Sinclair Lewis only! Now I don't know whether or not I should kick the stuffings out of you or out of myself! Somebody is going to get hurt – and I don't mean MAYBE! Ya, you'll be tickled to death all right – just wait until you see TEN mountainous volumes in front of you with not the slightest sign of a Sinclair Lewis – and I'll just bet you will want to mop the whole city with me! Pardon – excusez-moi! You see, Cesare, I'm too damn fast for you – I live in America and you

1 Since Chiuminatto signs this letter in pencil, it is uncertain whether the underlined words are by Pavese or by the letter's author. The same is true for the remainder of underlined words in the letter.

live in Italy. Ha! I jump at the slightest order I get, but it looks like you are an undecided corporal – I beg your pardon – general!

In this case I feel like the soldier who was going through his first morning in drill work. The seargent was bossing the troop, as usual, with 'Shoulder arms!' – Left shoulder –Right shoulder – at ease – Attention! About face, etc. The poor devil at the end of the line sat on the ground and looked sullen. The seargent came to him and used some very unmanly language! To which he replied, nicely and coolly – Listen here, seargent; when you make up your damn mind what you want, then I'll follow orders. What the hell are you tryin' to do, bawl me all up?' Ya, the sergeant was all wrong! (Excuse the spelling of 'sergeant' which in places was spelled by my machine and not by me!)

Now that I have already, unknowingly, sent you the desired Ten Volumes on a summer card, I am no longer entitled to take out books until those have been returned. I shall try, though, to see if I can get around the problem just the same at the library. In the meantime I have a copy here of *Free Air* of Sinclair Lewis, which belongs to the lady of the house where I am staying. She will let you have it gladly – if you send it back when you have finished with it. I'll get it off to you within a few days, and then I'll try to stir up the other volumes of Lewis which you have not – and there are still a goodly few!

Here is a complete list of Sinclair Lewis' works which are on sale in America. From the earliest to the latest they are as follows:–

The Trail of the Hawk .... Our Mr Wrenn —
The Job ..... Mantrap ..... Free Air ..... Main Street, which won the Nobel Prize ..... Babbitt ..... Arrowsmith ..... Elmer Gantry ... The Man Who Knew Coolidge ..... and his latest one which is — Dodsworth.

There are eleven in all and you have read but four, so there are seven more that you must have. Well, I do know that there are 75¢ editions for some of them, while *Dodsworth* and *Elmer Gantry*, being the latest ones are still in a $2.50 edition. What I shall do if I cannot get them from the library, and some I surely shall NOT be able to get for they are in a 1929 edition and even 1930, is, that I shall borrow them from friends or acquaintances and send them to you. How's this for service, eh? Speak up now! Cheer up, Cesare, every cloud has a silver lining, you know!

You have the other ten volumes from the library now and they will keep you busy. I'll give you the lift on Lewis most gladly and one by one, as soon as I can get them, I'll send them to you! Good luck and plenty of it to you! Be on the lookout now for this first one – *Free Air.* The others will follow one after the other like liquor-center chocolates!

Say, tell, Cesare, do you have to pay anything on the books I send you, either from the library or from the sellers, that is, a tax or fee of any kind? I always write 'Books to be returned to America' on the cover wrapping of the package so that you will not have to do so. Let me know, will you!?

Good news! Listen! I have just asked the lady of the house here if she will let me use her library card for the summer, and in this way I can send you Lewis' books! She said I might, so I just fell into some good luck. All I need find out now is whether or not the library will allow me to take out an entire collection of books from one list of one author! If not I'll send you as many as I can from the library and for the rest of the books I'll resort to the old tricks! Oh, boy, it's hard to fool the Yankees! You tell 'em, kid, you know your onions! (which means – you know what you are doing.)

Remember hereafter, too, Cesare, that I work FAST, ya, fast, that's the word! Why, when I typewrite I cover my typewriter with asbestos paper so that it wont catch fire! And when I write I use oiled paper! Get me, sonny, get me? Laugh that one off, will ya? We are now going to send King Richard the Lion Hearted to the Naval Conference in London.[2] We have prepared for him, through the courtesy of the Tailors' Association, a beautiful suit of armor with twò pair of pants! Well, well, – I guess I don't win the rubber dime!

So long, Cesare, and be good! Will write again when there is something new to say. As ever your Buddy –

Antonio Chiuminatto

Chicago, Illinois, June 7th, 1930
To Cesare Pavese, Turin

Dear Cesare:
I have just returned from the Post-Office, where I mailed you TWO PACKAGES, containing the remainder of Sinclair Lewis' WORKS which are

2 Chiuminatto is evidently referring to Secretary of State Henry Stimson, who headed the U.S. delegation to the London Naval Conference from 22 January to 22 April 1930.

unknown to you. I went to the public Library this morning and was successful in getting them for your summer vacation, though I took the books out on my landlady's card, since she was kind enough to help both of us out of the problem. See how congenial we Americans are! O hell, yes!

These books, like those Ten I sent you some few days ago, must be back in the Chicago Public Library on or before October 1st, 1930! You now have 17 books belonging to the Chicago Library, and even though you may, may not or might read them all, Cesare, try to oblige me once more and have them here on the date fixed for their restitution! Thank you!

I am glad, in one way, that I have sent you these 17 books, which represent just about all that you have desired so far in literature. It was possible to send them to you only through a Summer Vacation Card, so it is better that you have them all new while you can have them, even though you may not have time to read them as you would like! When this Summer Period expires on October 1st, I shall not be able to send you any more library books, for I cannot have that privilege here until I have been a resident of Chicago for at least one year! I shall only be allowed books for a period of two weeks, and this amount of time, as you will readily see, is not sufficient for me to send them to you.

I know, though, that there are several Private Circulation Libraries in Chicago, and I shall find out whether or not it will be possible to arrange with some of them in sending the desired books to you. Well, we wont worry about it now; when we get to the bridge we will surely find some way of crossing it! In the meantime, I think that you are MORE than well supplied! What say?

In these TWO PACKAGES I sent you to-day, you will find the following volumes of Sinclair Lewis, which, with those you already have, complete the list of his books before the American public! They are as follows:–

The Trail of the Hawk – Mantrap – Free Air – Main Street – The Innocent – Elmer Gantry – The Man who Knew Coolidge – and – Dodsworth!

Please remember that *Free Air* is NOT a library book, but belongs to the landlady with whom I am staying, and that you may keep it as long as you wish, just as long as you return it eventually! Get me, huh? The others are ALL library books!

I have done my fastest in getting them to you – and I hope that your efforts will be rewarded in an eventual essay! Let me in on that essay now, don't forget! And I DO hope that you will be able to profit from the other Ten Books, for I shall not be able to so favor you again, in which event I should regret it much. Well, it's all up to you now, Cesare; I like to think that I have done my best in doing my part so willingly for you. Here's hoping you have time to take advantage of the occasion!

You talked about red Indian pennies in your last letter, so I shall herewith list the relative expenses of the mailings to you. The first two packages I sent you cost – one dollar and eighteen cents ($1.18) and these two packages to-day cost – ninety-nine cents ($.99)! There is no need of my telling you that you DO NOT NEED to refund me the mailing money – it's understood that that part of it is always my gift to you – just a gift of generosity! Hell, YES! But since you seem to kick a hell of a lot about my generosity – I shall add that if your conscience bothers you so much about these expenses – why, go right ahead and repay me! Do as you like, now, and may God bless you!

Say; by the way, I wrote to Mr. Waldo Frank, personally, for a copy of his *City Black*[1] for you, but as yet have heard nothing of him or the book! Can he be on his vacation already? If I get it though, I'll send it to you.

And so far to-day your candy – these delicious liquor-center chocolates – has not arrived. I hope and pray that the customs house officers be not too thirsty in this dry weather! Oh, boy, I can just taste them already – and feel that heavenly liquor just ooze clean down to the end of the Milky Way! Talk about tickling me to death – well, I'll tell the whole universe! Ya, you tell 'em Adams, I can't Express it: (Taken from the famous Adams Express Company – fastest of all transportation companies).

Don't forget to write me often – and don't forget to say hello to Max, to whom I shall write as soon as I can! This damn Wop over there in Turin, by the name of Pavese, has kept me right up on my tip toes, these days! He's a great kid, though, ya, a regular knock-out! — Say, did you get those books from Mrs. Allegro? Keep me informed, young fellow, keep me informed – remember that I am your proud book agent – and Buddy –

Antonio Chiuminatto

1 Chiuminatto continues to confuse the title of Frank's novel *City Block*.

[Turin,] June 10th, 1930[1]
To Antonio Chiuminatto, Chicago

Dear Tony:
I've a lot of things to write about.

Here, before me, lie your three last letters, yet unreplied. I awaited in order to get the caboodle and write you accordingly. Well, I got the whole bunch of 'them' books safely. Naturally I want to thank you infinitely, but this is too little: I wonder if you have not received my suggestions about your wasteful expenses of mailing and my firm and business-like proposition to pay for them. 'Che diamine!' you are too awfully kind-hearted, but absolutely you must, next time, enclose in your letter a bill of all your stamp expenses. Get me?

I'm overflowing with merriment for the new books. I'll wade through them, certainly, however there be much other work to do.

Say, I'm becoming a true authority about American literature, I begin to feel chesty with my fellow-students, and especially with co-eds. But, let's on: it's you the fellow who is doing half the work.

As for the funnies you sent me,[2] it's again an awfuly kind idea and such a one as only you can conceive. With these texts, and with your explanations, I'll not miss the time and the target. You bet: in those cuttings there's slang galore: I'm fattening on it, day after day.

With all my heart: don't worry so much after Frank's *City Block* (not 'black' as you mistook it), it's a good hunch, the autograph's, but don't waste all your time about.

Also Sandburg and Co. I rec'd safely, and I'm here renewing my excuses for all that foolish ado I did.

I'm beginning now Lewis' *Our Mr Wrenn* always according that plan I wrote you about: to get a thorough knowledge of him in order to put down that essay on his general work, the first essay on him in Italy. There's a road open to immortality! I've some new ideas about Lewis I want to bid. Va sans dire, if I'll get the publication I'll send you the issue. You should have been midwife to it! You certainly remember I asked you for some more Lewis books on loan, as *Elmer Gantry, Main Street, The Man who knew Coolidge* etc. And it's a pity you selected the ten aforesaid ones

1 The rough copy of the letter is erroneously dated May 10, but it is obviously in response to Chiuminatto's letter of 16 May.

2 Reference to Chiuminatto's clippings from the *Chicago Daily News*.

having not yet rec'd my hint. However, now it's done; and I'll be contented with the three of four books I possess and frame the essay on them.

Should you find some reviews in newspapers and magazines about Mr Lewis, I'll be awfully glad to know them, or an extract from them. You understand ...

Lastly I thank you for your lecture on syntax about 'to explain to' and hope heartedly to receive some more.

Now, the blow-out: perhaps this winter I'll be in New York to teach (look me over) Italian literature or such similar things in Columbia University! I've been so admired (watch my smoke!) on account of my smattering of America that a professor in my University has written about me to Columbia's Dean who was searching for Italian students 'to cross over.'[3] I'm now waiting for a reply. 'Who Who? The Hooroo!'[4]

Yours

C. Pav.

[Turin,] June 21st, 1930
To Antonio Chiuminatto, Chicago

Dear Tony:
Gosh all fish-hooks! It's my lot to-day to be lectured by all. I've been lectured by the Board of Teachers of the University about the fondness of slang I showed in my degree (which I got safely, I'm Ph.D. now, ah!)[1] – late in the night coming home a little tight I found both your letters of 5th and 7th and worried myself infinitely about your lecture on comparative Italian and American fastness – at last, going this morning to the office to retire Lewis' goods I got together with them some curt advice about the best manner to pack things: 'Write to the forwarder, let him know, his frequent mailings of "books" have been noted, customs begins

3 See note 5 of Introduction.
4 These final words, apparently expressing Pavese's excitement, are not clearly legible in the rough copy.

1 Pavese was awarded his degree on 20 June 1930.

to feel obliged to open packages, so let him pack them more loosely (it's the word), it will be a easier "understanding."'

Get me? My buddy, you go on packing them in your wonted accurate way, if they get damaged, it is we must pay, no? Let custom-officers pry and ferret out – they are on the job for that.

Now, all this turns out to cast the blues on me. I'm very, very much displeased my contradictory orders have driven you in such a mess, and I can only excuse a little my rashness thinking how I did not know nothing about your welcomest mailing of ten books when I wrote you about Lewis!

And I feel the more worried as you also put down that your hurry and scurry gets you in wrong, and you worry about it and go fetching ways to repair. Certainly now that it is done, I've only to thank you a thousand times for your second expedition of books also and I'm beginning to wade through them which I cheerfully hope to succeed in, but, as far the general principle, you must not go fetching you so much trouble and hustle so, and disturb so many persons (e.g. your landlady) for your ungrateful buddy's sake. You see, till now I've only always answered to your kindest boons with always growing boldness. Now, I must stop, absolutely, and for the first time I'll try to write you a letter without asking for something.

You know, I got the ten and the eight ones. I'm now so overwrought I forget sometime to breathe, nevertheless, be sure, you'll get back the books on 1st of October. You'll read a corking essay on Lewis, it will beat everything! You wait and see! Va sans dire, you'll receive the review. I've something to say about slang, also, it will be grand and glorious. I'll teach a few fellers that are now overflowing Italy with vacuum-gabble about America, what people must say and how they must say it.

As for coming to New York, till now I got no reply from the University, but the thing seems sure and I've only to wait somemore. Hardly I'll know a bit, it will be a rush to inform you, you bet. Then I'll teach you slang. Tony, I want to write here how like all get-out were both your last letters. A card! All stuffed with delightful expressions and spirit. I'm studying them as regular texts, and I got already lots of style's stunts from them. You tell the whole universe, what a teacher you are!

When you'll receive this, you'll already have written me what about the sweets, of whose sound arrival I'm doubting, however, it was so hot, these days!

I beg your pardon if this time I write you a comparatively short letter, but I want extremely to begin *Elmer Gantry*. And, say, Tony, let me know something I can do here in Italy for you, otherwise I'll be too shameful to write you any more. Whatever thing, from buying you a Fiat to find out a bride for you, I'll be glad to do it for you, you have been too kind to me!

Chicago, Illinois, June 30th, 1930
To Cesare Pavese, Turin

My Dear Cesare:
I have just finished with copying an article of criticism on Sinclair Lewis, which I think will interest you.[1] It is by one of America's foremost critics. I am inclosing it herewith and hope that it will serve your purpose, give you some new ideas, if needed, and in a general way be of use. Oh, yes, I'm still on the job, all right!

I received your letter of the 10th and as usual was mighty tickled to hear from you. So you got the books safely, eh? Good! How about the Lewis books, though? Did you get them – in all eight books in two packages? Don't forget to let me know – boy, I'm keeping my eyes on those volumes so they don't go lost! You now have until October first to read them, or rather, that is the date they must be back in the Chicago Library.

What the hell are you crabbing about the expenses for? Don't you know a good thing when you get it, huh? Why, you great, big bookworm; here I go and make everything hunky-dory for you and here you come along and crab! Where d'ya get that stuff, huh, where d'ya get it? Well, for your further information – using the same 'che diamine' you gave me, I'll have to tell you that I DID give you the amount of stamp expenses in the mailings! Allright, kick in now, c'mon, kick in and make it snappy! C'mon, don't nurse those liras; hand over! (How's that, eh?)

So you might be in Columbia this winter, eh? Boy, you can just expect a visit from yours truly, say at about Xmas time. I'll be there with bells on; and don't forget the drinks! You're good in English, there's no doubt about it – and if you keep it up, why, say, kid, you'll be getting to

---

1 The essay on Lewis is from the volume *The Men Who Make Our Novels* by Charles Baldwin, originally published by Dodd, Mead and Company (1926).

heaven some day with your shoes on! No kiddin'! If you ever should be asked to write your 'memoirs' some day for one of these syndicated magazines, please don't forget to give me a look-in on the immortality!

I received a letter from Mr Waldo Frank, in his own handwriting – as follows:–

> 'I have no copy of *City Block* at present in my possession. I can either have one sent you direct from New York, autographed, or, if you prefer, in September from me, and sign it for you before I mail it. Kindly advise me which you prefer.'
>
> *Waldo Frank*

I have already answered him that I am in no rush and that if he sends me a copy, autographed, in September, that will be just as well. So there you are, Pavese, you'll be getting this one, too, early in the Fall and with the Big Boy's John-Henry on it, get me? It will be a prized volume for you, no doubt!

By the way, if ever you want any volumes like this autographed, just let me know, and I'll hunt up the authors, even if they are out in Africa on a hunting expedition! I'll get the autograph or die! Just speak up, sonny, just say the word – et fiat!

I'd like to kick somebody all around the States, damn it! Can you imagine it? Yesterday the publisher's launched new editions of *Jurgen*[2] on the market at one dollar ($1.00). For one, little, lousy, silver dollar and here it cost you $2.50 about two months ago! It makes me sore not to be able to guess when they are going to pull these darn tricks! Yes siree, you could have saved one dollar and a half had you bought it now!

I received your box of candy, for which I thank you most heartedly, Cesare. I think the officials in New York got most of the liquor-centered chocolates for I received seven of them in all, the rest being merely the good quality solid chocolates! They filled in the sides of the box with paper – the damn crooks! Well, I got seven pieces, anyhow, which still makes me feel lucky! I did enjoy them, though, immensely – thanks to you! The box, too, was lovely, though it was unnecessary to go to this expense for me. This kindness, though, shall not be soon forgotten, rest assured; moreover I shall double up on my efforts to be of service to you, trusting that you will know, then, how much I appreciated the gift!

---

2 By James Branch Cabell.

Some mighty fine books have come out lately here in Chicago, especially one *Wolf Solent* which is acclaimed as the greatest book of all time! It is by one Powys! All the critics are greatly interested in it. I priced it the other day while down town and Oboy – they ask Five Bucks for it! Two volumes! I think I'll wait until they have another Stock Market crash – maybe I'll get it cheaper then!

A few days ago I sent you a copy of the *Columbia News*, which is a monthly review put out by the Conservatory in which I am now a faculty member – look me over! You will find my kind, handsome physiognomy on page Four, under the heading of New Faculty Members! Kindly meditate – contemplate what is there upon shown! I too am among the pedagogues, Cesare, but not for long, if I can help myself any! I've got to do something to get a start – so here it is! They pay me $4.00 an hour for teaching, so all I have to do is get all the pupils I can! The concerts will come later on again – and this you may tell Mr. Max!

I have a friend by the name of Raymond Papineau, from Green Bay, too, who is now in Italy and who was in Turin, on the 4th and 5th of June. Did he get to see you? I told him to look you up and that you might be glad to see an old friend of mine! He is very interested in literature and music – and is a journalist, by the way in Green Bay. Tell me all about your visit with him – that is, of course, if you had it.

So long, for this time, Buddy! I'll write again when I have more to say. Drop me a line once in a while to make this vacation of mine more pleasant. Need anything more? Just let me know, kid, that's what I'm here for! As ever your life-long pal and Buddy –

Antonio Chiuminatto

Chicago, Illinois, July 5th, 1930
To Cesare Pavese, Turin

My Dear Doctor Cesare:
I received your letter of the 23rd of June[1] just this morning, in fact, just a few hours ago. I immediately went out of the house to buy me a new typewriter ribbon, so that I could make myself ever so much more 'clear' to you!

1 The rough copy of this letter is dated June 21.

I take my hat in my left hand, while I extend a hearty and warm right hand in congratulations to you for the successful outcome of your thesis! All hail to you, Doctor, and all good luck! You certainly deserved it – even if those bums of teachers were too dumb to fathom intelligence in slang! You should worry a lot and build a house on it!

Now, as for my lecturing you, well, I'll be flabbergasted! Say, do you ever see something serenely comical, or are you like the Englishman who laughs in his old age over the jokes they told him when he was a kid? I wasn't lecturing you in seriousness, but as a matter of American kidding; we're famous for that! We drive the poison home with a kiss!

It is never any trouble for me to do you a favor, Doctor; remember this! Any kidding that I may hand you by way of lecturing is always done in a most friendly spirit, and therefor, it is unworthy of you to take me so seriously, so much so, in fact, that you become 'infinitely worried'! Well, I'll be cow-kicked by a mule!

Say, will you tell the customs officials in Italy that little Professor Antonio Chiuminatto, 4421 N. Lincoln St. Apt. 3-A – Chicago, Illinois, United States of North America, says that they can and may go and soak their heads in a wine barrel! That's what they're getting paid for – to open suspicious packages and thereby satisfy their womanly curiosity! Any deviations from this path of duty is a transgression on the moral rights of citizens as tax-payers! Next time I might even tie a lovely blue ribbon around the package, with a tag on which I might even write, 'Kisses from you[r] little darling honey' or something like that! They are SO sentimental, God bless them – and so DAMN lazy!

Hereafter as heretofor, I'm packing packages in my own little way, and may the best man break his neck trying to open them! I'm not going to take any chances on having books ruined or even knocked around and then have to replace them with new ones. I have too much respect for your pocketbook and for mine! When the day comes when customs officials replace ruined books for me, why, then, I'll just walk down to the sea-shore in New York and throw them over on the shores of Italy by hand, but until then, boy, I believe in rope, cardboard and more rope! And how suspicious those Italians are; ye gods, what consciences! They are about as suspicious as the woman who just can't stand to have her husband smile in his sleep! Ha!

Say, please don't let up asking things of me in your letters; I'd feel about as lost as the fellows do whose girls quit sending them their love! It's a case, Cesare, of something like the good old wife of gone-by days. Whose husband made it a practice of giving her a good beating up every

Saturday night, just before his bath! Well, one fine Saturday evening he came home and took his bath without beating her up – and what happened!? Why, the poor woman just dropped dead, heart-broken, because her husband had lost all his love for her! That's just the way we stand now, old fellow, so don't fail me – my heart is weak! Just think what might happen on the day I get one of your letters without the usual friendly request; why, naturally, I'd feel as though you were through with me – and then I should think of the daisies in Flanders' field! Get me? Even the Almighty said – Ask, and it shall be given you! And he, too, was telling [the] whole universe! Pretty soft, isn't it?

While you mentioned something about my style, let me tell you an incident which brought my pride to the bursting point almost! Sometime ago I wrote a letter to a literary friend of mine in a city not far from Chicago. He is a noted organist and writer – mostly musical subjects, though. Well, some days later I received a letter from Miss Buckman, of whom you know, and she wrote me that this musician friend of mine had had a gathering at his home one evening and that they had discussed my letter, its style, contents and what not – and had decided that I was a worthy successor of Mr. Haliburton,[2] who is America's foremost writer of travels and travel incidents. Get that, eh? Some day you might have to critize my writings, if my swell-head continues as it is, and when you do, please be kind, brother, please be kind! And, Dr Pavese, while I make little use of slang in my letters and also in my speech, yet, I'm all there as far as knowing it is concerned! Boy, what a wicked tongue, when I get started! Yes, sir, Cesare, and a girl may love you at the bottom of her heart, but there's always room at the top for somebody else!

Just as present I am reading Theodore Dreiser's *Jennie Gerhardt* and while I find it interesting and even amusing, yet it strikes me as belonging to the old school – as far as plot is concerned. He is an excellent writer, no doubt, but I still hold him as out of the times, at least, from this reading. He sees beauty in everything, where Lewis, for instance, seems to like muck-raking!

I also finished reading *Costumes by Eros* of Conrad Aiken, which you too have! There are some exceptionally nice things in it, especially 'Your Obituary, well written' and 'The Necktie' along with 'West End' and a very few more, although Aiken strikes me as peculiar in these things. He

2 Chiuminatto is probably referring to the popular adventure travel writer Richard Halliburton (1900–39), author of such works as *The Royal Road to Romance* (1925) and *New Worlds to Conquer* (1929).

is inclined to throw his story over to you – as though it weighed to[o] much on him! As a writer – he's a rare example of a good one!

I have been trying to find some very recent criticisms on Sinclair Lewis for you, but as yet have found none. They all seem to speak of him as far as his *Babbitt* – and that's all. I'd like to get something on his complete works so that you could have something complete to work on, though I am quite sure that after having read his books, you will be perfectly capable of taking care of yourself. I should like to have you have an American bearing on the subject, too, that's all!

When you get to Columbia, let me know and I'll pay you a visit. That'll be a BIT of a Big day and I don't mean Maybe! Slip me the mitt, kid, and slip it fast! That's what I call bringing home the bacon!

By the way, I have something else in store for you, but is not yours just yet! A new novel has come out, more in serial form, though, than in novel form, and it is entitled *The Big House*. It is supposed to be the most powerful story of prison life and is an American plea for prison reformation. You will easily remember, I trust, of the prison disaster in Columbus, Ohio, some months ago, when over 250 prisoners were caught in the terrible conflagration and lost their lives – like birds in cages! Well, an author, by the name of Jack Lait has taken upon himself the responsibility of the plea in a serial novel which has been picturized, and which talkie is even now running at the McVickers Theater here in Chicago.

The book has not as yet been published, but by special concession the *Chicago Examiner*, a newspaper, is printing it chapter by chapter in its daily publication. The illustrations are taken from the various movie scenes. From the 20 chapters I now have cut out of the paper I can tell you that it is not an outlined novel – it is a serial novel, that is, a novel, of course, but worked out in fragmentary depictings, which, as a whole constitute the plot. I know that you will be interested in it because of the immense wealth of slang.

Every evening as the paper comes out I cut the chapter out, comment it for you and file it away. When the story has run its course I shall mail it to you.[3] Now it's nothing elegant as far as printing goes; it is just the ordinary newspaper paper and the usual newspaper printing – but it will serve your purpose – and cost you nothing! The book will undoubtedly cost arount $4.00 when it is published – but by that time you will have it

3 The newspaper clippings of *The Big House* are found in the Chiuminatto folder of the Einaudi Collection at the 'Guido Gozzano–Cesare Pavese' Center for the Study of Pied montese Literature at the University of Turin.

already! And there is slang more than galore in it! You would not want it anyway as a regular novel – and yet the slang in it can be of much benefit to you – so I am sure that you will be satisfied with it. Just wait for it – you're busy now anyhow!

Well, Cesare, this will be all for this time! Congratulations once more on the success – and best wishes for the future – in America! And hit Sinclair Lewis – show the boys up! And then don't forget me. – As ever your Buddy –

Antonio Chiuminatto

[Turin,] July 20th 1930
To Antonio Chiuminatto, Chicago

Dear me,
Now I'm writing, I've just finished my essay. Some amendment yet, and it'll be ready. You see, I've not only already read the whole of the Lewis you sent me, but also criticized him. In some days. I'll pack, get registered and mail the eight books. I'm already through the Cummings and Lowell and beginning the Ben Hecht of the first package. Look me over! I wonder if ever there was in U.S.A. such a snappy eater of American language.

To day I got your kindly gift and toil of *The Big House* for which I've only, as it is my habit, to thank you, waiting for some occasion to reciprocate. As for the toil – the 'comment' – I can only say that you got the same sharp eye of your previous lists in the choice of the difficult words and expressions and that you are the slickest teacher I ever enjoyed.

Thanks to you a thousand times. Say, you are a kind of bewildered and staring in your photo of *Columbia News*: the new dignity locate you in the Heavens? There's a swell bunch of hot mamas, seems to me, in the school and you are always the old good mixer-and-cake-eater (ah!)

By the way, the sweets you got were not the sweets I intended to send you. There must have been a larceny in the customs, or, as I think it highly improbable that people there could get chocolates to fill again the box, it must be that doggone moll there in the 'Sweets' who assured me they would have packaged, they have mailed, they done the whole thing and after, instead of a box of Perugina and Preferiti she reached out chocolate-centers.

I'll yet speak about this. But you are unguilty and, moreover, you are yet dry, so you expect in a month or two to get true 'wet' chocolates to repair. As yet, I don't know anything sure from 'my' Columbia, but I'm in corrispondence with them and hope and dream. Would it not be a grand thing, were it only for the frolick you and I would have in old Manhattan? But it will go, it will go, by jiminy! I bet on it my whole life's blood.

As for the Lewis I read, you know, maybe he's not the great corker? There are, at least, three of your books – *The Innocent, Free Air* and *Elmer Gantry* – which can match with *Babbitt* and *Our Mr Wrenn* and *The Job* I had already, were not less. He's a genius, your Sinclair. I had a lot to say about him and yet I've only expressed a bit of what I found and admired in him. It'll require a long stretch, before I get the essay printed – some months they say, 'you understand, precedently accepted writings' – but you will be, if not the first to read it, the last at least to forget it – it is your work.

And now, with your kindly premission, I go 'to hit the hay' as I am ossified by a whole day of poling on the Eridanus – commonly, by the 'tote turineise'[1] called the Po.

Good night old socks and keep remembering your

Cesare Pavese

P.S. I thank – I'll die thanking – you also infinitely for the trouble you took typing that article by Ch. C. Baldwin. I found it very useful and interesting and should like, in order to have it quoted on the review, to know where and when you found it: that is, the title of the newspaper or magazine, in which it appeared, and its date.[2]

[Turin,] July 31st, 1930
To Antonio Chiuminatto, Chicago

My dear Prof:
Here is at last another literary specimen of mine to enjoy yourself. (You seem to fancy them).

1 The young Turinese women.
2 Pavese will cite Baldwin in his essay of Lewis, but without the bibliographic data.

I'll begin shrieking Haboy for your corking lingo – you are the most wonderful slanger (does it go?), nay you are turning out a regular writer, a creator of speech. I think someday the manager of 'my' sheet will send me a best-seller by Mr Chiuminatto-Haliburton to review. I won't fail then to point out my previous friendship with the Big Boy.[1]

Do you know, Tony, that my essay (I beg y.p.: my and *your* essay) has done kind of a hit in the office of the manager and editor etc.? It will appear on the issue of September[2] – maybe we are not so slow in the Old Land, eh? – and, tear your hair! *they asked me for another of them criticisms on Sh. Anderson,* good old Sh. Anderson, whose complete works you will now have to find out, and borrow and send me. I hope you'll now compare no more your gracious self to the forsaken wife of gone-by days. Won't you?

Really, could you – which I think, at this season of the year, a little difficult – gather for me the works I want, I should be exceedingly grateful to your person.

I am expected to hand over my essay before New Year's Eve and so, you see, we have plenty of time to ferret out and mail and read the books.[3] I'm, together with this letter, mailing back to you the Lewis with thanks to your friend Cand. Cady, and in some days I'll also have finished and packed the other ones: I've only three more of them to wade through.

So you think about the following books:

Sherwood Anderson:
Windy McPherson's Son (1916)
Marching Men (1917)
Mid-American Chants (poems – 1918)
Winesburg Ohio (1919)
Poor White (1920)

1 Famed boxer Primo Carnera was known by this name. In his letters in slang, Chiuminatto often used this nickname.

2 Pavese's essay on Lewis was published under the title 'Un romanziere americano, Sinclair Lewis' (*La Cultura*, 11 [November 1930], 906–27; in the index the title appears as 'Sinclair Lewis, Premio Nobel 1930'). The article was included in the collection of essays edited by Italo Calvino entitled *La letteratura americana e altri saggi* (Turin: Einaudi, 1951), 5–29.

3 Pavese's essay on Sherwood Anderson, 'Rassegne – Sherwood Anderson,' would appear in *La Cultura* in May of 1931 (10, 5, 400–7).

The Triumph of the Egg (1921)
Many Marriages (1922)
Note Book (1926)
Tar (1926)

Dark Laughter I already possess, *A Storyteller's Story* you sent Max, *Horses and Men*, and *A New Testament* were in your last package and I read them. However, I should be gratified, could you in your future Anderson package also include *A New Testament*, as it is a very difficult and important work and such as I should like to glance at during the composition of my essay. Get me? Naturally *if you find out some unspoken of work of Anderson, reach it out with the rest.* And also, va sans dire, I should be your lifelong slave, could you send me some criticism on the subject, the important and not-to-be-done-without ones. And remember, pray, to always note the date and place (title of the newspaper) of the eventual ones. And yet, this is the last blow, I should like to get together with Anderson's, the following two books by Gertrude Stein *Tender Buttons, The Making of Americans* (Anderson has been influenced by her).

Now, we are arranged and you'll have to run about with a new pair of shoes. What do you think of your lil old flea-in-the-drawers of a friend? Make it snappy, Amuriccano.

You see, my kidding is a little heavier than yours and his gist is always some unending trouble for the fellow. This sort is the renowned European kidding. How do you like it?

Now, I thank you another time for the gift of *The Big House* which is truly a gold mine of slang, a thing to be studied by heart. My admiration for your wonderful new language (about which I wrote 'something' also in my essay) has yet increased since the pleasure of your unforgettable conversation and to my eyes you are now the hero, the saint, representative of a new religion.

I adore words. For instance 'here is at last the promised *doremi*' what's more wonderful than this? And there are score of it!

As for Columbia I don't yet know anything sure. Now pardon me my long silence and have a friendly wallop on the shoulder by your.

P.S. Would you mind sending me a good explanation of the words: *bromide* (*bromidic*), G.M. (after a hour) *dope-fiend* – *up-de-dee* – I don't *film* well to *panhandle*?

Chicago, Illinois, August 1st, 1930
To Cesare Pavese, Turin

Dear Cesare:
Your letter mailed on the 21st reached me yesterday afternoon after a span of only ten days. There seems to be some darn good service on these coal-boats, eh? Pardon me, I mean, steamers!

Since you asked after that article of criticism I sent you let me tell you that I copied it from a volume of criticisms entitled – *Men Who Make Our Novels* by Charles Baldwin. The book of criticisms was published in 1926. It is a regular volume treating on all our contemporary authors and their works to 1926, of course. This is all I know of the book now without going down to the library for other information. I think, though, that this will suffice you.

Just as soon as I can find time to go back down to the Central Library I shall hunt up some more articles of criticism on Lewis for you – some of the more recent ones – as I am sure there must be some.

There is much criticism against Lewis in America, especially on the part of the Jesuits, who accuse him of corrupting the morals and in a general way of encouraging materialism. Speaking of books of Lewis' kind, the Rev. Daniel A. Lord of the Jesuits, noted American writer and critic, says in one of his writings entitled *I Can Read Anything – All right, then, Read This*! – 'Dirt is dirt whether it is written by a Boccaccio or a James Joyce or a Cabell, and all the smug hypocrisy in the world will never make it anything but DIRT.' He claims that men like Lewis can afford to walk in smut up to their necks, because that is their nature, first of all, and then, too, they receive handsome profits for it. The fact is that many of Lewis' books are on the Index.[1]

According to the Rev. Lord, S.J., depicting a life devoid of virtue, a life that is imbedded in materialism, may be realism, it may be true to life, all right, but it is bound to show us the castaways, the outlaws of life who cannot by any means enrich life but only reduce it to the commonplace. Writing of prostitutes and gangsters may be profitable, especially if you have a wicked pen, but it is never literature, never something that will remain. He has predicted that before this generation dies out Lewis'

---

1 Chiuminatto refers to the *Index Librorum Prohibitorum* (Index of Forbidden Books), a list of books once forbidden by the Roman Catholic Church's ecclesiastical authorities as dangerous to the faith of its members.

books will hardly be known – will hardly be read – they will die a slow and natural death.

Better still is the opinion of the Rev. Conroy, also of the Jesuits, who is undoubtedly an acknowledged author, an outstanding critic and a man of exquisite literary tastes. He claims that our 'best sellers' – novels by such men as Lewis, Hemingway, Cabell, and others – are like so many compositions of jazz music – but that not ONE in a million is a classic, not one could stand on its own two feet. Being like a piece of jazz music it appeals to the immense public in general – especially in these wayward and modernistic times – but that like all masterpieces they are different in as much as real works of art were made for the select minds and these too easily attractive volumes were undoubtedly written by simple minds for kindred minds. They are men whose literary ability is astute, he claims, they have realistic and wicked pens – but back of them is not even a single grain of substance – not a single thought that could ring true to tone – just a jazz theme nicely jazzed up for public enjoyment for some short time.

What say, Cesare? – I read *Farewell to Arms* some time ago and I must admit that it is downright dirty – and that in many pages you cannot excuse Hemingway's smut on the grounds of frankness. So does the teamster swear and curse – and he's frank – but you know what you think of him. There were times when I liked Hemingway, especially in some of his war scenes – but his dialogues are rotten – and the love affair between that officer and the English Red Cross Nurse is just too simple to consider. I haven't gained anything by reading him.

Say, I wrote and told you about those candies, those chocolates, not that you might get a hint to send me some more, but that you might know just how things were. If this letter gets to you on time, please don't trouble yourself to send me any more – I appreciate your willingness just as much as though you had actually sent me them!

If you get those books back to me in these days yet – why, say, I'll go down to the library and pick you out some four or five more and send them. At the rate you're going you ought to be able to give the whole library the once over yet this summer! Eat – hell – you don't eat them – you just inhale them, my boy! I'm almost afraid to pull any slang on you now; you may even correct me! Listen, though, Buddy; it surely is a pleasure to feed a guy like you. I don't have to use a spoon on you – a shovel is better!

Just keep right on remembering that you can get all the damned books you want – singles or in quantities. That's what I'm in Chicago for

– and by the way – Chicago is now the fourth city in the world with a population of over three million and a half! Look it over, will you? And I'm teaching in it! That makes it a better place to live in – what say?

Oh, boy – I'm just laying for that essay of yours – and my hands are already itching for it. I don't want any credit for it – but I will appreciate having a copy of it – all to myself! And with your John Henry, too, by the way! (Signature) So let's see you make it P.D.Q. (Pretty Damn Quick) (Alla svelta).

I may have plenty of time this month to myself – so I may even get some good book, with plenty of slang in it – and comment the whole thing for you. How's that ? I'm only promising, remember, as yet!

Write me again, old top, and accept all my best wishes. Here's hoping to see you on Old Manhattan and soon. If you have any need of books let me know – there are plenty of one-dollar editions now, and the library is full, too. Take your choice! Your Buddy as ever –

Antonio Chiuminatto

[Turin,] August 19th, 1930
To Antonio Chiuminatto, Chicago

Dear Tony:
I got your letter of 1st August and as I'm mailing back to you the other books of the Library I take the occasion to unite here a few lines, just a few, for you.

I shall be much gratified to receive other pieces of criticism, about Lewis; but, don't worry too much, because I cannot change anything on the drafts of my essay. Worry rather yourself, if worry you must, about Anderson.

I'll write about the ideas of the several Rev. Critics you quoted when I'll answer to your next letter. Now I'm in a hurry, I must make P.D.Q.

Important: On the 1st of September my address will change: the new one being Via Lamarmora 35.

By the way, I pray you, but take it leisurely, to look after the association conditions[1] of the following reviews: *Transition, The Scribner's*[,] *Harper's Magazine*[,] *This Quarter, Poetry, a Magazine of Verse.*

1 Pavese means to say 'subscription,' as he will note in his letter of 22 September.

And please don't cease to pull on me slang galore. I feed on it, do you know?

I beg a hurried pardon and (*in cauda venenum*) give you a last order: borrow or buy it, send me *Congo*, or *The Chinese Nightingale*, or better than all, *Collected Poems* (Macmillan 1923), by Vachal Lindsay.

Your always ashamed and never reformed friend

Chicago, Illinois, September 2nd, 1930
To Cesare Pavese, Turin

Dear Cesare:
Now that I have my storm-windows on (eye-glasses) I can begin to write. I have two of your epistles to answer now; the last one arrived just this afternoon. Some crusty cocky took the stamps off the envelope and here I am saving them, too. It must have been the mail carrier; I don't like the looks of his face anyhow – and his neck's too long! He has a face that only a mother could love – and the poor sap's an orphan at that!

Buddy, old timer, I might have answered you long before this, only that my mother was with me here in Chicago on a vacation. She just left for Green Bay this morning, so – Whoops! I'm free again! (I wont get home until morning – and maybe not at all!) Remember that song? Well, now that she has gone back I can fall into my regular stride again. I was home in Green Bay myself from the 15th to the 23rd of August – but since my mother then decided to come down here I also returned. I wasn't keen on staying around the house all alone.

I received the Lewis books – all of them, and in good condition. The package, though, was a sore looking sight; it surely was banged up some. Had it not been for the rope I hate to think what might have happened to the books. I shall not take them back to the library, though, until I have received the others you have; I'll make one trip only down to the Loop.

Thanks for the dollar-bill; now just what was it for – do you know? Stamps – mailing – or both? I do wish, though, you wouldn't trouble yourself like that. Being a musician I do like the sound of the good, old do-re-mi; those iron men, paper soldiers or what will you – always come in mighty handy. What say, Doc? And listen, Big Boy, don't you call me Big Boy, Big Boy!

Your request of books of Sherwood Anderson has gone into both my ears. I already have a complete list of his works, minus those you have read, of course, but how to get them is worrying me – and I don't mean Maybe! I can't get them from the library any more; second hand book stores have very little of him and very few people have more than one of his books. Unless I'm fortunate enough to land on some fool's luck somehow I'm afraid the only way to get them will be to buy them. Nevertheless, Cesare, old boy, you'll get them – sooner or later; just give me time.

I know that there are 95¢ editions of Anderson and still others at $1.25. These are not bad prices at all, a-tall, but wanting the whole works, the whole caboodle, is what counts. For the present, leave it to me; I only was in a pinch, Cesare, once in my life – and that was when a sweet little thing threw her arms around my neck and said, 'Mark Anthony, I'm your Cleopatra.' Still speaking of Anderson I shall try to get the ones you listed, along with *Hello Towns* which came out in 1929, and *The Modern Writer* of 1925. And, by the way, Cesare; how about Anderson's Short Stories? He has contributed quite a few, you know, to various magazines.

Speaking of short stories, I just cut one out of September's *Hearst's International Cosmopolitan Magazine*, 1930.[1] It is by Sinclair Lewis – and will be herewith inclosed. I don't even know what it's all about – since I ran across it just this morning and got it for you. With my compliments, then!

I'll look for Gertrude Stein's two books, too; don't worry.

Now for the slang explanations you asked about.

Bromide (bromidic) – È una medicina che si dà per male di stomaco o mal di capo ... come avviene, per esempio, in chi si ubbriaca [*sic*]. Da noi si chiama 'bromo-seltzer,' ed è effervescente.

G.M. – vuol dire 'Good Meal' (un buon pasto). Quando il dottore le ha prescritto la medicina, le dirà pure quando potrà poi mangiare a voglia Le dirà 'After an hour or so, take a G.M.' (Dopo un'ora dal più al meno si faccia un buon pranzo, un buon pasto.)

---

1 The short story by Sinclair Lewis is titled 'Bongo,' which Pavese mentions in his letter of 28 October.

dope-fiend – gli addetti ai narcotici, come i cocainomani, quelli addetti alla morfina, all'eroina, ecc. Tutti i narcotici, nello slang, sono chiamati 'dope.' Eppure tutte le droghe. 'Fiend' (demone – schiavo delle droghe). 'Dopo-fiend' – schiavo di narcotici.

I don't film well – vuol dire – che 'io non riesco mai bene nelle fotografie.' Da – 'film' che è il 'lastro.' Si dirà pure delle pellicole cinematografiche – oppure dei 'talkies.'
I have my picture taken every year, but I don't film well.

To panhandle. – leggere la vita con insistenza. (per [p]oi definirlo precisamente dovrei vedere la frase onde fu tolto.)

Say, Cesare, if you ever get to be King – give me a Dukedom, at least, will you? And whatever you do, don't reform; just keep asking. I admire the fellow who comes out into the open and fights. Like Carnera! Push-'em-over, Big Boy!

I have finished commenting a book for you; *Laughing Boy* by Oliver La Farge. It was the Pulitzer Prize Novel of this year. No slang, though. It is about the Navajo Indians of the Southwest at the time of American colonization – and I am sure you will like it – that is, when I can get the book and send it to you. Until then I'm holding up the comments.

I'd like to hand you a lot of slang, all right – but not this time. I have so darn much mail to answer that I'll have to make it snappy first. The next book I get on slang for you will probably be one on gangster life – and then, O Boy – you'll get enough to drown in. Then, too, I'm making up a list of modern slang which I shall send you sooner or later. Get a load of that, will you? – more slang!

Well, Cesare, say hello to Max for me. By the way, I have to answer a letter to him, too. Until the next time I'm your Sherlock Holmes! But I'll sign my name –

Antonio Chiuminatto

[Turin,] September 22nd, 1930
To Antonio Chiuminatto, Chicago

My Tony:
There's only a thing that's worrying me: I cannot make you the proposal

to 'give us the *tu.*' 'Twould sound grand and glorious, however, would not it? '*O thou who art* ...' (here I intended to write some extraordinary funny and clever superannuated phrase but darn it, it failed me and I'm here cutting the most deplorable figure).

Sincerely, our friendship lacks only this to become perfect. I want you to promise me that, would you ever have something to say to me in Italian, you will use the 'tu' like you do with Max. I don't know he is prettier or smarter to enjoy such privileges. Now to the point.

As for Anderson, I knew it was difficult you could succeed. I want you not to worry too much and here I write a note of the comparative importance of them books.

Mid American Chants. The Triumph of the Egg. Winesburg Ohio. Hello Towns. A New Testament. (They are all on the same degree of importance and not-to-be-done-without. You can buy some of them, also, preferably by second hand.) After them come in descending order: *Many Marriages. Poor White. Marching Men. Note Books. Tar. The Modern Writer. Windy McPherson's Son.* At last, Gertrude Stein's. Vachel Lindsay is another thing: you look after it with leisure and borrow or buy it, we have plenty of time.

Say, Tony, *I'm a fool* as sounds a tale by our Anderson in *Horses and Men*: I wrote 'association conditions' without glancing at the dictionary and naturally I was wrong: I intended to say '*abbonamento,*' '*subscription*': I should like to have someday a list of the prices of these magazines (you have the titles) in order to subscribe to some and be so more up to date with your doings. Can you understand, now? I'm very sorry of this unkindness by my part: to write an incomprehensible thing, and I assure you I'll henceforward be more careful.

Thanks to you for your happy intentions about slang. I'll be hanged if I am not owing to you my whole learning. Someday I'll try to reciprocate.

I called on Misses Franchi: they said me a lot of kind things about you and offered me a protector in America: whom I don't as yet want, as my dealings with Columbia are as yet unfinished and, at least, for this winter, I think there will be nothing new.

But. Patience is also a virtue.

Say, old socks, Max tells me you are unsatisfied with your America. How comes? I know that one's country is always more captivating when abroad, but you must not forget that coming abroad is also intended to augment one's understanding of the native country. And you, who are in the tremendous situation of being both an Italian and an American, you must try to comprehend the two nations, try to raise above the petty difficulties. Moreover you must not forget that we Italians are two distinct nations, the North and the South, and that we are the Northern and that the Chicagoans gunmen[1] are the Southern and there is a deeper difference of race and history between us and them that nothing could repair.

As for the money-making America think that all great nations were in the beginning money-makers, also Italy, when in the twelfth century a bunch of republics, and look in Anderson and Lewis for an escape from that.

Lewis will teach you how to understand and love the money-makers, the Americans, how to love them across irony, across that human tenderness which comes out from artistic contemplation: after all, the Americans of Lewis are good, very good people, and dear, also, in their somewhat childish psychology. And you've seen in *Arrowsmith* how this childishness can become in a nothing a true human and brotherly suffering.

And in Anderson you find your own problem uttered: Americans are money-makers, they cannot be artists or such: but you see in the very person of the author that artists can after all be born in U.S.A. and create a *new* art, which come directly from your *new* life: factories, humble people, tortured intellectuals, or artists themselves. You know: Anderson is somehow an Italian like you: his grandmother was Italian. You must think of this: you are middlewestern like your greatest contemporary writers (and not only money-makers), you are a son of two races and so you enjoy the odds of both: don't turn out a piker, a traitor, a four-flusher, an outlaw of the culture.

I expect something by you about this. Now good-bye and a manly wallop by your Buddy.

Chicago, Illinois, September 22nd, 1930
To Cesare Pavese, Turin

Dear Cesare:
I imagine I'll be hearing from you pretty soon, nevertheless, I'm writing. I received all the books in good condition and now they are all nicely

1 A reference to the rampant gangsterism in Chicago that prompts Chiuminatto to respond in his letter of 7 October.

resting up on the shelves of the Public Library, so much the wiser for their trip and experience abroad! What lucky books they are – and they don't even know it!

And I'm having one hell of a grand and glorious time trying to get the Anderson books for you! Just about now I feel like Napoleon about half way through the battle of Waterloo! The library makes no more concessions to me, the book stores won't rent them out and my acquaintances are so limited here as not to be able to get even ONE book, let alone a collection!

As a last resort I went to the famous Brentano book store – and asked for a complete list of Anderson's books, with the LOWEST PRICED EDITIONS! Here's what I got – so you're getting it – too!

Windy McPherson's Son	— $3.00
Marching Men (Out of Print)	
Mid-American Chants (Out of Print)	
Winesburg, Ohio	— .95
Poor White	— .95
Triumph of the Egg	— 2.00
Many Marriages	— 2.00
Horses & Men	— 1.00
A Story Teller's Story	— 1.00
The Modern Writer (Out of Print)	— 2.00
Dark Laughter	— 1.00
Notebook	— 2.50
Tar	— 3.00
A New Testament	— 2.00
Hello Towns	— $3.00

Now, Cesare, I just aint got the heart to figure this sum up – so you calculate the do-re-mi – huh? Those are the lowest possible prices – at the present writing! I'm still doing all I can to get them – one way or another – but it surely looks tough, what I mean! Wanting the entire collection, you see, makes it damn hard to get around now. I could have gotten them from the library on the vacation card – but now your just S.OL (Shot Out of Luck). (S.O.L. means 'to be shot out of luck – and you know what that means!) In short, you're S.O.L – P.D.Q! (Shot Out of Luck – Pretty Damn Quick).

I ran into a second-hand store the other day where I could have gotten a few volumes at reduced prices – but O me, O my – you want the collection, see – and if I had taken them where the devil could I get the others? That'll give you some dark laughter now! I've been able so far to do everything for you – and it fairly gets my nanny to be hampered now – it sorta cramps my style, see! Damn the gas company, anyway, – and the parish priest! Ye gods and little fishes! Ya, that's the way I feel, all right, all right – and I don't mean maybe or IF!

I'm letting you know just how I stand – still hoping I'll find the solution. If I don't, Cesare, don't blame me – it will be very evident I did all I could under all the conditions! In the library at Green Bay, for instance, they only have two volumes of his – so that's N.G. too – (No Good!). In the meantime I'll try to get Stein's two books for you and send them as a prologue!

Cheerio – old top – something has to happen. Until the explosion I'm your bomb –

Antonio Chiuminatto

Chicago, Ill., October 7th, 1930
To Cesare Pavese, Turin

Ciau Cesare:
Come stai, caro? Get that, eh? Hot stuff, what say? Say, I've been waiting until now to get a break from you like this and now that I have it I feel great! Place the mit[t] and let's shake; it's a go! Thou must also remember that in writing to me it's 'thou,' too! Oh thou fair faced son of Northern Italy, thou art verily ritzy; thou are truly magnolias, I mean, magnificent, pardon me!

Buddy, old socks! I thought sure as hell that you had forgotten me, that you were peeved about not getting quick service on those Anderson books. But along comes your letter of the 22nd of September now – and so all is well, all is quiet on the Western Front! Thou are verily of a comprehensive nature.

Cesare, there was absolutely no way of getting those books for you without cash, without the customary American do-re-mi. The Library was simply out of the question; the book stores would rent them but at prices that would be more convenient in the buying. Speaking of renting books from any book stores the prices are five cents (5¢) for the first day and three cents (3¢) for every day thereafter ... And no exceptions are made! Figure it out yourself now just how much it would cost you to rent the Anderson collection for only two months! I gasp for air at the mere thought of it.

I wore out a pair of shoes trotting from one second hand store to the other looking for Anderson volumes. Very fortunately, though, I know where I can get some of these volumes at good second hand prices. I already have my eye on *Winesburg, Ohio,* a second hand copy which is practically as good as new and for the price of sixty-five cents (65¢). It's a buy, I tell you – and you'll get it.

Now that I have the final dope on these books from you I'll immediately proceed to put into action with the customary pronto service. Within a few days one or two volumes, at least, will be on their way to you. It is also understood that I shall borrow whatever book or books I can and only buy them when all other methods fail hopelessly, definitely, sadly or otherwise. And this goes for Gertrude Stein and Vachel Lindsay.

By the way, that dumb sock of an author, Waldo Frank, promised to send me his autographed copy of *City Block* sometime last month already, but has fallen down on the job. I hope he's still alive, though, and prosperous. Just as soon as I get it – so will you!

Dimmi, caro Cesaruccio ... did you get the short story of Sinclair Lewis I sent you along with a letter of mine? I imagine it should have reached you by the date of your letter to me and I am merely wondering now whether or not you just forgot to mention it. I wanted you to get that, by all means.

As for the list of good magazines and their subscription prices, well – you'll have the information soon. I may even send you a few of them as samples. Please don't apologize; they are easy to get since people who have read them through only once are perfectly willing to give them away. And even if I were to buy some, the prices are not prohibitive. I'm at your service, you know – first and always, right or wrong! This little bit of enthusiasm comes from our American motto, which says, 'America, first, last and always, be she right or wrong.'

I am indeed sorry to hear that your plans with Columbia have not materialized as yet. I am sure they will, though, Cesare, so just be patient. And remember that if there is anything at all I can do for you from here, just let me know, see? When I shake the ashes, Boy, I shake 'em – and I don't mean maybe! I'll be hanged if I don't see you in America yet!

Say, Max got me all wrong on my feelings towards America. I merely wrote him my impression of Chicago and life as it is here. I have no kick to make personally save in a very general way. What Anderson says of America, what you say and what I said is all perfectly true – but that doesn't necessarily mean that I'm dissatisfied. I'm merely looking at a condition from a cultural standpoint, if I may be permitted to say so. To be personally dissatisfied would be an injustice to thousands of real people, thousands of educated people, thousands of artistic souls right here in Chicago!

I'm all hot and bothered about these damn Sicilian gunmen who have never done a damn thing but ruin the reputation of Italy. They are pimps, procurers and brothel keepers; they are assassins, usu[r]ers[1] and muscle-men, which means that they use threatening means to an end; they have become listed in America as 'public enemies.' Racketeers, just about all of them, they traffic in dope, liquor, women and whatnot!

It's all well and good for you to remind me that Italians are distinctly in two classes, the Northern and the Southern. But who the hell knows that but us Italians and about 10% of the Americans? The general conception of the Italian in America is based on the Sicilian make-up. Being an Italian in Chicago to-day is not so pleasant; people look at you askance when they know you are Italian, as much as to say, look out! And the general run of America will tell you that they are afraid of Italians, that they would not even rent rooms to an Italian. How do you like that, eh?

Last week I was beyond myself with indignation, damn it! The Police Department openly published a list of 26 'Public Enemies'[2] who were to be arrested on sight – and believe it or not, Buddy, old boy, 22 of them were Italians. And this is the case in every metropolis in America. I have the list here which I am going to send to Miss Franchi, as usual, but I'll quote it to you with the qualifications. Here goes:-

'Scarface' Alfonso Capone – Commander-in-Chief of Chicago rackets and responsible for at least fifty gang killings.

Antonio Volpe – Capone gangster with several killings to his credit.

Ralph Capone – brother of Al and beer boss of Cicero, Illinois.

---

1 Underlined in pencil, presumably by Pavese since he asks Chiuminatto for an explanation of this word in his letter of 28 October.

2 On 24 April 1930 the Chicago Crime Commission posted in public the names of 28 criminals, creating the first 'Most Wanted' list, headed by 'Public Enemy No. 1,' Al Capone.

Francesco Rio – A Capone watch-dog and notorious hoodlum.
Giacomo Ghebardi[3] – Capone machine-gunner.
Giacomo Belcastro – Capone pineapple-man.
Rocco Fannelli – Gunman and bomber, a terrorist.
'Wop'[4] Lorenzo Mangano – Boss of the Capone gambling syndicate.
Giacomo Mondi – Secretary of the Capone gambling interests.
Giuseppe Gennaro – proficient murderer, hi-jacker, bomber and what have you?
Samuele Campagna – One of Capone's toughest.
Filippo D'Andrea – City Hall Agent of Capone.
Carlo Fischetti – a Big Shot in rackets.
Giovanni Gennaro – brother of Giuseppe and of the same caliber.
Solomone Visione – Graduate of the Giacomo Zuta school of hotelkeeping.
Francesco Nitti – Director of the Capone murder squads.
Domenico Aiello – Lieutenant of the booze rackets.
Giuseppe Aiello – brother of Domenico and boss for the Moran gang.
Ernest Rossi – Another two-gun man of Capone.
Giovanni Armondo – A pleasant boy from Maxwell Street at anyone's orders.
Domenico Bello and Domenico Brancato – Aiello gun-men.

Hot stuff, isn't it, eh? And the list keeps growing day by day with the lovely surprises that two out of every additional three are Italians. Isn't that a swell list, though, with swell recommendations, to be published in every newspaper of prominence in America? Who wouldn't feel hurt – indignant? This is why I kick to Max – and not for myself.

There is no deep cultural atmosphere here, either, of which I probably kicked a little in writing to Max, too, but that did not mean that I was dissatisfied. I was merely commenting. My possibilities in Chicago are very promising, to say the least, and I love the city for its opera, its concerts, its lectures, its debates, its museums, its library – and God knows for what else! Mine was merely the indignation of an Italian over what I have just told you.

And still speaking of this, Cesare, I was going to spring a surprise on

3 Chiuminatto is probably referring to Vincenzo Gebaldi, better known as 'Machine Gun' Jack McGurn.
4 Mangano's more familiar nickname was 'Dago.'

you, a pleasant one for you, too – but now I'll make a break of it and divulge the so-called secret. I am at present commenting a gang story by the same author of the *Big House* – namely, Jack Lait. The story is entitled *Put On The Spot* and deals with the most intimate workings of the racketeers and the rackets. He wrote this story just very recently, in the hope of arousing public indignation against the 'public enemies.'

It is full of slang, more so than his other story! It is far more interesting and vital. And it will give you an exact picture of gang life in Chicago and in America in general. You'll like it! As a matter of illustration it is full of ACTUAL PHOTOGRAPHS OF GANGSTERS WHO WERE MURDERED, gangsters who turned out to be pikers, double-crossers, stool-pigeons[5] and whatnot. In another week or so the story will have run its length in the paper and then I'll send it to you with the comments, all stuff that you can digest in big doses. Yes, I'm always on the look-out for something of use to you. It certainly is a corker, Cesare, a real darby! And talk about slang – why, say, you'll get enough from this story alone to last you a lifetime!

Well, this is all for this time, old fellow! I have in mind, too, just what I'm supposed to do for you – don't forget it. Write me as soon as you can again – and until then think of me as your pal for life –

Antonio Chiuminatto

P.S. – I'll look up the definition of 'bromide' and 'bromidic' and let you know next time.[6] I still think that the use of these words is figurative, meaning such as adjectives like 'bitter' 'upsetting' 'revolting,' etc. which is the effect of 'bromide' as a medicine. However, I'll make sure!

[Turin,] October 28th, 1930
To Antonio Chiuminatto, Chicago

Dear Tony:
And so we're getting along pretty well, my boy, ain't we?

I'm shamefully late in replying to you, almost hopelessly late. Anyhow,

5 Underlined in pencil, presumably by Pavese since he asks for an explanation in his letter of 28 October.

6 Chiuminatto either forgot that he had explained the word 'bromide' in his letter of 2 September or wished to find a more specific explanation for his Italian friend.

here I am. Surely, I got the Lewis' short story and the two next Andersons, the *Testament* and the *Triumph.* You bought them, I think, and I'm now waiting for the bill stuff, do you know? Buy some more, buy all you can. I'm sure you'll do things better than I.

As for 'Bongo,' the short story by S. Lewis, maybe it ain't the old cookie! Here we have a little George F. Babbitt, in the shape of a circus bear lost in the funniest predicament: a clan of wild bears shocked with Bongo's civilized effeminacies, and what not. In it, however, our Lewis is no more much of a slang-slinger, but never mind. Perhaps it is I that have got so deep-rooted a slang-culture not any more to feel the novelties.

I thank you for the gift. Ditto be said for all your other designs, your troubles, *Put on the spot* etc. I'm on this side of the Atlantic gaping: not only your kindness is enormous but also it is everlasting.

Now rejoice, old-time, ferret out a prescription and with bells on get yourself sousy, cockeyed do death! Last week I rec'd the draughts of *our* essay to correct![1] In another week it will appear and you'll get it in three more. They procrastinated the whole, on account of its length: about a score of sheets! Fivehundred 'caviglie'[2] to guzzle and destroy! Your lire! I'll toast to your health till my own will be practically gone. Hand, hand over only more books and I'll sweep the whole of the peninsula with essays galore! Slap it in the face of 'em, Big Boy, slap into them!

I got also the Trio Chiuminatto,[3] the all-round-the-world-famous three Brothers and I wondered at the sturdy Jesuit. Fine stock ain't it? And you, the handle of them all! I hope to see you breathing someday in such a medium: 'twill be a glorious sunrise, then!

But let's come down to earth. I want you to explain to me: *usu*[r]*er, stool-pigeon* and *pine-apple man,* you darned Halliburton! By-the-way, I bought here a translation of Halliburton's *I conquer new worlds* (is it so?)[4] Not so bad, my boy, not at all. I should read some more with pleasure.

Take with leisure the Magazines stuff (have you got the list?) and Lindsay and Stein, and if I can be of some usefulness to you, ring only the buzzer, and I'm ready. Got me?

A hundred millionaire-pupils to your fiddle-craft and *one* she-pupil.

---

1 On Sinclair Lewis.

2 'Lire' in Turinese jargon.

3 Probably a photograph of the Chiuminatto brothers, one of whom was a Jesuit.

4 The original English title is *New Worlds to Conquer.*

Chicago, Illinois, November 11th, 1930
To Cesare Pavese, Turin

Dear Cesare:
So you're still alive and kicking, eh? I was just wondering what in the devil had happened to you. This is Armistice Day, so we'll smoke the old Indian pipe of Peace!

Say, I've been so darn busy in the past month that I hardly had time to think. I meant to write you but as it is you wrote me. From to-day on now I hope to take things a little easier, which means that I'll be able to give you your due attention.

So you got the books, eh? That's fine! The *New Testament* will set you back just exactly $1, one solid plunk – and you may consider yourself darn lucky to get it at that price. The *Triumph* will make you dig in for an even $1.25 and this was so excellent a buy that I was tempted to keep the book myself. You're what I call lucky – and I don't mean MAYBE! The full bill as it stands, then, is for $2.25. You have no other worries.

I had to run this town foolish in order to come into contact with these volumes ... but for you, old timer, I like it. If I ever come to like my sweetheart like I like you, well, say, I'd jump off a 40-story skyscraper into a glass of water for her. Yes, I would — NOT! Within a few days, to come back to the subject, I'll send you some more books of Anderson, just as soon as I find time to get around to those joints where I saw them. The last one of Anderson's books you're going to get will be *Marching Men* – because the lowest second-hand price I can get on it is $6.00! Think that over, will you? As for Stein, Lindsay and our Anderson, just be assured that you're going to get them!

I was going to send you *Put on the Spot,* but now I'll have to wait. Some of the chapters are missing in my collection, so I'll have to get the book when it comes on the market and comment from that. Too, there is a sequel, *Gangster Girl* which I may also send you. Just stick around until you get a red nose; you'll get it all sooner or later.

So the essay is ready for the March, eh? And what a price! Put her there, Buddy, right in the mitt; you're good! If I had your brains I wouldn't work any more! I'd retire on my good looks! You might add, if you're still in time, that Sinclair Lewis has been named for the Nobel Prize, which he has accepted. I just read an account of this very few days ago!

In my next letter I'll try to include a list of the magazines you asked about; I'll have to go to the library first. And I'll renew my promise to send you some shortly ... I mean, magazines, of course.

A 'stool-pigeon' is a spy (una spia); such are called detectives, secret service men, and the likes. The word comes from 'stool' (sediolina) and 'pigeon' (pigione) [*sic*], the bird that always flies home. In this case, no matter where the spy may be, he always goes back home to police headquarters and reports his finds. Some gangsters, for instance, after years of notoriety, turn stool-pigeon to save their hide, but if found out they are put on the spot, as was Lingle, the newspaper reporter.[1]

A pineapple is a hand-bomb (una bomba a mano) used by gangsters to force their way into control of legitimate business. Pineapples were used not so long ago here in Chicago, to force beauty shop owners to contribute to gangsters for protection and higher tariffs. These hand-bombs are called pineapples because they look much like a small pineapple (l'annanas) and are used like a hand-grenade. Some beauty-shops, to continue, refused to be under control of muscle-men, men who want to force themselves into a legitimate business for profits. The gangsters succeeded in getting most all beauty-shop owners to join a sort of league, under the regulations of which the prices of services were raised considerably. Girls and men working in such shops were obliged to pay a certain sum a month for the privilege of having their jobs protected, and of this sum 20% went to the gangsters, who had promised to see to it that there would be no violations of the regulations. A few shops objected and one lovely night, around midnight, some pineapple-man just threw one of those nice little things into the doorway and blew the shop to hell! These shops just had to conform to the dictates of the gangsters, otherwise their business would have been ruined. One shop owner went so far as to rebuild his shop for business, and the second day after he was back to work another pineapple was launched from a passing automobile, ruining him so badly that he was unable to get back on his feet and had to work by the day for some one else! This is the gangster world of Chicago, supreme and all-powerful! A pineapple man, then, is an individual who is hired by the gangsters to throw these hand-bombs or pineapples as needed and where needed! A 'gunner' instead is a gangster who is paid to do nothing else but use a machine-gun or a revolver as he is told, for which he gets a monthly salary from his chief and a stipend in the form of cash for every man he bumps off – something like the 'boia' in France. He is the paid killer, in short!

Well, Cesare, this will be about all for this time. I want to get caught up on my mail and then I'll write you again. Don't forget the essay – and also remember that little by little you'll get the Anderson books, for as

---

1 Alfred 'Jake' Lingle was a corrupt crime reporter for the *Chicago Tribune,* who was gunned down by the mob on 9 June 1930.

low as possible a price. I'll assure you that when I buy one of these books it's at the very very best that can be done. Anderson is still living, you know, and his volumes are costly – even second hand – but so far I was able to find two of them for you, in very good condition, too, for half-price. I don't think you could do better anywhere in America! My full and whole-hearted services are at your disposal!

How's the old burg over there this Fall, eh? I'd like to be there with you just about now – say, in the Mugna.[1] How are the mammas? Have you any of them feeling 'that way,' I mean, in love?

I'm coming along fine – but I haven't any she-pupil yet, much to my regret. Better luck soon! I gave a concert last Friday and got away big, you know, like a house afire! Oh, it's a gay life, Cesare, if you don't weaken!

S'long and good luck! Step on the gas with an answer now and let's see you knock my eye out with another letter like this last one. As ever

Your Buddy
Antonio Chiuminatto

[Turin,] November 26, 1930
To Antonio Chiuminatto, Chicago

Dear Tony:
I got your last letter of 11th. Nov. And make haste to reply. You'll receive separately the everlasting essay with the due dedication.[1] I was greatly favoured by the Nobel Prize and many a guy, who should otherwise have ignored my (b.y.p. your) work, has been obliged to sling his five lire on the counter. I am the only person in Italy to-day who knows all about Lewis. And so I'm highly priced on the market. Our plodding begins coming home, does not it?

But, there is sad news. Buddy, you know, my mother is dead.[2] I should be lonely as the devil, were it not for my good married sister with whom

1 Cafe Mugna.

1 At the bottom of this rough copy of the letter, the following line is written: 'To my dear, dear Buddy in America, who let me in a new world.' It is probably the draft of his dedication to Chiuminatto.
2 Pavese's mother died on 4 November.

I'm dwelling now. Of course, I'm pretty well... I only wanted you to know.

Leaving dirges aside, I get along thanking you for your kind troubles. Only, about that terrible Anderson-fellow, be careful – if you are yet in time –: wipe from the list *Winesburg, Ohio* and *Poor White.* (I found here a cultured lady who lent them to me.) Of course, if you have already bought them, it is my absolute will to have them and pay for.

As things are now, I should be satisfied upon receiving only more *Mid-American Chants* and *Hello Towns* (absolutely both). I think I could manage to get my article on that.

Do you know, my boy, I'm translating *Our Mr Wrenn*? The Nobel Prize's awakened Eyetalian publishers and I'm drudging now six hours a day about this book. New worries for you. Of course there is something here and there I'm afraid I don't quite understand, and so I'll send you someday the very book with all difficult words underlined ... will you then be so kind, as to send me, a last time, some of your thorough explanations? Honestly, let me know before, whether you have the time.

Surely, your bargains are all genius strokes and I can only compliment myself for having stumbled on such an agent ... I beg your pardon, I'll pay you next time. I've now not the time to get the greenbacks and I want you to have the letter.

Thank you for the explanations on gangster life which truly is turning out every day more as the lovely Mafia, and don't take much trouble about *Put on the Spot.* Take care of your health. You are lucky enough, gangsters did not put an eye on fiddling-teaching the way they did on beauty-shops.

Miss Franchi wrote you about the 'Lega d'insegnamento,'[3] she says to me. But, as yet, you don't know anything about my (your!) new English class. I keep in the same room perhaps, where you had yours. What brazen-facedness! And say, among my she-pupils there are some exceedingly good-lookers, hot-scorching-mamas, we should say. My dear, old timer, I feel swoozie, while begetting English nonsenses in their youthful minds (ah!). I'm seriously thinking about love, do you know, 'that way,' love and death, all this stuff, going wild, my boy. Nope, be sure, we'll yet meet in lil ole Manhattan.

3 See note 2 to letter of 29 November 1929.

P.S. Say, book-clerk, would it not be possible to let Sinclair Lewis, – I mean, the actual Mr Lewis – have as a humble token of my admiration a copy of the everlastingly blooming essay? Try and find out his address. 'Twould be great, would it not?[4]

Chicago, Illinois, December 6th, 1930
To Cesare Pavese, Turin

Dear Cesare:
I may not have written to you for quite some time, nevertheless the same is true of you. What's the matter: in love? Miss Franchi tells me that you are teaching at the Lega[1] and O boy, I know those girls – and how! When I heard you were teaching there I almost wished myself back on the old job again. That would be swell, eh?

I suppose you have been wondering why I haven't sent you any more books. Well, Cesare, it's like this: I've been saving my pennies to buy those confounded Christmas presents that are a great conventionality with us Americans. I assure you, though, that you'll get your books soon now, if you will only be patient.

Speaking of books, Mr Waldo Frank just sent me his copy of *City Block.*[2] Really, I don't know how to handle this proposition now. I'll tell you why. I ordered it last May, you know, when you told me to do so – and here he sends it at Christmas time.

It's a lovely volume of some 300 pages in sketch form, marvelously written, though I don't like his choice of subjects, which are dreary. This is the only edition in English, published by the author himself, since the book was forbidden public circulation. There are only 1225 editions in all of *City Block* and this one is numbered 116. Moreover, as you remember, I asked Waldo Frank for his autograph: he got very generous, instead, and sent me a dedication with his signature. It runs 'To Prof. Antonio Chiuminatto with the best wishes of Waldo Frank.'

---

4 The entire postscript is crossed out.

---

1 The *Lega d'insegnamento.*

2 This copy is located in the Pavese library at the 'Guido Gozzano – Cesare Pavese' Center for the Study of Piedmontese Literature.

He wrote me that the price of this volume was 7 dollars – a special price he would make me since I told him I would eventually send it on to Italy. I wrote him that the price was a bit too stiff for me – so he opened up his heart and sold it to me for 5 dollars, which I sent him yesterday.

Here's the proposition, Cesare. You ordered the book, but without the autograph in my name, so you're not obliged to take it. I shall send it to you within a few days; you may read it as many times as you like and then return it to me. If you decide that you want to keep it, that the autograph and the price are all right as they are, well – that'll be a go with me, too. And please give me your full impression of this book, since I find it hard to fall into step with it. I repeat it's a lovely volume and powerfully written, but his choice of subjects is so extraordinary I don't wonder the book was forbidden circulation! At times it's almost depressing. Remember, now, suit yourself as to what you want to do – buy it or send it back; either choice will suit me!

I'm still waiting for your essay, you know, so shake a leg! And how did you like the *Triumph of the Egg*? Within the next ten days I'll have some more of Anderson's book on the way to you.

I still have to finish commenting *Put on the Spot.* It shouldn't take me long, though, since the book has already come out. If I could only lossen [*sic*] my do-re-mi I'd be all right, but we're too near Christmas now and a lot of people are dreaming of presents and more of them! Thus, you see, my book change has to stay with me. We'll fix that up, though, old Scout, don't worry!

The 27th of last month, you may not know, was Thanksgiving day. Well, the folks in Green Bay celebrated by having the garage burn down with two cars in it! How the fire started nobody knows, but the fact is that we lost the garage and both cars. Luckily enough we have insurance on them but there's still a loss. That's what I call tough luck, see!

Tomorrow will be a big day in American football history, Cesare. The Green Bay Packers, from my old home town, North American Professional Champions, will play the Chicago Bears in a title match. Our team has been the victor since 1927, having at that time taken the championship from the Bears which they have never been able to recover.[3] Over 5000 fans from Green Bay are coming to Chicago tonight on the

3 The Green Bay Packers became NFL champions in 1929, the first of three consecutive championships.

special train, my brother included – and what a glorious day tomorrow will be if WE win! The Green Bay Packers are the most powerful professional football team that American history has ever known, having suffered but ONE defeat in three years! And that one NOT by the Chicago Bears, either! The advance sale of tickets shows today that over 117,000 people will see that game tomorrow – and I'll be one of them!

The most interesting thing about this game, as far as I am concerned, is that the real fight will be between Italians. The Chicago Bears have one young fellow, Giuseppe Savoldi, who is acclaimed the greatest football player turned out in America since the famous Jim Thorpe, American Indian, and if anyone can make the Packers lose the game, he is the one![4] On the other hand, the Green Bay Packers have two powerful Italians, Bo Molenda and Francesco Carideo, both shining stars.[5] The former has the reputation of being the greatest kicker of a football ever seen on a campus and Carideo is known as being the greatest field general when it comes to brain work! Oh, Boy – Cesare, that is going to be SOME game – and I don't mean Maybe! I'll give you the dope on it when it's all over – and we are the 1930 Champions!

We had quite a bit of snow here last week, but so far this week it's been almost like summer, like Indian summer as we call it! Only a few more weeks and I go home for Christmas; two weeks' vacations. Maybe I'll get some work done for you, then, what say?

Ya, I'm still teaching and going strong! Business is on the bum in America just now, but we're hoping it picks up. There is so much unemployment that the problem is really serious and needs attention. I still have my few lessons every week which keep my head above water, at least.

How about some news from you now, eh? C'mon – snap out of it – and give me a break! I'm still on the job for you, remember – so give me plenty to do.

Say, we're having a play in Chicago from the Italian; it's called *Death*

---

4 Late in 1930, just after the college season had ended, the Chicago Bears signed Notre Dame University's All-American fullback 'Jumping Joe' Savoldi before his college class had graduated. Savoldi played three games for the Bears and then retired to pursue a successful wrestling career. The Chicago Bears' roster included legendary stars Red Grange and Bronko Nagurski.

5 Frank Carideo was a first-team All-American quarterback in 1929 and 1930 and during these years led Notre Dame University to two undefeated national championships. He was not, however, on the Green Bay Packer roster in 1930.

Takes a Holiday.[6] What do you know about it? It was quite a hit – according to the critics.

Good luck and good-bye until next time, Cesare. Let's hear from you soon. As ever, your old Buddy

Antonio Chiuminatto

Chicago, Ill., December 18th, 1930
To Cesare Pavese, Turin

Dear Cesare:
I received your lovely letter and the essay, which I was so anxious to have. But first of all, I want to express, most sincerely, my sympathy for the loss of your Mother. Just as I came to the front after my years of study I lost my Father, and you, almost under the same circumstances, your Mother. Be sure, Cesare, I can sympathize with you and most heartily do! Remember the evening you sat with me in the café San Carlo – and Jack Hilton's Orchestra was at the Torino? Well, that was one night already through which my Father was slowing [*sic*] dying. Knowing you, I know you'll look ahead to realities, in spite of this loss, but once in a while you, too, will take time off to cast a lingering thought back into the past, your Mother's past. There is more good even in that than you may now realize. But why am I talking to you in this tone? Buck up, old fellow, and smile with the world!

I must congratulate you on the success of the essay. I find it perfectly marvelous – and I defy some of our own critics to show me their knowledge of Lewis and his works as you have done. I have translated your essay into English and plan to read it to some of the Lewisan fanatics, who will still learn a thing or two. If I can have it published in some of our literary reviews, I shall tell you how much I was given for it – and then use that money to buy you your books. How's that? It will take some time, of course, but that's my plan. The criticism that Lewis and his personages are provincials will not be taken so gaily, so cheerfully by these Americans, but we'll attempt it. Too, *Arrowsmith*'s Leora is not a likable type with us – which will show you contrasting viewpoints of environment.

---

6 English version of Alberto Cassella's *La morte in vacanza* (1923).

I am more than ever interested now in Anderson for you. I have checked off my mind the books you spoke of – and I am double-checking the ones you are still to get. My Christmas money ought to turn the trick for you. Don't worry, though, I'll still find a way to get the whole collection to you, so that you can do as much justice to Anderson as you did to Lewis. If you'll just be patient – or as impatient, rather as I am!

As for *Mr Wrenn*, my big opportunity as a friend has arrived, I guess! Whoopee! Say, Buddy, just send me the whole book, marked, and with it your translation – so that I can cross-examine the entire work, not to criticize your handling of it, understand, but to help you find the 'perfect' translation. I won't take any credit for it – except from you, if you choose to give it to me – and I should like to know that translation is the one and only one. No one else need later attempt a 'better' translation. Get me? And it can be done, for in the 'listening' Italian is as good as English to me, though I may not write it as well. I can help you much here – as Tirotti[1] and I once attempted with *The Scarlet Letter* but on which Tirotti weakened. If you'll send me the complete work – book and translation—I'll be all right for a perfect handling of the situation ... And you won't regret it. I'll put my whole time at your disposal, too.

I've already planned to look up *Our Mr Wrenn* in Green Bay on my two weeks' vacation for the holidays. I'm leaving for there next Tuesday morning and I'll be returning on the 5th of the New Year. I'm going to keep you in mind, though. This proposition of *Mr Wrenn* interests me immensely – and I'm only too glad to be in on it with you. Get the recognition, Big Boy, get it – I'm with you on that!

So you have an English class where I had mine, eh? What is yours, first year? I was lucky in my last year there to have a third year class, a small number of pupils and mostly intelligent. It was pleasant work. Here's the same good luck to you, Cesare – but look out for those scorchers! I think some of the other teachers had all the good-looking mammas; they got the real breaks; I didn't.

Well, well – so you're seriously thinking about love; some little tootsie has put you on the spot, eh? Put her finger on you! Well, if she's got you feeling 'that way' I give her credit – she must be good – and HOW! I wonder if she knows she's mighty lucky to get a fellow like you? Go to it – Cesare – wedding bells always sound good to your own ears, you know! I feel sorry for those other mamas in the Lega; it'll be hard on them. A

1 Chiuminatto's Turinese friend.

good man should be generous, you know, but there you go and turn out selfish!

Well, Christmas is here again, Cesare, and I'm trying to think of some way to celebrate. Whether it'll be with water-guns or knives and forks is still hard to decide. Nevertheless I am going to paint the old town red – a blazing red! I think I'll smoke cigars, carry burnt matches in my pockets and spit against the North wind! That ought to get 'em, eh? I'm getting to be so hard, any way, that I have to sleep nights with one eye open to keep a watch on myself!

I wish I were back in Italy for these holidays. They don't mean much in America except buying presents and getting drunk. This is the week, you know, I swear off my girl friends! I'll renew their acquaintance again the second week of the New Year. It's the American plan of economy, that's all.

I lent your book of *City Block* to a very interested friend, so I'm afraid you wont get it until after the first of the year. Frankly, I don't think you'll need it before then, and this fellow would like to read it – since it is a very uncommon book, indeed, as affairs of purchasing. I mean you can't buy the book anywhere –which makes it so desirable.

I'm going to the opera this evening to take in Tannhauser. Somebody got generous and gave me a six-dollar ticket, so why not! All I have to do is dig out my Tux and look natural! Someone may take me for Hoover or McCormick.[2] And, by the way, I'm going to take note of the soup-and-fish suits to-night, just to see how right you are in the criticism on Lewis! We think we are natural, you know – even if we kick like Babbitt. Dress suits are getting to be a fad over here right now – worse than football, almost!

When in Green Bay I'm going to try to get what books I can for you from the library on a three months' plan, as before. That's why I've been holding out of late; they ought to have something, at least, and that would always be better than nothing. If one could only wait, how nice it would be! Do you know you can get every darn Lewis book now for 75 cents (75¢)? Yes, sir –the Nobel Prize made his books of the popular kind. I wish something like that would happen to Anderson, too – and in a hurry, if you ask me?! (Why the question mark?)

Be good, Cesare, and keep in touch with me always. We can be of some help to each other yet; I'm tickled pink over the new prospect, you

2 Colonel Robert Rutherford McCormick, newspaper baron and owner of the *Chicago Tribune* from 1920 to 1955.

know. Mit[t] me, Big Boy! Stick her here, right in the ole glove! Now pump!

Until next time – your pal

Antonio Chiuminatto

[Turin,] January 9th, 1931
To Antonio Chiuminatto, Chicago

Dear Tony:
It's a rotten world this, ain't it? Now that you are so keen about helping me in the translation, it all turns out the other way round.

You know, I already mailed the ms. to the publisher and I got only that copy of it and, when I'll receive the draughts to correct, I must send them back in two weeks. So I cannot, as it is my fond desire and your friendly offer, send the whole for you to look over.

But I won't even trouble you with the book, for there are comparatively little cryptic sayings (*Our Mr Wrenn* is the first and so the least slangy of Lewis' works) in it and I found here a Webster's Dictionary which explained to me almost all of technical words. Yet there were your previous lists of phrases which served me a good turn. And so I want, now, nothing more than the explanation of this title of a song *Waal I swan.* (I think it has a spelling quite of its own.)

Certainly I regret that you cannot cast a glance on my Italian in order to improve and fix it but go on and speak to publishers!

But there's consoling news: perhaps I'll undertake two more translations (as I don't as yet know which) and then ... I'll take advantages of you.

Here is at last the mazooma of the *Egg* and the *Testament*: you seem badly injured by Christmas gifts ...

You read about these two books in my essay (if I'll ever put it down) and so, I think, soon. It would suffice to me now to have *Hello Towns* before the month has ended. Wipe from the list, if you're yet in time, *Tar* which I got here.

About *City Block* you surely must send it (when you will have it back) and as you are such a bosom-friend of mine the dedication will be better yet than done for me.

And so you liked the essay, eh? I'm mightily glad, but keep an eye peeled.

I'm a little devil of a writer and I don't say 'provincials' in a bad sense: I mean Lewis' people are healthy, unsophisticated and strong. Get me?

But I'm tickled to death by your proposition: to have some ideas of mine, printed in an American review! I'll sit on the top of the world.

Lastly I got acquainted with some opinions of your foremost critics about the Nobel Prize. They all say it's an offence to America, a shame, etc., but I should like to have some of them highbrows here to teach them how to defend themselves. These guys seem to ignore that almost all great American writers were discovered in Europa before. So it was with W. Whitman, so with H. James, so with Lewis. In USA the average people read and like them but they cannot gainsay the laureated asses who are, as in the Old Country, the *learned* men; the profs., the scholars.

And it is perhaps the greatest feebleness with you Americans, who are so healthy and youthful and forward looking in everything, that you so much respect university men, stuffed with non-digested classical learning, the pettiest and damnedest buttinskies woman's love ever produced. Oh, how I should like to beat someone's block off in this quarrel about Lewis! I feel myself Italian to the marrow, a wop, (you remember Dante Alighieri's sentence) 'a color che così ragionano si vuole rispondere col coltello e non con le parole.'[1]

But I must stop otherwise I'll put on fire the sheet.

Say to whomsoever you meet making fun or saying that Lewis is clever, but no creator, that a not-so-stupid-after-all Italian reader maintains that he (the 'whomsoever') is 'fesso,' un cretino, un coglione, nay, not a *coglione* for to be such would require a degree of virility the speaker certainly has not.

How do you like this?

We are yet the Renaissance rabble in Italy, ain't we?

As for love, don't be afraid: 'know mammas and no kiddies' is my motto.

I like exceedingly your plan of economy about girl-friends and I'll try it, but, I fear, it will succeed only the first time.

And send books books books I'm here roaring for books, for *Ameri can* books to guzzle. By the way look after a tract, that must be published in a magazine named *Form*: it is by a George Frederic Nieberg, entitled *The American Slanguage.* I – and methinks you also – should like to glance it over.

I don't know anything about *Death takes a Holiday*. Perhaps the title has

1 *Convivio,* IV, 14, II.

been changed, and then ... Moreover, I'm quite disinterested in theatrical shows. I prefer movies (another heresy that would send afire your learned people).

Chicago, Illinois, January 23rd, 1931
To Cesare Pavese, Turin

Dear ole Doc:
Let me tell you, young fella, there never was a snappier guy in all these 48 states than I am! Here I get your letter in the morning, and in the evening I send you the answer and the books you want!

I received the two dollar bills intact – corners and all – for which I thank you sincerely, heartily and cheerfully ... Hell, yes! And I've already spent them for other books. That's me, kid, that's me, all over! What do we care about expenses, eh? We've got a lot of 'em! And another thing, Doc old Buddy, if you only knew what pleasure it is for me to get letters from you, you'd write more of 'em, too!

Business before pleasure! I have the honor of telling you that on this very evening – aye, before another sun arises on this dismal globe – a packing of books will be enroute to you. In the package you will find the following:

Sherwood Anderson	— HelloTowns	— $3.00
	— Many Marriages	— $1.00
Waldo Frank	— City Block	— $5.00

What I have already written you about *City Block* still holds good, id est – if you want to buy it – one look at the price will be just as good as a dose of morphine – and if you don't want to buy it, just read it and return it. I shall be equally contented in either event.

I had to buy *Hello Towns* in a NEW edition, for the simple reason that there is no other edition available. And from what I hear in authoritative circles, there will be no other edition of this volume, due to the fact that this book, in particular, is not a rapid seller! Many volumes of this edition, and the only one so far, are still unsold. *Many Marriages* is now to be had in the Dollar-Edition, so I bought it, also new. Believe it or not, Cesare, I chased all over stores until I was blue in the face and sore in the feet, looking for second-hand editions of Anderson. There aren't only a few – and those his earlier works which you already have read. With these two volumes you have his collection just about complete, I think. If I am not mistaken, you have read every one of his books now but these following ones:

Windy McPherson's Son (1916)
Marching Men (1917)
The Modern Writer (1924)
Notebook (1926)

You have done well, indeed! Should you want any of these I can always buy them for you, understand, though I fear there is no other way of getting them to you. Remember, too, that with the first of June I shall again be able to send you all the books you want for three months, just like last year. Prepare your list now – do your rushing early! And with this we open up another account; blue ink, $4.00 and red ink $5.00 (which means a credit of the former and a debit for the latter, which MAY or MAY NOT become a credit later).

And now, Cesare, remember your strength; My Gawd! Be good or I'll have to slap your wrist! Why the very idea – calling American critics 'coglioni'! As you said, I don't mind the 'fesso, cretino' and so on and so forth, but I object to the other appellation out of respect to – well, you know!

I fear, though, Cesare, that with your being perfectly right, you will find hardly a single critic who likes Lewis in America. As for myself, I like Lewis as a creator of language, a creator of expression more vivid than we have ever known. He is powerful – and vast. But I, too, will come to the defense of America, claiming that Babbitt, Gantry and Arrowsmith are not typical personages, characteristic Americans, as might be inferred from a reading of those mentioned, but I want to tell you – they certainly don't constitute the majority! But I will say – and repeat – that as a writer Lewis is unique – and that in the mere matter of his art, writing, I am the only one in any argument any where over here 'colui che lo difende a viso aperto.' (With apologies to Dante.) I am not always in favor of his ways of attacking characters, though. For this reason I'd like to see some Review over here publish your essay – that is, if God will give me time to translate it and time to refer myself to the texts for the extracts you have made use of in the essay! An European viewpoint, which we never get over here – I wonder why! – might strike a few nails on the head!

I'll try to look up that article on 'Slanguage,' too, when I can, and then send it to you. I also discovered while at home in Green Bay that

Lewis has written another Short Story for the Cosmopolitan; if you're interested yet, let me know and I'll send it to you. Yes sir, Cesare, when you roar for books, yap for them and cry for them, the plea falls upon my ears as that of the infant pleading for a piece of bread to its mother! Now I ask you – how can I overlook you? Damn it – old socks – if I could only send you our entire out-put I'd do it tomorrow! I ran across one book of Gertrude Stein the other day – and it only cost TWELVE DOLLARS – and – well, when I awoke they were fanning me and giving me a drink of water! I forgot to price her *Tender Buttons.*

'Waal, I swan' is a Southern farm expression for saying 'Well, I'll be darned.' Or 'Well, I'll be damned' or a million other such expressions of real wonder, surprises or incredulity. When we are extraordinarily surprised, for good or for bad, we generally exclaim 'Well, I'll be damned!' meaning such things as 'Well, I can't believe it' or 'Well, can you imagine it' and the likes. In the country – the real provincial class – they exclaim with a 'Waal, I swan' and the type is usually that of our Uncle Sam! I don't know where the 'swan' originated, of course, but I've heard this expression so many times I more than know what it means. If you were to translate it with an 'Mah, guarda lì!' you'd come about as close as possible to the right solution. The fact is, I don't see any difference in meaning, at all!

I'm in a hurry to get these books off to you, so I'll have to come to a close. Before long you'll have some more books if I can locate them. And you'll probably get more news next time, too. Too bad I couldn't help you out on *Our Mr Wrenn,* but if you can use me in other works don't be bashful. And don't forget to write me often – as often as possible. Ya!

With all best wishes ——— toodle-oo!

Antonio Chiuminatto

[Turin,] February 11th, 1931
To Antonio Chiuminatto, Chicago

My Tony:
Hot letter I got, hot books, hot bill, too – I'm burning all over, fortunately the 'merla'[1] is here at hand and I can cool myself out.

1 The 'Blackbird Days.' Pavese refers to a popular belief that the last three days of January are the coldest of the year.

You're right – how can you get along bothering about me and 'Sme,' such a lazy and exacting fellow? Someday you'll send me a pineapple registered and not to be returned.

No, no, be sure, I'm only kicking sometimes out of jollity, in my humble endeavours to express my comradeship in a lingo which is not mine.

As for the books – they are O.K. – morphine[2] and all – and here's the dough. So you, not only open up the account in the two inks, but already wipe it out. How about snappyness, eh?

I'll say something about the contents, when I'll have at least glanced them over: now I'm chocked with a flood of English books from a certain highbrow friend I got.

However I'm sizing up *Hello Towns* and see it will cause me to change something in the essay I already wrote. I fancy this fellow Anderson exceedingly, you should read something by him: he's someone.

About Lewis, I've nothing more to say. I see, we've got to be talking, not writing about: we are only this way coming to a misunderstanding: I think, the whole point is not the rendering of characteristic Americans but of men, whomsoever they be. It is not that personae become great creations by means of their being truly American, on the contrary, by means of being great creations by an American, personae become truly Americans: Babbitt, Gantry, etc. are such a living, such a truly speaking and breathing lot that they must necessarily also be true Americans, full of the rich blood of the country! And, after all, in Lewis there is so much good people as bad ones. But, avast of it! My plans of crossing to Columbia heave in sight again and I hope we'll settle this matter by living talk.

Thank you for *Waal I Swan*. That's the real stuff! I've here a whole family of Yankees – Bostonians them all – I asked them about it, and after much blabbering and 'webstering' they all agreed they didn't know what the saying meant. It's not just the thing. Someone suggested the following spelling: 'Well I'se one' and translated 'Bene, sono uno ...!!!' Isn't my Buddy the cold card!

Heartily I hope to meet him before long in his own den. I've got now only to elude the draft and I'll be on my voyage for him. And so my old asthma is turning out a wonderful stunt.

I forgot: about Anderson, don't trouble any more: only if you'll someday stumble on the *Notebook* (1926) pick it up. I'll send you next time a hint of summer books: but I would not abuse of your kindness.

---

2 Pavese responds to Chiuminatto's words about Waldo Frank's book (23 January): 'one look at the price will be as good as a dose of morphine.'

And so you like my letters? Out of affection, I think, for, as for English I'm quite sure you're shrinking all over, in reading them. Miss Franchi already pointed out with the feminine care some blunders of mine in the corrected tasks of the Lega. Waal I swan, I must say.

Hello old socks auf wiedersehen.

Chicago, Illinois, February 25th, 1931
To Cesare Pavese, Turin

Dear Cesaruccio:
Did you say 'snappy'? Well, I'll tell the world! When I opened that letter and a flood of dollar-bills gushed forth I was speechless! Couldn't you find a single five-dollar bill over there? Or is it just your keen sense of exactness that makes you choose all one-dollar bills? That was a hot bill right, if you ask me, but I was just as much put out making it up for you as you probably were to have to pay it. Such is life, though. Some books, old sweetheart, just have to be paid for 'in full.' Only exceptional books in America cost three dollars or more and they are of the kind like the one of Waldo Frank, personal publications, in short. The whole trouble, isn't it? – is that you deal in stuff that is ultra-modern and you also pay the price for being in love!

Now then, I'll get you Anderson's *Notebook*. I think I can get a second-hand copy, but if not, I know where to get a new one. Too, I have a pleasant surprise for you. I just bought Ludwig Lewisohn's very latest novel, in fact, it has come on the market only this week. It is entitled *The Last Days of Shylock* and treats of the personal life of Shakespeare's Jew from the time of his leaving the court-room in Venice, after his condemnation. It is a defense of the famous Jew as well as the whole name of Jew itself, but I have my doubts about Lewisohn's success in re-establishing the Jew, Shylock! It is marvelous English, a very flowing style and colorful, not to mention that occasionally Lewisohn CAN paint a powerful picture. The one of Shylock's forced baptism in San Marco is exquisite in its excruciating details; the other of the martyrdom of 24 Jews under the Holy Office, at which Shylock is a spectator, is also very powerful. The point is this – that, within a few more days, when I hope to have finished it, I shall send it to you for a reading. You need not buy it, for it is a personal copy of mine. Should you want it, though, we can make matters very simple; just send me two dollars and fifty cents and I'll buy myself another copy!

Ben Hecht, if I have not told you, has also published a new novel, called *A Jew in Love* which I understand is *sexy*[1] and drawn out in details. However the case may be, I'm going to get it and give it a reading. Should I then buy it, I'll send it to you for as much. I mean a mere reading of it, understand. You know, Cesare, I don't buy very many books, first of all because they are expensive and secondly, because they are not in my line. I feel the need of building up a musical library, instead, when there is money. But I do read, making as much use of the libraries as possible. Why I said this merely to inform, if you have not already read it between the lines, that everytime I DO buy a book, I'll be only too glad to forward it to you for a reading, after which you will send it back to me. Distance must be no handicap to our friendship, you know!

And now for another surprise. I think I have found an excellent review that will publish your essay on Lewis! Whoopee! Before I accept, though, I am going to try to get as much out of some other review with a larger circulation, such as Scribner's, for example. *America*, which is a widely read and widely circulating Catholic review, through the added efforts of my brother the Jesuit, has agreed to publish it a little later on, due to the fact that only recently they published an article on Lewis, and secondly, because they think your essay just a trifle too long for their usage. But they will publish it later on, as I said, when they can give it the necessary space! How's that, eh? All I have to do now is get busy and make a good translation – which, I trust, is within my power. By that time, who knows but I shall have Scribner's consent to it, or some other review's acceptance, just as worthy.

O, I tell you, Buddy, ole timer, I'm sticking with the ship until it sinks! All this ought to prepare a warm reception for you when you get here. So you are coming, eh? Whoopee, once more! Just wait until I get out my bottles, my cigars and some good, hot coffee! Still prefer Lucky Strikes? There they are, right on that ash-stand, you know! And we possess the spirit of dyed-in-the-wool bachelors! O Mamma – please don't tempt me!

So Miss Franchi has corrected some of your exercise papers, eh? Well, to be truthful, she DOES know her grammar, and HOW ... but what I object to is the woman who is so damn pedantic that she stinks! Pardon my phraseology, but that's how it makes me feel! And to think I wrote

1 Underlined in pencil, presumably by Pavese.

her and expressly WARNED her against any kind of pedagogy in your regard! I told her that you knew the American language like very few Italians ever will, SHE included, in spite of the fact that your pronunciation and knowledge of grammar might not be on an equal footing – But – But – I also added – please do not play around with dynamite! I warned her, as I said, about trying to correct you – but since I know how woman is – and 'inter nos,' Miss Franchi, in particular, I just knew she WOULD correct you! I also added, by the way, that if she DID correct you, she would soon learn what a scholar, what a real gentleman is, – for you could still take it right on the chin standing up! Not only, but that you would profit from the correction, like all intelligent people do, especially when they are FORCED to take one. Which is more than SOME people will do, and you know what I mean! Well, shut my mouth now, if she isn't good! 'Parlar con i morti'! (Pardon me, Cesare; this phrase 'Well, shut my mouth' does not mean 'parlar con i morti' as you might think. It is the American way of saying 'Well, I'm speechless' (mi manca la parola') I wrote 'parlar con i morti' because after all I wrote Miss Franchi about you, she still turns right around and plays kid-teacher stuff! If that isn't a woman every damn day of the week, awake and asleep!)

The whole trouble is, you know, that in the two years I taught at the Lega, I gave her written comments on the whole grammar, which are dogmas almost; I always set down examples, when I could, as unchangeable facts. She still has those comments, and unfortunately, if you just run off the track a trifle now, she has you right on the head! It isn't her courage that is correcting you; she knows that back of her reason she still has my doctrines, which as far as that goes, I can vouch for myself.

But, Cesare, old boy, never be it said that I left a friend in need! NOW GET THIS! I have a copy of the same grammar she uses and I'm going to translate every damn exercise in it for you, with all the possible ways of a single translation.[2] You will judge for yourself the reason of syntax or grammar ... and if still in doubt ask me! I'm the berries on grammar – just as pedantic as she is, when it comes to that – and SHE knows it. She'll suddenly be surprised to find out that she has nothing to correct you on any more! How is this for a 'pineapple,' eh? And this little piece of work – if I may still be permitted to assume it – will be of considerable assistance to you in your public and private work.

And now, Cesare, addios! I'm with you to the last drop of Christian

2 The translations of the grammar exercises are located in the Chiuminatto folder 'Guido Gozzano – Cesare Pavese' Center.

blood – so you should worry a lot and build a house on it! Ha! They NEVER get around to ME – not if I can help it! Mum is the word, then, 'zitto'! I'm your old Buddy as B/4 –

P.S. And don't be bashful about that list of books for the summer months, see! The library does the work, not I! The books belong to them, not to me! Don't weaken, sonny, don't weaken! Sursum corda! Et cum spiritu tuo! Aufwiedersehn! Ciau – toodle-oo!

Antonio Chiuminatto

Chicago, Illinois, March 12th, 1931
To Cesare Pavese, Turin

Dear Cesare:
This very morning I have received a letter from the Reverend Wilfred Parsons of the Jesuits, who is Editor-in-Chief of both *America* and *Thought* magazines, with offices in New York City. I wrote him last week, sending him extracts of your essay and giving him an outline of your published work, telling him that I hoped he would see fit to publish it in *Thought,* which is a cultural magazine. I herewith quote you his entire letter:

> Prof. Chiuminatto: – I wish to thank you for your interest in THOUGHT and for your kind offer to send an article from Dr. Pavese. We have, however, adopted an absolute rule that we do NOT publish translations in THOUGHT of articles that have already appeared in other magazines anywhere.
>
> From the quotations you give me, I judge that the essay is a VERY BRILLIANT ONE, but unfortunately it is impossible for me to break that rule.
>
> If Dr Pavese cold submit through you another article on the same subject, we would be glad to consider it.
>
> *Wilfred Parsons, S.J.*

There you are, Cesare! Anyhow the great Jesuit admits that your essay is a 'brilliant one,' so you have scored a point! I sent him three solid pages of extracts in English – good English, let me say – so he could judge it thoroughly.

The idea now is this, Cesare. Half of the other magazines seem to think your essay is far too long for a single publication and they do not care to run it twice. This does not mean, though, that I shall not try to get one of them to publish it in spite of all – no siree, I'll still try. Here, of course, we have *Thought* and you'll thereafter see yourself in America. (Father Parsons has not read your essay entirely – so he can not know it well enough to argue as to what you wrote). Just touch up your old essay here and there and send it over. Take your time, too, there's no hurry. If you think this plan is worth while, go ahead; if not just forget it. I still insist, though, that it may be the means of your getting other calls for essays, though, later on. With your present essay on hand, I don't think it will take you long to 'make' another. Could you send me a typewritten copy, when you do, so that there will be no doubts as to what I must translate?

I'm with you now, Cesare, so take advantage. I may be the only one you know in America – but this old Buddy of yours is going to be the whole of America to you if he can! Follow my instructions (ahem!) and you'll see yourself in lots of magazines over here very soon; I have faith unlimited in your ability and so I'm going to convince America of it. We'll work together and in so doing nothing but good can come of it. Say, you've got some of these half-wit critics beat so many different ways they'll never catch up! Some of the essays I have read in magazines on Lewis are childish, yet they get published and command a good price! How about you – I asked myself – Holy Moses, a good man must have and especially so when that good man is a Buddy of mine! Now that I have finally succeeded in getting one editor-in-chief interested in you – and that's not so damn easy, if you ask me and you ought to know yourself – I'm going to use him as a stepping stone to better things, if such there are. I got all the Jesuits in the University of St. Louis with my brother to shake a leg on you, until I finally succeeded in getting a personal recommendation to Father Parsons, so that I could write him a 'PERSONAL' letter (S.P.M.) and know that he would get it – and not his secretary or some other numbskull. He has answered me personally, as you see – and most encouragingly ... which is your credit and not mine. It's a 'brilliant essay' he says, so consider yourself flattered by an outstanding editor in America ... even though as a religious he stays in the background. And he'll publish another essay of yours on Lewis, if he is assured that that essay has not appeared elsewhere. I made the mistake of telling him it was published in the *Cultura* merely to impress him with its seriousness and worth – but that's all right; we'll get out of that, says I to you and says you to me! Well, I'm at your complete disposal now – so do as you care!

I was going to send you *The Last Days of Shylock* but so many have asked to let them read it that it is still in circulation. But you'll get it some day in the near future. I have had to order a copy of *Notebook* of Anderson, not having been able to find a new edition, let alone a second hand one in all of Chicago. I am told that Anderson had the volume recalled to his publishers in New York – and so it was to them I had to apply for a copy. As soon as I get it now I'll send it to you. I have also read *A Jew in Love* by Ben Hecht and consider it a nice piece of psychology on sex and sex relationships. It is very smutty – or dirty, in other words – just a novel to make money. It's a long story of a Jew who goes from one mistress to another, prying into their mental and physical affairs – all bed-room scenes for the most part. I don't think you'd be interested as for literature, but you might for other reasons, if you want to read it.

I'm still waiting to hear from you lengthily. In the meantime I'm giving you something to keep you busy – another essay on Lewis.[1] And I'm going to be busy working on a concert I must give with the organ! When I do give it, it will be in the huge church of St. Patrick in Green Bay – where the people thirst for good music makes itself evident and I am selected as the drink-giver – the water-boy! But I'm sticking right with literature, you see, also, I'll have to pull you up into the limelight now. (How I love myself, eh?)

Cheerio, old pal! Lots of luck and write me soon. As ever

Antonio Chiuminatto

[Turin,] March 18th, 1931
To Antonio Chiuminatto, Chicago

Dear Tony:
Had I not already used up all possible expressions of wonder and 'speechlessness,' I should now send you a whole dictionary of compliments about your new enterprise – the translation of a grammar – but, things being as they are, I say only 'Buy you another typewriter.'

And what's worse, you're meaning business and your translations are getting home, one by one, all thorough and perfect. Yes, I'm staring

1 Unidentified essay.

speechless. Someday you'll present me with your own violin and you'll go, after, tramping and bumming round.

Honest, don't be so kind, otherwise I'll be obliged, when I'll cross over, to become your everlasting slave.

The same I say about books in general. I didn't know a simple request of mine would have raised such an activity on your part. Hand them over, surely, but take it more leisurely.

I want also to thank you very much about the probable publication of my essay. T's grand to be read in America without ever having been there! But keep an eye, I don't know if Jesuits would like such stuff as mine. There's a page about *Elmer Gantry* I think would pickle their eyes. However you're a knowing fellow. Do what you think best.

And, I pray you, whatever you could want – books, reviews, musical or not – broadcast only your s.o.s. and it will be got. I want to reciprocate.

And here is my summer list. (You select from them):

Thornton Wilder, *The Woman of Andros* (I read the other two ones)
Vachel Lindsay, anything
C. Sandburg, *The American Songbag, Smoke and Steel, Cornhuskers* (not *Chicago Poems*)
Countee Cullen, *Caroling Dusk*
Cabell, anything except *Jurgen* and *The Cords of Vanity*
J. Moncure March, *The Set-Up*
Glenway Wescott, *Goodbye Wisconsin* (not *The Grandmothers*)
Langston Hughes, *Poems and blues*
L. Lewisohn, *The Case of Mr Crump*
William Carlos Williams, *The Great American Novel* or anything else
Scott Fitzgerald, anything

As for Miss Franchi you are a damned good psychologist. Pedantic, it's so! She knows, however, her rules, and in this field can yet teach me. But I'm looking forward to the day when I'll speak American as no Englishman will ever be able. As for now, thanks and thanks for your translation. But don't don't trouble yourself.

Dear Tony, I'm so crowded with work that I must steal to my sleeping the time to write you this letter and so you'll pardon me, if I come so briefly to a conclusion. I'm teaching philosophy (!!) in a Lyceum out of Turin, and teaching Italian in Turin, and so I must leap from a waggon to another and from table to bed without a requiem.

---

1 Pavese may be referring to Hughes's *The Weary Blues.*

I hope (and have good reasons to) this requiem will be someday for me America itself – the business land that I think, instead, to be the pacefulness and dreaminess land (I'll demonstrate it another time) – and with the vow that this requiem will be sung with you, I am now yours devotissimo

[Turin,] March 26th [1931]
To Antonio Chiuminatto, Chicago

Dear Old Tony:
I want to thank you infinitely for your swell results about my journalistic career.[1] You bet you are a Live-Wire! Now listen, I'm enormously glad to be given a chance in USA, with the hope to enlarge subsequently my field. Moreover, I think, American review-world is not like ours so divided in quarreling groups and it is possible to appear in a sheet without dyeing oneself with the color of this same sheet. I say so, with an eye to the religious tinge *Thought* certainly has got and my essay certainly hasn't.

So I'll begin to put down a new essay on Lewis. There's also another reason to rewrite the old one, apart from the rule of *Thought,* and that's this: I've got to speak to an American public, no more to Italians. And this changes things a little. I don't promise you the new article for too soon, as you know I'm already breaking myself down with work, but certainly in the month of April, it'll be done.

Now, I want only to congratulate you and arrange businesses. If some mazooma will come out of our united literary strivings, that is, if *Thought* will send you some doremi, we'll go fifty-fifty. Are you game?

Say, Buddy, in a fortnight, my *Anderson* will appear!

Take your time, as for *Shylock* and *A Jew in Love.* And more time take about summer books. Perhaps I'll already be over there, by that time. In April I'll know the sentence.

I'm glad to hear from you good news about the fiddle – mightly glad. And so you also are hanging on, eh! Well, we'll yet turn out the Phenomenical Twins, what d'you say?

---

1 Reference to Pavese's essay on Sinclair Lewis that Chiuminatto translated and sent to the Reverend Wilfred Parsons, editor-in-chief of the Catholic review *Thought.*

Now, I beg many – too many – pardons, and must come back to my unrelenting works.

So keep an eye on Father Parsons and you'll soon get the stuff.

Chicago, Illinois, April 24th, 1931
To Cesare Pavese, Turin

Dear Cesare:
I've been so darn busy here of late that I haven't had time to write a decent letter to anyone. Please notice you're only getting a note yourself – for this time.

I got your card yesterday. With regards to *Notebook,* let me say that it is another of those volumes you will take or leave, as you see fit. The price is $2.50. It is a volume I should like to have myself, very much, but if it is as important to you, just keep it; if not, though, as I have said, just send it back and I'll be more than glad to have it. Either way is a go with me!

Along with this note I am inclosing some more translations from the grammar. File them away with the rest – and make use of them, if you can! I'll finish the grammar little by little – and it'll be a pleasure to do it for you, I assure you.

I'm waiting for your essay on Lewis. As soon as I get it, I'll stay awake nights to translate it, if I have to – but Father Parsons will have to publish it or I'll break his holy and sanctified neck! We mean business, don't we?

So you're almost due for America, eh? Well, you can't make me sore by coming, understand. Should you be in lil ole Manhattan this summer, give me a ring on the phone, a telegram or what have you – and I may call on you. Wouldn't that be grand and glorious, Cesare? We got together over there and now we'll get together over here – one for all and all for one!

According to your specifications I'm holding up books and all other interests of yours. Should you not be coming here this summer –unfortunately – let me know in time so that I can still handle all things to your advantage. Remember, too, that if there is anything at all I could do for you to facilitate your coming to these good, ole States – just say the word, Buddy, just say the word! When you met up with me, you met up with a funny personage, Cesare; he's just funny that way when it comes to friends, see? My poor, old Father used to tell me, 'Tony, fight for your friends and they'll fight for you' – and that's just what I'm doing for a Buddy of mine now! Want me to start a revolution for you, Cesare; just say the word, Big Boy, just say the word! And what's happening to Mila? Is he letting me down, or am I letting him down? Tell him I'll soon be writing again, though.

Caroling Dusk[1] is out of print and simply cannot be had, except by advertising to private owners who wish to sell. The library may give it to me on usage, though. Some of the other books are in Dollar-Editions if you should want them.

Well, Cesare, toodle-oo and cheerieooo! Keep in touch with me – that's all. Best wishes to you and Max – from your old pal –

Antonio Chiuminatto

[Turin, May 1931]
To Antonio Chiuminatto, Chicago

Dear Tony:
At last I succeeded in putting down another essay on that guy.[1] Say it's not so damn easy to rewrite on a topic! I had to plug along like a dog, believe me. But you'll soon get it and this matters, all other things 'are silence.' Now let Father Parsons decide.

And I'm not due to America. 'Tis sad, honey, but 'tis so. On 1st November I'll enter under the arms. That doggone doctor found me able-bodied to war and peace service. Eleven months! Till June 1932. Adieu America! And I had already rec'd the Columbia acceptance! Surely Daddy above is a funny guy, you bet.

So you can forward the library-stuff, according the list you already got, I beseech you, enclose *Caroling Dusk.* I want it before all other books.

As you say you like so much Anderson's *Notebooks,* I'll mail it back, it's truly interesting and worthwhile, and I'm only sorry I read it after my *Anderson* was already in proofs (by the way, it'll appear before long).

1 By Countee Cullen.

1 Sinclair Lewis.

Together with the *Notebook* and the new essay on Lewis you'll get a novelty, my own translation of *Our Mr Wrenn*! You'll judge by your own eyes.

Say, you're really tough, my boy, when it comes down to brass-tacks. You get along with the translation of that whole grammar (methinks you'll spend less time and fatigue in writing a new one). However many thanks and ... *a buon rendere.*

As for Mila he's turning out a regular four-flusher. What's more, he picked out somewhere a light-hearted widow and he's now sowing as many wild oats as you can conceive. Speak about writing to cronies! I'm not even myself seeing him, you know.

But that's more news. A desperado-publisher will perhaps undertake my old study about your older Whitman and so make me a world-famous scholar about American literature. Should it turn out good, I'll be ... hanged ... no, I'll be sure to find a new place somewhere in scholarly America and so, after my damned term in the army, hug and kiss at last my unique friend, over there.

Now, I stop to hurry and get typewritten the everlasting essay.
Toodle-oo and come over sometime.

Chicago, Illinois, May 28th, 1931
To Cesare Pavese, Turin

Cesare, ole Buddy:
I received your long waited-for letter about two hours ago, and since then I have shaken the meanest pair of legs you ever saw! I have already been down to the Library, have gotten permission to take out your books now, before the first of June, have already picked them out as they were there roosting on the shelves and now have them right beside me at home here to send to you! How's that for 'Friendship with a Heart' and 'Service with a Smile,' eh? They'll be on their way to you before tomorrow!

The rules and regulations are the same as last year; you must have the books returned before or on October 1st, 1931! A few of the volumes you asked for I could not get – but should it be possible to get them in the cource [*sic*] of time, I'll send them to you on someone else's card. (My friends all cater to me, you know.)

Now, then; *The Case of Mr Crump* by Lewisohn has been forbidden

Library circulation by the Municipal authorities – so it can't be had in any way at all, through the Library. The book is out of print – But – a new edition has come to light now – for the price of $5.00. If you want it, let me know and I'll get it new; or a second-hand copy, if I can. This is the only way in which you could possibly get it.

Caroling Dusk of Countee Cullen may not be taken out of the Library, since it is out of print and the Library possesses an only copy ... i.e. you may not take it for more than two weeks. This, then, is another volume you will have to buy, new or second-hand, should you really want it. Let me know.

Hence, in the choice of books, I have kept myself strictly to the authors suggested by you. If any others are desired, just let me know and I'll still see that you get them. (There are plenty of library cards in circulation, you know.) These, then, are the books you will receive:

Countee Cullen	———	Copper Sun (1927) – (Poems)
J.B. Cabell	———	Something About Eve (1927)
		The Way of Ecben (1929)
Carl Sandburg	———	Slabs of the Sunburnt West (1922)
Thornton Wilder	———	The Cabala (1928)
		The Bridge of San Luis Rey (1927)
V. Lindsay	———	Golden Whales of California (1920)
		Every Soul is a Circus (1929)
Scott Fitzgerald	———	The Great Gatsby (1925)
		Tales of the Jazz Age (1922)
Glenway Wescott	———	Good-bye Wisconsin (1928)

I was just wondering whether or not you have read the *Golden Whales of California* – but I think not – so here goes it to you. As for the others, I'll keep an eye open for you! Have a good time in reading them, and give a thought to your old pal ... n'est-ce-pas?

I have not as yet received the essay or the translation of *Our Mr Wrenn* but I can assure you that I shall be tickled to death to get them. As for your essay, it'll get prompt attention – and publication, ... if I have anything to say about it ... And I think I have.

So you're in the Army now, eh? You have my heartfelt sympathy, condolences and what else? It's too damn bad, Cesare, but buck up, old timer; it can't last forever, you know. If we both live, we'll still meet again in the U.S.A.

So Mila is becoming a fourflusher, eh? Oh, Cesare, have a heart; don't be hard on the poor fellow: 'Errare est humanum,' you know! And with all those swell looking dames – ye gods – how can a man resist? Now I ask you in confidence – is that the way to feel about him? Think of love, my boy, think of it ... that loveliest of all lovely pastimes between fools! Well, I was a fool once myself – and I'm looking forward to it again! Ha! So it's the Merry Widow, eh? If he wouldn't only forget his pals, the four-flushing fourflusher of a fourflusher!!! That ought to hold him, eh? Kiss the boy for me, right on the forehead, and tell him to pass it along!

Sunday, the 31st, is my birthday; I'm suddenly 27! My Mother will arrive in Chicago from Green Bay on the 30th, and on the 31st we shall leave for St. Louis, Missouri, where my brother is receiving his Degree in Philosophy at the University. He is the Jesuit, you know! He now becomes the Reverend Doctor Lorenzo! O, these Chiuminatto boys – all hot stuff, under the collar and above it!

Spring is here, Spring is here, cried the poet, as he took the back off his watch. (The watch spring!) Well sir, Cesare; it's lovely of evenings now, so I take a stroll occasionally down to the Lake, around Lincoln Park. Sometimes I even have a young lady with me – but no wild cats, understand! I'm not that kind of a rooster with that kind of a hen!

On May 2nd, I was elected presiding judge of the State Examinations for College Musical Graduates. I had to listen to 11 pianists, seven orchestras, 4 violinists and six girls' glee clubs! – and then award first, second and third place! I also gave a talk in the auditorium to the vast crowd of spectators, for the most part, musicians and teachers. All my expenses were paid to De Kalb, Illinois and I received $30 for the day's work – so that's that! Ci siamo o non ci siamo? I'm stepping up in the world, if only very gradually. I have more pupils now, more friends, am better acquainted with the city – so I really can't kick! My only regret is that I haven't a million dollars, a solid million bucks! D—n it! With my money, then, and your brains, we could own the world, what say? Ha!

By the time school starts again in the Fall, you'll have the remainder of that translation from the grammar – but, poor fellow – you're in the Army now – and we have music for that! And if you see any wild oats around, just pick a few for me!

I am always glad to hear that your spirit is not weakening any; I really sympathize with you on the Columbia shake-up. BUT – it'll make our meeting over here so much the sweeter – and we have candy for that! Just don't forget to write me as often as you can – even oftener, if you can! I fairly revel in all your letters, for they have brought me ever so much closer to you, as close as I'd like to be to you.

Now we'll have to get the books off – so here's wishing you a lovely vacation. Toodle-oo to you – and write me soon! As ever – your old pal –

Antonio Chiuminatto

P.S .... Under separate cover (naturally!)

I am sending you two more books – as follows

Herman Melville —— Mumford
Marching Men —— Anderson

I know you want 'Melville' badly, so I am tickled to death I could still get it at the library. I am also sending *Marching Men*, since it is one of Anderson's books that we were unable to get through the year – and which you really should read, at least.

You should just see our library these days! Books are going out by the tons – since you may take out any number of them at all on a vacation card. That is why I always get permission to take yours out before the 1st of June; I know I shall still have more or less of a selection to pick from. Yesterday, instead, Cesare, I called for some ten books out of which I got these two – and I consider myself lucky. In such a city as this, no matter what book you want – at this time of the year, there is always someone else, too, who wants the same one. It's just a question of getting there first.

Now, then; as soon as you have finished reading those eleven – get them back to me pronto – and I may send you another ten or eleven – if there is time enough left. And through the year following the vacation period, I'll do my best, as ever, to keep you in reading material.

[Turin,] June 14th, 1931
To Antonio Chiuminatto, Chicago.

Dear Tony:
I got them eleven books, a cocktail of American life, wonderful! You're so snappy in your doings. I must watch myself, for sometime I'll want something without giving you notice and at once you'll send it to me. I think you're like Mississippi, but break the banks and after speak about catching it again!

By now you'll have rec'd the translation-package[1] and so must know about my last desire: since you seem to revel in tiring yourself out in good-doings to your friends, would it be the straw on the camel's back, should I beg of you to look after that *Melville*? You know, my new translation is from *Moby Dick* by Melville and the book of Mumford would do me exceedingly good.

But 'let's be nice' as said the robber after trimming again his necktie all bespattered with blood, let's be nice, says, and let's be satisfied with the former advantages taken of the victim.

And so you were Prexy already, this Spring? And what's more you're getting doremi? My best wishes on this path of manly achievement. And my compliments to your brother, the Doctor!

Which reminds us of Father Parsons and the hot stuff he will someday have to cry over. I thought it yet over, and I don't think my stuff will do for his magazines, however 'trying' is the word, and you're such a diehard! I'll serenely be on the look for the issue.

And so you also are that way again old bac?[2] Say, I was always master of my moods, but I began suddenly some weeks ago and – perhaps it was a trick of inhibition, I don't know – now I'm 'crushed' on four pink faces at once ... I always mix up names and lookings, out of overworking, and there's a fifth one looming on the horizon. Not so bad, eh?

Well, in the army there are going to be more. But maybe it ain't a sun-of-gun of a job! (There's no joke with 'gun,' for, you know, we carry muskets).

And at last here's my *Anderson*[3] which has been much discussed here, but you see, he's always hale and hearty and on the path for new adventures like his writer which however does not even succeed in coming out of his debts, let alone coming out of the Old Land.

Adieu.

P.Scr. What d'you Americans mean by 'your are perfection to a T'? (Here I should like one of your page-long explanations).

---

1 Included in this package is Pavese's revised article on Lewis that he and Chiuminatto hoped to publish in the American review *Thought*. For whatever reason, Chiuminatto's translation of the essay was never published. See note 4 in Introduction.

2 Bachelor. In rough draft of letter, Pavese cancels 'helor.'

3 Pavese's essay on Sherwood Anderson.

Chicago, Illinois, June 29th, 1931
To Cesare Pavese, Turin

Dear Cesare:
Ave Triumphator! Your letter arrived this morning – just a while ago; so did your essay on Anderson. Speaking of that essay now – did you find it necessary to make so condensed a mass of it? It's rather compound, you know – not like you at all – or is it just my imagination? It may all be that I am used to reading you more in the mood of exposition rather than in that of investigation. However, I like it immensely – only it doesn't strike me as being a full picture of Anderson; at least, the picture seems to have no frame around it. Now you'll pardon me, old man, for this insinuation – but you were a bear-cat in Lewis – and I never take anything less from anyone. I think you know what I mean, though! Don't work too hard, Cesare!

As for the translation of Lewis – I am well on the way with it. I have been extremely busy this past month, since it was the last of the school year, you see. Then, too, *Thought* is published only every three months, so there is no use in hurrying. Day before yesterday saw the close of the year at Columbia, but, fortunately or unfortunately, as you will, I was assigned to Summer School teaching – so I'll still have six weeks of it. I shall now be teaching aspiring young things – women, of course – in the art of playing and teaching public school music. I'll still have plenty of time for your essay, though, and by the end of July I plan on having it in the hands of his Religious Majesty the Jesuit! Don't feel pessimistic, Cesare; I still have a certain amount of the gift of gab – or as Shakespeare calls it – the tongue of persuasion! Besides, there are plenty of other reviews you know!

Tomorrow I'm going down to the library to see if I can get you those other books *Melville, Caroling Dusk* maybe – and whatever else I think you can use. I shall use my landlady's library card – so all will be well. And you're translating from *Moby Dick*; what the hell! can't you find anything better than that to work with? We know the book to be listed as one that NEVER should be read! And here you are trying to spread its gospel! Cesare, Cesare, ubinam gentium sumus?[1] But I suppose you know better – so lots of luck to you.

1 'Where in the world are we?' From Cicero's *Oratio in Catilinam Prima in Senatu Habita* (First oration against Catiline).

It's so confounded hot here that in the last three days there were 251 deaths from heat! Yesterday over 900,000 persons tried to find relief on the beach! This morning the thermometer registers 101 degrees Fahrenheit! And we are not promised any let-up. How I wish I were on a North Pole expedition now!

So you are lost for an explanation of 'perfection to a T,' eh? Well, just bring your troubles to me. Now, then; you must know that certain workers, like carpenters, cabinet-makers, etc. use a measure, an instrument, they call 'T-square.' It is a long ruler-like instrument topped off like a 'T' – sometimes only on one side, like this: ⌉ – It is used for squaring off perfect measures, obtaining perfectly straight lines – since it's of perfect angular form. When you measure two given sides of any rectangle, for instance, with a T-square, the imperfection of construction, if any there is, immediately comes to light. Hence, the expression, perfection to a T.

From this origin of the expression, we have adopted it in many ways. For instance, we say that our new suit of clothes fits us to a T – meaning that it is a perfect cut, therefore a perfect fit. Get me? We say that any idea or other suits us to a T – meaning that we are in perfect accord with that idea. Examples:

> His musical arrangement of that symphony is perfection to a T. Dr. Pavese's essay suits me to a T; I agree with it all around. The lady's beauty is perfection to a T; she has everything. Your idea of a good time suits me to a T; let's start in. These shoes fit me to a T.

Get it – do you? We also speak of a 'T-bone steak' since it is that piece of meat, the steak that has in its center a bone that has the form of a T – almost. Sometimes we call it a small steak.

And here I thought you, Cesare, were perfection to a T when it came to slang – yet I discover that there is a phrase you don't know. Imperfection of construction; hence, no perfection to a T yet! Ha! Is that clear now? Just remember that your hat can fit you to a T; so can your shoes, your gloves, your shirt, your false teeth and your glass eye! Not to mention, also, your love affairs!

Here are a few slang expressions you may not know:

A poker-face – far l'indiano. Deriva dal giuoco di 'poker' nel quale giuoco non si legge mai nella faccia quello che può contenere la mano, faccia tosta, indifferente, che dice nulla – ma che può far danno.

To have hot-pants – aver voglia di coito. 'pantaloni caldi' – e non so se mi spiego! 'Hot trowsers' è piu' elegante – ma sempre di uso fra gli uomini, si capisce!

Impatient virgin – dicesi ora delle donnine cercatrici di emozioni.

And when you must – please write 'Printed matter' – NOT – 'printed stuff.' 'Stuff' è già più slang. Printed stuff – dicesi di Rabelais, Hecht e Melville. Ha! Mai di Pavese, certo! Il postino ha creduto che fossi un comunista russo quando mi consegnò la posta!

I'm going to kill someone over there in Italy – you know it? After getting the *Rassegna Musicale* for months and months – here they come along now and send me a bill for 40 liras! Because I have accepted them! I thought Max was sending them to me – not the company! I don't care, understand; I'm glad to read Max – and musical subjects, in general, – but I do like to know where I'm at – just how I stand. Here's where you can do me a favor now, Cesare, if you will, please. Will you give Max the 40 liras to pay my bill with – and ask him to renew my subscription, too, while he's at it – and we'll fix things up between us the next time you owe me something; how's that? The next time you buy a book, say – we'll just deduct 40 liras! Thank you again and again – and once more! That'll save me a lot of red tape, see!

Well, here's wishing you a lot of luck with the 'pink faces.' Just make sure they don't turn blue with rage – and then all will be hunky-dory – meaning, well, well and very well! Lots of luck, Cesare, from your old pal evermore –

Antonio Chiuminatto

[Turin, July 1931]
To Antonio Chiuminatto, Chicago

Dear Tony:
Your letter was an oasis in the wilderness, these hot days. 'Tis bracing in the maudlin dejection of Italy to get something of a handshake from over there. Among all I liked best the opportunity to render you a favor, at last. I cannot immediately ask from Mila what's the matter about that bill, for he is now scrambling the Alps, but as soon as I can I'll fix everything. However I think things are so: Mila presented you with the first year of the *Rassegna,* afterwards he forgot about it and now the company is sending his annual form letter to all subscribers. But you must not trouble about: I'll quarrel and pay what is required and you get along

reading our Lothario's *stuff.* Who, by the way, is quite indecently misbehaving. I think the mountain-term is a veiled elopement with the Merry Widow.

And so you're kicking about Melville, eh? Not you alone, not you alone. Italian publishers also are kicking, but I got a crush on that fellow and would it cost me my life-blood I'll push him along. I find *Moby Dick* an extraordinary piece of writing, and so on, but, be cheerful, I'll not worry you with an offhand lecture on his personality. I've got other chances: before long, I scribble one of my famous essays about him and you'll hear.

Speaking about essays, I must say on defence of *Anderson* that the manager of the review granted me just that number of pages and nothing more (on account of the everlasting Lewis) and so I had to cramp my style and ideas to death!

Many thanks also for your undying interest in the translation of Lewis, about which I've only the doubt of coming short of all America's expectations.

The lovely list of slang phrases touched my heart and I'm already studying them by ditto. Come over always, buddy, with such things sweeter than candy box! By the way, I'm impatiently awaiting for the heat to let on, and then I've an idea to send you some more liquor center chocolates. But this time I'll attend personally to the packing in order to avoid changelings. (Procrastination is only for a more merciful climate's sake, you know liquor centers are easily dried.)

In some days I'll mail back to you the eleven books on summer loan and if you'll be able to renew the gift I'll be tickled etc.

So it's all hunky-dory with you? You are Summer School teaching? Will hustle in the world, also by my part, who am now a totally lounging fellow, quite all of a philosopher, spending hours before the mirror to admire my perfect looks. (I'm waiting for the Army to spoil them.) Good-by.

P.S. Naturally I got Melville and Anderson and I thank you. As for new books, keep always in mind the list you have, insist on the authors named there (especially Cabell, Williams, Hughes, Sandburg) find out new ones, and use, in short, your own wisdom.

The Bibliophile

[Turin,] August 28th [1931]
To Antonio Chiuminatto, Chicago.

Dear Tony:
I hope you'll have received the first package of books I sent you on the 6th of August. Here's another set and so the whole is on its way home again.

Many good things I got from them: you're truly a grand booster of USA abroad. All I knew in this line I must own from you.

I worked manly this summer and before long you'll get 'printed stuff' to testify of it.

Say, there's corking news for me and you to know: I'll not go *under arms*! I'll acquit myself with some pre-military courses, on Sundays. And remain a civilian all the time.

America looms again in the skies.

I spoke at last with Max (by the way, he's reduced to a shadow of his former self, sex-appealed too much on him), we'll arrange the *Rassegna* affair. On the August issue there's a good article of our chum on music and movies: it means something here in Italy. America plays a standing role in it, you bet.

Please accept some bootleg hootch[1] to start your dreams with, hope will get you in good shape. 'Tis so, you feed my mind with books, and I try to reciprocate by feeding your sins: who has the best of it?

Wishing you a happy father of many a spiritual child, here's my paw.
Toodle-oodle

Cesare

P.S. They are three the packages I'm mailing to-day: two of books and one of liquor-centers. Perhaps the last will get injured, let us hope.

Chicago, Illinois, September 8th, 1931
To Cesare Pavese, Turin

Dear Cesare:
I have just come back to Chicago after a month's vacation in Green Bay.

1 Liquor-filled chocolates.

Yes, to be exact, it was a month and 4 days! I find your letter here; also the package of 4 books. I am sorry that I cannot send you any more books from the library; before taking even another single volume out, you must have returned every other one you have. Rules and regulations, you see! But don't worry; I'll see to it that you get what books you want in one way or another.

I had a lovely vacation – a real, hot time in hot weather! And I didn't do a damn thing but loaf or play around, everything from swimming, motor-boat riding, fishing, tennis, diamond ball, to moonlight parties with women! And some indoor bridge parties!

I had planned on finishing my translation of your Lewis, but I blush to confess that it is still unfinished. Cheerio, though; I'll get it done yet if I have to take it to church with me!

Thanks for the help on the *Rassegna*! It will be appreciated, I assure you. So Max is going hay-wire, eh? Which means all wrong! Well, at the call of Nature who is the man so strong as to resist? And when you have Latin blood in the veins – O boy! – mountains, snow, sunshine, a cabin and you and I – the 'you' meaning 'la femme'!

My heart goes to you in appreciation of the kindness you extend to me! So it's liquor-centered chocolates again, eh? I shouldn't like to have you put yourself out, Cesare; but if you insist —well, thanks, ole top, thanks. I'll drink a couple to your health and to your career, military and civil.

Just as soon as you have returned all the books on the summer loan, I'll look around for the ones you weren't able to get. I'm still promising to be right on the job, you know. As for *Moby Dick* – go right ahead; I know it's a great piece of work, all right, though I don't quite coincide with you that greatness is always great. Ben Hecht is great, too, you know; great junk, great trash!

When in Green Bay, Cesare, I presented some letters of yours to a High School supervisor – a lady. We agreed that your feat of mastering English and slang was nothing short of phenomenal, considering your limited surroundings. The surprise was general that such a feat could be achieved; I was at the time showing the fallacies of American education, the superficialities of it. And by force of argument I convinced the teachers that we are weak in our results among students. You were the example, see! So give yourself a pat on the back – and remember that there's music for that. (Whenever we use a slang expression taken from some title of a song, we add 'There's music to that,' meaning that it has been sanctioned by the nation.) You will find authors using this form of expression – so now you'll know why. In other words, 'there's music to that' is another way of saying, 'And I don't mean Maybe!'

And now I'm back in the harness, ready to pull. I have just this week yet in which to line up my classes – and then business will become serious. I'm not kicking, though; I had a swell vacation, so why should I? I even spent many a day out at the Neveu cottage on Lake Shawano, where all is quiet, plenty of trees, wild birds, water and moonlights. It's the great Wisconsin summer resort – and the Neveu family, druggists of our city, are dear friends of mine, so much so that the oldest daughter would like to become Mrs Antonio Chiuminatto! They have three pharmacies in Green Bay and it's too bad I didn't take up medicine, eh? The girl isn't so bad at all – a-tall; she's not a stage beauty, by any means, but she is refined, young, healthy and wealthy. What more could a man want, n'est-ce-pas? But I'm not in the market as yet for a wife, see – so I'm stalling ... holding, off and some more off! When that fatal day comes, Cesare, only God knows when, though, you'll get the invitation to hear the church bells and to eat a piece of the cake!

I have just been reading H. L. Mencken's *In Defense of Women* which is, in reality, an attack on them. He's not bad, though – and certainly not one of our poorest writers. I have just about made up my mind to quit reading novels and read something more substantial instead. I think I'll go in for travels now, with such other subjects as music and minor sciences. The more novels I read the less I seem to know about morals and sociology! I'll leave all that stuff to you.

Yesterday was Labor Day and we had some celebrations around here; speeches, parades and what not! Most of them had the tone of 'Work' 'Jobs' 'Bread,' etc! If you know what I mean! This country is on the rocks right; if something doesn't happen soon we'll witness a veritable revolution such as we have never seen! And we'd deserve it, too.

Well, Cesare, keep in touch with me now that I'm back I'll try to give you anything you need, you know. Until the next time then – au revoir. Your buddy – as ever –

Antonio Chiuminatto

P.S. I have a hunch that next summer will find me in Turin. How's that? My mother and brother are planning on going over – my grandmother is still living, you know – and so I'll have to go along. Even if the others shouldn't go, for some reason or other, I still think I'll go alone, then. Just for a few months, see. So if you don't hurry and meet me in Lil Ole Manhattan – I'll be seeing you in the café Mugna! Wotta visit, eh. Wotta visit! Wish me luck, Cesare!

Chicago, Illinois, September 22nd, 1931
To Cesare Pavese, Turin

Dear Cesare:
I have your letter of the 5th. The remainder of the books arrived this morning – and I am writing you so that you will put your mind at ease. The box of 'candy' has not as yet arrived – but when it does – I'll be too drunk to write you about it, until maybe a week later! Whoopee!

This afternoon I shall return the books to the Library – and as usual the librarian, who is a friend of mine – yes, a lady – will want to know what I thought of them. I'll have to drag out my line of bunk and spread it gently, if you know what I mean. I have read Wescott, Wilder, Sandburg and a few more, so I think I'll get by.

And I'm still trying to work on your translation. But I met with bad luck! I can only do such work in the evening – please – and one evening the gentleman who lives downstairs came up and kicked because I pounded a typewriter for hours at a time, daytime or night-time. He has a daughter who is a nervous wreck and he said it affected her so that she was restless and ill at ease. He not only asked me to desist, but commanded me to 'lay off and do your goddam typewriting some other time'! How then, Cesare, when they talk to me like that I get huffy myself, see – so I ups and says to the punk, says I –any time you think I'm a tramp and truck-driver like you are, you've got another thing coming! Just consult my calling card on the mail-box – ground floor to the left! And with this I slams the door in his face, slams I!

But the ole son-of-a-So-and-So goes to the police and they serve me with an order whereby I am forbidden to typewrite after sunset. And this is supposed to be a free country – my eye! The police tell me that I'll be able to typewrite again upon further notice – after they have investigated things a little – but if they haven't investigated that 'little' yet, I hope to Hell they don't investigate a 'lot'! I told them that as far as I knew, apartments were not meant to be hospitals or sanitariums – but I guess they were, at that – judging from the results. What about radios and phonographs, eh?

Anyhow, Cesare, please be patient. I'll do what I can for you – when I can, I promise that. My evenings were the best time to do it in – but, of course, this small time sap had to butt in! It even gets my English! I feel slangy to the point of a Sinclair Lewis. After another month or so I ought to be able to peck away again of evenings! He says, says he 'This is no goddam office building' and I says right back, see – I says 'Ya, and if it was you wouldn't be here – except as the janitor' – just like that, says I. My only mistake was that I slammed the door in his face – so he went over and opened the door of our District Police! And that bunch of retired farmers, ditch-diggers, booze-hounds and loafers are not telling me what to do – or rather, what NOT to do! Pazienza, caro; pazienza! Ci sono dei momenti nella vita quando è difficile credere che si sia in un mondo anche poco intelligente!

Wotta break you get from the Army, eh? Wotta break! Well, let's get down to business and boost some more. I'm not boosting America, understand; I'm trying to boost a friend, a Buddy, see; don't get them mixed! First it's Cesare Pavese and then comes the rest! And next time you write give us a line-up on your books and your English teaching. I have to get my face into all of it, you know.

I'll give you some more translations from the grammar, now that I think of it – so just tell me what year you will be teaching – what lessons – page so-and-so to page so-and-so, see? And if there are any urgent volumes – speak right up, sonny, speak right up!

So Max got too much sex-appeal, eh? How about the others who get too much sax-appeal – or don't you have any good saxophone players over there? Sax-appeal has outdone sex-appeal over here – ya!

Hey, I hear we have a man in the University here who is also a man of letters – from the University of Turin. He was sent here on a scholarship two years ago – and is about ready now to go back. A Calabrian! I don't know his name – but I'm going to try to find out who he is, what he does, etc. I understand he is going back to Turin – and in that case I'd like to have you meet him; he could give you some first-hand information – what say? All I know about him is what an Italian family told me – and I've asked them to shake a leg and have him meet me – as we Americans says. Not a bad idea, what say, Cesare? And besides I want him to know about you, see?

I'm back on the job and in a big way! Yes, brother, in a big way! My whole class of last year has come back to me – and so far I already have five new ones. What a vision of dollars and cents! (I hope it isn't only a vision, though!) This teaching business takes up just about all my time – just when I had planned on doing a little more studying, myself. I like progress, see! Pro-gress, as the English would call it! But I still have time for you – remember! When my friends get to be the last thing in my life, then I'm quitting progress – and in a big way, brother, in a big way! Just a weak sentimentalist, I guess! But I like liquor-centered chocolates.

Some more slang! — To take off — incominciare (espressione derivante dall'aeroplano. La gita giù per il campo prima di darsi all'aria, si chiama il 'take-off'). Esempi:

Are we going to the theater? Well, let's take off!

No, it's too late to take off now; let's just coast around. (To coast around – andare con il motore chiuso – come fa l'uccello senza moto delle ali). Il desiderio spento (dall'esempio) sarebbe il motore chiuso, quindi 'let's coast around,' O al caffè – o al parco, per esempio.

Static (il rumore della radio) dicesi ora per la chiacchierata che non valgono nulla. Quando qualcuno Le conta delle stupidaggini, dica pure che è 'static.'

Don't talk so much; it's all static to me!

Get another station, you've got too much static! (Cambi discorso; c'è troppo rumore noioso.)

And with this I greet you with an au revoir: 'À la prochaine, mon ami!' Here's the mitt to you, Buddy; clamp it! And if you have any love for yours truly, don't wash your hand! 'S long – ole timer – 'S long!

Always –
Antonio Chiuminatto

[Turin,] October 15th, 1931
To Antonio Chiuminatto, Chicago

Dear Tony:
I waited for some days to reply to your last, in order to receive a note about the 'candy.'

Now I'll despatch myself. I hope they'll be arrived safely and you already too drunk to think about friends. 'Twould be the greatest pity and nuisance, had they been marred or miscarried. Well.

About Policemen, don't make a break like our Max,[1] you know. It's easier to get in than come out what it comes to Big Houses. The S.J. has time to be tackled. A slap on the back, however, old fellow.

Now, don't hope I'll worry your gracious self with grammars and linguist stuff. Your time's too precious to waste it that way. And after all, I'm going to strike a great idea on the Lega. This year I'll teach English not

1 Reference to Massimo Mila's first arrest for political motives in 1929, while Chiuminatto was still in Turin.

on grammarian's notions but 'reading': I'll ferret out a primer somewhere and have it perused by my brunettes all Sundays God ever made. I think it more in my line and profitable.

I'm waiting for the guy from Calabria – excuse me, Illinois, – and high time indeed it'll be to hear him talk in a Southernly way of my Piedmontese – again pardon, – Chicagoan buddy. Hand him over, he'll be properly treated.

Get along with your Vision of Dollars and a good achievement may they prove also, but don't turn out a quitter, on account of them. Get me?

Thank you for the slang gift. None knows where you with liquor centers and with slang will land. What with the two of them working together?

Now about books, you must look after some good *literary* magazine or review, the biggest on[e] in USA, the most informed and highbrow. Notice me its subscription conditions. I'll send you the caboodle and you'll handle the bargain. So, I'll be up to literary going-ons in God's Country. Plenty of books for you to buy will be the issue of it.

But don't get on neighbours' daughters' nerves according to your ways. Too many nervous daughters over here I myself got already on.

Good-bye, Paganini.

Chicago, Illinois, October 29th, 1931
To Cesare Pavese, Turin

Dear Cesare:
What could be sweeter? Your letter just arrived and I happen to be taking a morning's rest – a badly needed rest, I assure you. It seems like ages since I heard from you last, and unless I'm mistaken, it's been quite some time since I wrote you.

Did I get the chocolates? Cesare, how can you, how dare you remind me of that greatest of all pleasures? Did I get 'em? G'wan; quit the kidding! I'll say I got 'em – about three weeks ago. Right now I have only about ten pieces left I am saving for my brother; he will be here day after tomorrow. The candy arrived in perfect condition; not one piece was either crushed or dried. It was a perfect piece of work all around – and did I enjoy 'em! Boy, Oh Boy! I never had so many friends coming over to visit me as I did in the early days after the package's arrival! Ha! It was grand of you, old Buddy, to be so kind – and I could not only send you books, but even write them for you now! What a treat it is over here to get a mere taste of choice liquors! Something, you know, that doesn't make you see snakes or white elephants!

I'm sorry I kept you waiting this long for a notification of the above fact, but believe it or not, as Ripley would say (the man who writes up the caricatures of extraordinary facts) I was busy. You see, I'm not a quitter as you reminded me not to be! About a month ago I entered a contest for a scholarship and won it! Congratulate me, Buddy, congratulate me! Yes, sir; I am also a student again and a darn serious one. I am taking coaching lessons on concert repertory from Prof. Ludwig Becker – and for the rest of the year I get a 12 dollar, one-hour lesson, free of charge! How's that? And just about now I am buried up to my neck in Wieniawski, Bach, Rovelli and Halir. And next season will be some more concerts, see? And maybe the Chicago Symphony Orchestra.

That's why I have somewhat relented in my writing, not only to you, but to all others. I had to prepare for the contest – and that was no small job. And I had to compete with individuals who had real merit – even if they didn't possess the quality talent I do. (Pardon the self-love, but it comes natural-like now!) The age limit was 28 – and since I am only 27, I thought I'd take the dying man's chance – and, fortunately, it turned out well! And I am happy to get the opportunity – because education, even on the violin, is never a thing of the past. Now, though, with all my teaching, it keeps me on the hop, skip and jump – believe me!

No, there's no Big House for the troubles I get into. The cop starts to lecture me and I immediately lecture him, see? After all, this is a free country – in speech, at least – as long as you don't offer personal violence or insult. But that matter has been straightened out; I may use my type-writer until 9:30 P.M. And that means Post Mortem to me! And all the girls with nerve strain can go and get themselves psychoanalysed!

I'll find out just as soon as I can about the best literary review in America – which I think is the *Mercury*.[1] And when I do I'll buy a copy and send it to you. On the cover you'll find all the information you want about subscriptions, payments and conditions. And whenever you want books, well – you know me. Just send me the glad word – and I'll trot right down the stairs and into God's sunlight to get them.

---

1 *American Mercury*.

I haven't done any reading of late, at all – only because every minute of my time has to go into memory work and study for my project. I see a chance of getting into the $100-a-week class, so I'll not pass it up. Besides, my brains crave progress and more of it!

Sunday afternoon, Nov. 1st, the Green Bay professional football team will play the Chicago team in Chicago, for the North American championship. Our team, from the good, old city of Green Bay, Wisconsin – became nationally famous two years ago, when it won the American championship, against such cities as New York, Chicago and Philadelphia. And they have been the champs ever since. My brother is coming to Chicago for that game, along with some other 7,000 fans and a band. Wotta game that'll be! They have already sold over 55,000 tickets – and be assured that there will be as much team spirit on the field as in the grandstands! This is why I kept saving those pieces of chocolates for my brother!

I also received another copy of the *Rassegna* – this morning. Evidently, everything has been put aright, eh? You will let me know how much you paid, and I shall make deductions, additions and divisions over here.

Just to give you an idea of the forces of slang, let me quote to you an article on the students feeling in Columbia University against the professors. It reads: 'Columbia students, through the Spectator, school paper, have launched a war against professors who "murder the King's English." Twenty-six professors were listed as horrible examples. One student wrote: "Many of the professors around here are just plain dumb when it comes to speaking correctly. I know one who used 'don't' for 'doesn't' 17 times in a single lecture." And another wrote: "We are tired of sitting in at lectures where the English language is murdered with impunity. There is a certain amount of grotesqueness in the situation. Can you wonder that we are more than a little militant?"'

Hot stuff, isn't it? But that's the way it goes – slang even in the lecture-rooms of our Universities. I myself have heard more than one professor say such things as 'O, you ain't got nothin' on me!' or 'No, it don't make a bit of difference.' I agree with you that they know their subjects – or they wouldn't be at Columbia – but is that all that is necessary, after all?

Well, Cesare, I have to let up once more! Thanks for the lovely gift, again – and write me often as to what's what and who's who! I'm your Buddy ever and ever, you know. Au revoir –

Antonio Chiuminatto

[Turin,] December 24th, 1931
To Antonio Chiuminatto, Chicago

Dear Tony:
Surely Americans are kinder than we. I got your wishes and never thought to send you any myself. Here they are then, posthumous as always. I hear from you that all your boosting in the world raised you to dizzy heights. Good-luck on your career.

Say, how's thing in Ole Chicago? When will you build an Institute all by yourself? Remember your Buddy when you'll be a big executive and send me word to come over and bum some residence in USA.

Now, that's the winter season we'll have to let up books-sendings. So, you'll enjoy some peace, aint' it? Once in a while look after the *Mercury*, if you think that's good. I wrote something more on the *Cultura*[1] and here it is. Don't get too worried over it.

Do you know I got a victrola? I've a ground of the cutiest American trifles I ever heard – The Revellers, The Footwarmers, Ted Lewis, Whiteman etc. Now, you'll have another office: should you hear about some hot American record send me title and composer and orchestra. Get me? Especially *blues* and *saxs*.

Chicago, Illinois, January 6th, 1932
To Cesare Pavese, Turin.

Dear Cesare:
Your letter of Xmas day and the *Cultura* arrived this morning. I certainly was glad to hear from you after this long lapse!

I returned only yesterday from my Xmas vacation at home in Green Bay. And I had a swell time – so much so, in fact, that on New Year's Eve I went to a house party at 8 P.M. and came home the next morning at 9 A.M. How's that for celebrating, eh?

The first thing I did yesterday was to mail you a copy of the *Bookman*. After much investigation I was informed by Prof. McCole of Notre Dame University that the *Bookman* is by far the best literary review in America.

1 The essay *L'Antologia di Spoon River*, published in the November 1931 issue.

And so that's what you'll want, if any. I have also found out the annual subscription price is four dollars ($4.00) plus one dollar ($1.00) for mailing. It is a monthly publication which sells for 40 cents, which is a reduction of 10 cents from last year. Prices are coming down in America due to hard times. If you still care to subscribe for this review just let me know and I'll see that everything is put in order for you. And just how do we stand financially, since I think I owe you now? Yes, I.O.U. all right! I have mailed you the December copy – and before the January copy makes its appearance you'll have time to give me the dope, see.

So you have gone in for American records of the jazzy kind, eh? Well, Cesare, if you only know how to pick your records all will be well; if not, you'll get more damn junk than you could think of. Here, too – all modesty aside – is where I can help you to choose numbers that have more that musical value. Within the next few days I shall get a catalogue of the Victor Records, mark the good jazz numbers that I know will interest you and then mail it to you. That's the best way to get things done right. There are some excellent things in jazz music – but God knows how few, too!

I suppose you have 'Dinah' sung by the Revellers, eh? Now that's a swell record. It's a perfect picture of the South and in a great way gives you the soul of the negro. Another number I think you should have is 'Saint Louis Blues' which is the song of a negro prostitute deserted by her 'man.' She sings in what is known as a barrel-house of the South, a dive frequented by both whites and blacks. In it you will hear all the nostalgia of a broken heart, all the longing of a negro heart, which is as sincere as it is childish. It is among the very fine things we possess. So is 'Ole Man River,' if you haven't it. If you shouldn't be able to get records over there, let me know and I'll get them here for you. What's more I'll send you the words along with the record, and my comments, if necessary; in this way you'll get the full import of the record as a whole. Va bene? You are now speaking MY language, you know – so that puts on a new cloak of understanding.

Just before I went home I took a girl friend to a dance at the Edgewater Beach Hotel, where Whiteman and his Orchestra are now playing. He is permanently located in Chicago now, you know. Ted Lewis and his Orchestra, by the way, are now making an appearance in one of the theaters here. Whiteman of course, is still THE orchestra, but have you heard Rudy Vallee, Guy Lombardo, Wayne King or Ted Fiorito's orchestras? Very good! Ya, we'll have to get together on this. It will give you a better understanding of some of our literature, too.

And how about books? isn't there anything you'd need? Don't be bashful, you know – I can still get them. Have you read anything of Willa Cather; she was mentioned for the Nobel Prize, though she didn't get it. Just now I am reading her *My Antonia*, which is very good!

And now that I have read your essay on *Spoon River* (Jan. 7th), I note that you mention *My Antonia*. I am just about to finish this volume. Where the devil do you get all those books? Your translations from the *Anthology* seem to me to be very, very good, Cesare! You might give us a translation of the whole book, what say? And as usual, if you need any help here I am! I'm going to get me a copy of *Spoon River* and then I'll tell you just what I think of your translations. But the ole boy sure knows his p's and q's, eh? Which means you know your letters!

Say, you haven't given up the idea of coming over here, have you? How about Columbia? Better give me some more details; I may be interested in seeing you get over here, see? Next year, you know, will be the World's Fair, and I must have you as a guest. Maybe we can arrange it, eh? All you have to do, Cesare, is arrange to come over, which shouldn't be hard considering all the privileges that will be granted. You can room with me at a minimum expense and in the meantime I'll see what I could get you to do. I know some of the Professors at Notre Dame University – and I am sure they would be glad to give me a hand. Think it over! Even one year in this city would be an education to you! It shouldn't be any trouble to get a passport for the World's Fair, diamine! And in a year's time you ought to be able to make expenses all around! C'mon; Cesare, we've got to do it now that you are still batching it – a bachelor, I mean! If you want to come over right now, let me know and we'll see what can be done about it. With your excellent preparation, you need some of this free air in Chicago. You'd have a modern library at your call, a world of slang for the asking – and an environment that has a bit of all America. You'd be one of the snappiest critics over there, when and if you were to go back. Get yourself to come over as a student if necessary; I could arrange that nicely – and even at that you could work, see! As I said, I'd room with you – unless you object, of course! With six bucks a week it's a cinch! Then you get the restaurant habit, see! Eat when you like and only as much as you like! I'm all for it – and I'll give you both hands; so shake a leg! You ought to be able to teach Italian, at least, even in a night school; money is money, you know, when you have a bigger purpose in sight. Our motto then is 'America Soon'! Remember it!

Here it is the 7th of January, 1932 – and you'd actually think it were

September; no snow, no cold weather and plenty of sunshine. This country has gone nuts, financially and thermometrically! Now it is, indeed, the land of artist Bohemians!

Julius Rosenwald, the great Chicago Jewish philanthropist, just died last night. In his lifetime he donated over sixty-two million dollars to charity! That doesn't sound much like a Jew, does it – but that's what he did! With more men like him in this world we'd have a better place to live and weep in! We are expecting to see a phenomenal funeral to-morrow! He was part owner of Sears & Roebuck, the great general merchandize stores of America. Requiescat in Pace!

Well, Cesare, keep the thread of our plans and write me often. Anything you want – books, records or what have you – just remember me! And here's wishing you plenty of good luck and happiness in this New Year. May it be the year in which we meet again – in Chicago.

Toodle-oo and take it easy! Always your pal –

Antonio Chiuminatto

[Turin, January 1932]
To Antonio Chiuminatto, Chicago

I thank you for the *Bookman*. 'Swell' magazine! I succeeded in having it bought by a publisher of Turin (he intends to translate American novels) and so, without expense I'll look it over and keep informed. He just intends to translate *My Antonia*.

Can't you find out for me some novel by Faulkner, the new famous writer of Southern stock so spoken about just in the *Bookman*? If it's not too costly, buy it offhand and let me have it. Otherwise send word about. We'll set accounts after this.

Now, as for the records, I have 'Dinah,' I have the 'Chant of the Jungle,' 'Lady Play,' etc. all by the Revellers. By Whiteman I've 'Blue Hawaii' (!!!) and 'Just Like a Melody.'

I'll buy the 'Saint Louis Blues' just on account of your advice. I think I'll find it by Ted Lewis.

Send me the words of all these records, if you can, and – sure – your comments. I'll be tickled. And put down always all novelties in this field, *names* and *comments*. I'll tell the world.

Say, you have an idea to treat me, over there in the States. Don't say it twice, ole boy, don't. On March, if all's well, I'll be free from the army, and after that ... don't get too chummy with me, don't ... I'm the guy to accept.

We also, have a phenomenal winter, all sunshines and perspiration ... only not the righteous perspiration, the worker's, I mean. We are all fired, and perhaps that's the reason we want to fire ... guns ... you know.

Chicago, Illinois, February 21st, 1932
To Cesare Pavese, Turin

Dear Cesare:
I am already answering your letter, you see! I was also glad to hear that you have arranged to see a copy of *The Bookman* each month; it is supposed to be the best thing of its kind on the American market. You see, I always manage to get the best even when I don't know what it's all about myself! Ha!

I had to buy a copy of *As I Lay Dying* by Faulkner, since it was impossible to get a copy in any other way. I still have some forty pages to read and then I'll mail it to you. The reason why I am reading it is because I discovered that you're going to need some comments on the English, which is all in the Southern drawl, dialect – and poor English, at that! Southern conversational English, is what it is![1]

While the rest of the world may accuse Faulkner of being a genius – I can't say that I DO! Not from this single reading, at least. I consider him an excellent writer – even profound – but I don't like his choice of subject matter. However, that's for you to decide! Books are an avocation for me – not a profession!

The book will set you back $2.50, if you want it – and if you don't, just send it back. I can always find a place on my shelves for it.

And I have another proposition to offer you. I can send you two books at a time from the library with a month's permission. If you could read the books in a few days and then send them right back, you would not have more than 25¢ or 30¢ of fine to pay on them. Which is still more

---

1 See appendix for Chiuminatto's comments on Faulkner's novel.

convenient than buying them ... that is, if you CAN get them at the library. The month's reading permission will take care of the trip over and back again – giving you a few extra days to read at the price of three cents a volume per day! If you are interested – just send me the names of any two books you'd like – and we'll try it out, anyhow!

So you have the 'St Louis Blues'! I'll say it's a darby; it's the best thing we have in jazz inspiration – if there is any such thing. You ought to get 'Ole Man River' as played by Paul Whiteman and his Orchestra. I spent two hours listening to records yesterday afternoon at Lyon & Healy, but I couldn't find anything worth while – that is, anything beyond the ordinary dance-hall numbers. 'The Song of the Bayou' is quite a hit, too – and you may be able to get that over there. If you are interested in American composition – more than jazz – get the records of the Mississippi Suite as played by Whiteman; there ought to be a booklet of information on it, too. It's really lovely in its Southern setting! I am not promising you any rush service on records; I follow jazz music too little to know all about the records that are out. But as I hear a good one I'll let you know all about it – and I still KNOW a good thing when I see it or hear it!

How would you like a pick of Negro Spirituals – as sung by Paul Robeson? Or some comedy records by those great negro impersonators, Mack and Moran? The Two Black Crows, they are called! Or some organ records of jazz as played by Jessie Crawford? You will hear the famous Barton organ on these records – organs that you do not possess over there. Among the old records of Paul Whiteman you will find 'On the Waters of Minnetonka' which is a gem! It is an American composition of Indian setting and is really a lasting number (Record 21796). 'I kiss your hand, Madam' as played by Jack Hylton's Orchestra is also a darby! So is 'Black and Tan Phantasy' as played by Duke Ellington and his Orchestra! As for anything else I do not want to precipitate, see! I want to hear the records for myself and then I'll quote to you, later!

And the proposition I made you about coming over here is still good, you know. I'm lonesome for some good company, see? Next year will be the World's Fair year – and you certainly ought to be here.

We still aren't having any winter. Every day is a summer day. This has been the most surprising season in all my life. The unemployed are surely getting a break – with no coal having to be bought. How is it over there?

Well, Cesare, this is about all. I'm mailing your book this morning –

the 26th. I just hope you like it; I DON'T! If you find out that you like it, let me know why, will you?

And with this we'll say toodle-oo. As ever your pal

Antonio Chiuminatto

[Turin,] April 2nd, 1932
To Antonio Chiuminatto, Chicago

At last I'm here answering you. As for Faulkner you're right: he's a tremendous bore, till now at least: I didn't as yet get through the whole book. I buy it however as a curiosity and enclose here the dough. I cannot remember whether I'm yet owing you something: please look over your accounts-books and send me a notice.

Thank you for the explanation you put down for me: it was very useful. So you're not forgetting old ways?

Say, just this evening I'm swept along by the wanderlust. I swear here to you that I cannot any more stay here in Italy. My army-duty is over at last. I've no news of my old fixing with Columbia, and don't speak about blues, boy! I dream, hope, long, die after America. I must come.

Till now you've been so kind with me: try to make me the last and greatest favor, call me in USA. You know, we cannot come over without an employment from over there. It's now your task of friendship to find me an employment, however a nominal one, something to get the passport. I'm ready to teach Italian or to marry the horridest heiress, only I could get there.

Apply to the University, whether there are possibilities to find a place as an assistant, as an usher, as a what-you-call-it. Only, help me through. Otherwise I'll try revolution in Mexico and bootlegging through the frontier.

Now that I've cooled myself out let us speak of records. Yours consels are very precious but nothing of what you point at in your list is found here in Italy.

But avast ... I hope I'll buy my next records right there in God's Country.

On any day – even to-morrow, I'm ready to pack. Only say the word, boy!

Pav

Chicago, Illinois, June 3rd, 1932
To Cesare Pavese, Turin

Dear Cesare:
I have your letter of April 5th,[1] with the inclosure, but I was just wondering whether or not I already answered it. I have my doubts, so I'm now just to make sure.

I was glad to hear that your Army service has come to a close. That ought to give you more free time for worthier purposes. Now that June has arrived I was going to send you the usual run of summer vacation loans on books, but I do not know what books you want. Let me know before August, at least, and I'll get them for you; the loan is good, you know, until the first of October.

I have been doing some hard thinking about getting you to come to America, and as yet, at least, I'm at no definite conclusion. The times are so rotten here, too, that nothing is a good proposition any more. However, I'm looking forward to better times in the Fall, which will also be preparation time for the World's Fair of next year. If I find the least opening for you, I'll lay your name before the Italian consul Castruccio, and do all I possibly can to see you over here. We'll have to be patient, though, because these are not things that can be arranged over night. And with all the unemployment in America, the problem becomes just that much more complicated.

We are planning on opening Italian classes at the Conservatory next year, mostly for those in the vocal departments. It won't be much work for the first year – and they are planning on giving the work to me. If I can possibly arrange to use that as an excuse for you, be assured I'll do it. The only reason why I would take the classes is because I can always use some extra pennies, but where musical instruction could occupy my whole day, I'd gladly give it to anyone else, and certainly to you, if it could so be arranged. Anything, in short, to get you here, after which you could move with greater ease, n'est-ce-pas?

Personally, I can't imagine what is going to become of this country! Yes, it's all that bad and even worse! Now that there is no work of any kind money also stops circulating. I'm having a hell of a time trying to collect my fees! And everybody else is, too, that I know of! Well, there is the World's Fair next year; that ought to push things around a little anyhow. And it will be a good excuse to visit us, even if you can't stay. As

1 Rough copy is dated April 2nd.
2 Giuseppe Castruccio, Consul general of Italy in Chicago, 1928–35.

things pick up, though, there'll be some way of getting you over here. Just take it easy!

Spring is here and all we get is rain! I haven't been able to wear my spring hat yet, darn it! Maybe I can wear it on my vacation in August, at least. Yup; I'm going home for the want of something better to do.

We have plenty of lakes up there in Wisconsin so there is plenty of swimming and fishing. The only music I shall play will be a radio program or two – and that's all.

Hey – what about our friend Max Mila? He's still alive, I hope. Why, the son-of-a-So-and-So hasn't written to me for ages. Shake him out of it, will you? If I should ever disown him as a friend of mine, tell him it'll be his head-ache.

I was planning on going to Italy this summer for a short vacation, but I have already discovered that I'm short on the finances. After we get to the Russian system of money then I may be able to travel on my looks! How funny human nature; I'm tired of America and you're tired of Italy! You and I are like the married woman and the old maid; each one thinks the other is getting all the fun out of life! Some Senator a while back asked what might be the cure for this depression – and the answer was 'Give America right back to the Indians – that is, if they'll take it.' That's just how I feel about it!

Now that my greater period of liberty is near at hand, don't forget to give me a list of what you want done and what you want to know; books, records and the likes! I'll have lots of time to get around.

Just keep up the old spirit, Cesare – and all will be well. Drop me a line occasionally – at least a little oftener. There's nothing like a steady contact to keep the old fires burning, see!

Give my best regards to all who ask of me – and write me soon. Lots of luck, old pal, and stick it out!

As ever –

Antonio Chiuminatto

[Turin,] July 24th, 1932
To Antonio Chiuminatto, Chicago

Dear Tony:
I didn't as yet reply to you, for the reason that I was planning a little holiday on sea on board a sailer and so it was impossible for me to send you

the wonted list of summer books, being as yet uncertain about my future adress. Now the sea-travel has gone to pot, but my adress will be wavering just the same. I'll tramp through Italy, and so it'll be useless to have you troubled about books. I'll not be able to receive.

About your economical worries surely you're no worse than we big men, that every morning wait for a flood or something fiercer.

Thank you for your good will about getting me over there, but I see the difficulties and apart from some fit of hysterics I can quite clearly see that there's salt water between.

I've philosophy enough to perceive that I also, after some time, would be tired of God's Country. I already taught philosophy. I don't know what I've not yet taught: leaving aside Italian and English, I can remember Latin, Geography, History, French, Greek. Here's a brazen-faced bum, you can say! I've already seen the dregs of teaching, waiting to see life's.

Good holidays, old boy, on your Wisconsin lakes.

Chicago, Illinois, November 14th, 1932
To Cesare Pavese, Turin

My Dear Cesare:
I had been hoping to hear from you for ever so long now, especially since I was told in your last letter that you were traveling around in Italy. But since I have heard nothing more from you, I shall write in answer to that letter of some months ago – in hopes that we can soon get back upon our old footing.

Miss Franchi has sent me the clippings of the criticism of your latest translation, that of *Moby Dick*. I am taking this opportunity to congratulate you upon a work of no small proportions. More power to you, old boy!

Now that Hoover has been defeated – and I certainly am glad of it – I hope things pick up around here. We are still in a very bad way financially, morally and whatnot else. Anyhow, the Democrats have promised us beer for Christmas, with the result that beer is all over now just awaiting the final permission to be sold publicly! What'll you have – light or dark, or Pilzener or Munchner!

The defeat of Hoover, as you may know by now, was one of the highlights of American history. No other president was ever so thoroughly ousted. And America, so republican in spirit, has suddenly become solidly democratic. You may be interested in knowing why.

Well, we Americans feel that Europe must pay its war debts – and that there must be no talk of cancellation unless all countries completely disarm. In the face of the actions of some of the nations, we want to arm and arm heavily! Hoover has been too partial with Europe, to our loss, and we have told him so ... in the last election! We need a president who is not to be talked out of action by slick European diplomats! And while I am an ardent admirer of Mussolini, I feel, as an American, that he must be made to pay his debts, too! Europe has run away with Hoover in these four years, especially England, and we'll have no more of it. So last Tuesday, America, in one of the most overwhelming elections in history, has ousted its president! Think of it; out of 527 electoral votes Hoover got the enormous sum of 57! That ought to express our resentment.

Roosevelt, the president-elect, is the grand-son of our former president, Theodore Roosevelt – and if he turns out to be anything at all like his grandfather[1] – God help European politicians! He is every inch an American – at least we hope he will continue to be so in the presidency! He is against cancellation of debts – and HOW! He is against prohibition, too. Under him we hope to restore prosperity, first of all; then we hope to be able to disarm all nations, with the accent on France. If we can't do that, we hope to build the strongest army and navy in history, with which we'll collect war debts if it's the last thing we do! So right ahead, Roosevelt; up and at 'em!

My dear Cesare, we have finished with apologizing to Europe for being Americans! We have rights and we're going to get them!

Two weeks ago I had the pleasure of meeting, in a Sunday afternoon musicale and reception at Columbia, the noted American pianist and composer, Charles Wakefield Cadman. I used to discuss him with Della Corte – and now after all these years I have met him! Very nice, isn't it?

And how are you, old fellow? Let's get chummy, c'mon! How about books – how about slang – and how about getting into some work on your English teaching! I mean, how about taking up your problems with me – so that I can have an occasional hour with you over my typewriter, huh? I'm still at your service, you know – and I only wish I were a consul or something like that so that I could do more to get you into America. Books, by the way, can now be had second-hand at very reasonable

1 Theodore Roosevelt and Franklin Delano Roosevelt were distantly related, fifth cousins.

prices; the market, there, too, has taken a slump in price. I need some more activity with you – so get busy and think something up!

And how is my old pal Mila? I shall have to write him one of these days, but if you see him, tell him to drop me a card at least and say hello!

In the field of music we are still having such appearances as those of Kreisler, Heifetz, Horowitz, Paderewski, Martinelli and others. There is no opera this winter, but an improvised company is going to try to give us second class opera, at least. This is all the result of the doings of Samuel Insull,[2] whom I hope they get back here and put into prison! He has just about ruined this city.

Well, Cesare, this is but a note to tickle you into some letter writing. So let's have it! Give my best regards to all who should ask of me and accept my best wishes of friendship for yourself. Here's hoping you have a pleasant and successful year in English at the Lega – and let me know ho[w] it's coming along.

Until next time, then – I am as ever your old pal –

Antonio Chiuminatto

[Turin,] December 1st, 1932
To Antonio Chiuminatto, Chicago

My dear Tony:
At last I got something from you! I thought you were dead. But it seems Roosevelt's hit knocked you on the head and caused you to remember old friends. If that's politics, all the better.

I don't know whether to congratulate you for your righteous burst of patriotic feeling. But, to mix some water in your *new* wine, I must say that I *don't* think Europe will pay: after all Europe already paid in the World War with all its dead, wounded, and maim'd, and it's only right *you* also pay with money. Moreover if we pay you, we'll be ruined and so your trade and exchange will be lessen'd too, not to say destroyed. As for our Premier you fancy so much, I should suggest you Americans

2 American public utilities financier, whose Middle West utilities empire collapsed in 1932. Insull went to Greece, then Turkey. Extradited (1934) to the United States, he faced fraud and embezzlement charges (1934–5), but was acquitted.

come over and carry it back in God's Country: Italy will be delighted to pay his war debts that way.

Speaking seriously, I'm glad you're not forgetting me. As for books, slang and so on, you are but too kind: it's your old need to be of service to someone and I'm getting crammed of English Literature to hold some professional examens and by those gentlemen the American one is ignored. But it will not be long before I pull your wire for some service. So, be merry.

Old Max is yet playing the Merry Widow. How do you think it will pan out? I'm about sure, he will marry his musical comedy and then she will turn out a tragedy.

By the way, I've got a very stingy fellow as a publisher and I've already spent on critics and friends the whole lot of my due copies of the translation.[1] So now that I know you are yet kicking, I cannot at once succeed in begging from him a copy of them to mail you; but be sure on the first occasion I'll remember it.

Chicago, Illinois, December 16th, 1932
Cesare Pavese, Turin

My Dear Cesare:
Your letter could not have arrived at a better time. I have just taken to-day and tomorrow off in order to get my Xmas shopping done, which includes, among other things, a suit of clothes for myself. Early next week I am leaving for Green Bay and the holidays, where I shall join my brother, the Jesuit, at mid-night Mass; he will be on the altar and I shall be playing in the choir! I am looking forward to about ten days of good times and good eats!

Sometime to-day I am going down town to buy a few books as Xmas presents. I shall look around carefully for a copy of Hemingway's *In Our Time* – and if I find it, you will have it a few days after you get this. Looking for some book or other for you makes me feel like an old friend again! Atta boy, Cesare!

We are having a helluva time here with war debts! Since France has

---

1 *Moby Dick.*

repudiated us, we have attempted to impeach President Hoover; in other words, kick him out! He is the second president in our history against whom such a drastic action has been suggested. It's all his fault, what with his pro-English spirit and his banking tricks.

Italy is the only country that has come in as a lady! She paid up even the day before the official date for payment. Three cheers for Mussolini, who is an acute statesman, believe me! He has it all figured out that he will let France and England do the dirty work; if they win, he will, too – and if they lose, he will have lost nothing by playing safe now! That's what I call keeping your head on your shoulders!

And France will get it in the neck like she never got it before – since she thinks she's so smart. Right now we are planning a boycott – one little end of which will deprive France of 600 million dollars a year in tourist trade alone. Not only, we will sell French bonds – and then let the French worry about paying someone else! This is once when France's diplomacy got all wet – and the whole country'll get plenty soaked now, believe you me!

It's all well and good that you Europeans got killed, mutilated, gassed and what not – besides running into heavy expense – but don't forget for a single minute that we, too, have thousands and thousands of dead, crippled, shell-shocked and what else have you? Besides, we, too, are paying war debts – paying them – understand – not repudiating them! We are not asking for war debts – since just about all of them have been cancelled to Europe; we are asking for the payment of after-the-war loans, which we gave you for reconstruction purposes.

We have no incentive to cancel right now. We have 11 million unemployed, business is shot in the head, international business isn't worth a damn because of the tariffs – so what was it you said we had to lose? Be yourself, Cesare, please! What money we have is still damn good because it's all in Europe! If those countries all repudiate, don't you think for a minute that we can't make them suffer for it; in the meantime, you had better pray that they all do like Mussolini!

A new American regime will go into effect in March, and I promise you that American common sense will suppress that hypocritical diplomacy so prevalent over there. Guns have even been flashed in our Senate against the French action! And England got cold feet at the last moment – and decided to pay! Roosevelt is just lying in ambush – and all he has to say now is 'Let them either pay or repudiate; we'll take action afterwards.' You boys over there are playing with fire and you think it's funny! Well, he laughs best who laughs last, you know!

When you have time look up Mr Philbert Deyman at the Lega; he is my old American chum – and is now teaching Spanish there, I hear. You could have a nice conversation with him.

About your translation, Cesare – there is no hurry. I don't remember having made so bold as to ask for one – but if ever you should see fit to send me one, you may be sure that I shall appreciate it.

If you know of any good Italian novel that needs translation into English let me know, will you? I could find time now to work for a few extra pennies. With translation rights reserved, capisci! If you know of any young and aspiring authors who have written something recently – and something that has some value – get them to let me translate it for sale over here. This public reads a tremendous lot —not to say what, of course – but still a lot; it may be worth everyone's effort in such an undertaking.

So Max is still on the band-wagon, eh? When you see him again, give him my best regards and wishes – and tell him to shake himself out of that state of coma – and drop me a line or two.

I have just received a lovely Xmas present from the family with whom I am staying – a set of the complete works of Plato – in a deluxe printing! Now I shall become a classicist – Ha! If the rest of my gifts go according to this one, I'll have to ask that we have at least a few more Christmases each year!

And while I'm still near the subject, let me remind you that I have moved from my old address. Just about three weeks ago! I am now living at this address: 5906 N. Kenmore Ave. – Apt. 2. – Chicago. It's only about a block from the lake shore – so next summer I'll be able to jump out of my window into the refreshing waters of old Michigan! If you ever get around this way some time, Cesare, just drop in! No, not the lake; the house! Ha!

Since the first of the month we have been having real, honest-to-goodness Winter. It's way below zero and so windy that the cold comes right to your address! I feel sorry for the poor devils who are unemployed and who have to walk sidewalks to beg for a few pennies to get a cup of hot coffee. Some of them have even been beggin old stoves, which they set up in some sheltered corner – and around which they gather to keep warm, by burning newspapers, boxes and anything else they can find or beg! Yes, 11 million of them, too! The same ones who contributed all that money so that you fellows over there could assassinate each other very amicably ... at our expense! Anyhow, we have already called Napoleon a great big bum – and are now waiting for the French to get mad –

so damn mad they'll tear down the Colonne Vendomne! If I were the French, though, I'd put a line and pulley on that obelisk; it makes it so much easier to get back in place, afterwards! Pagliacci!!

In closing, Cesare, I hope you have a Very Merry Xmas and a Most Happy and Prosperous New Year! And many of 'em! I hope, too, that through the new year we shall carry on this good work of letter writing.

My best regards to all who may ask of me – and until next time, with all best wishes for lots of luck to you, I am as ever – your pal –

Antonio Chiuminatto

[Turin,] January 24th [1933]
To Antonio Chiuminatto, Chicago

Dear Tony:
Now that I'm out of danger with Xmas and New Year turkey-stuffings, I can write you off a good old letter. As for politics: here's to you, hoping to encounter you at my machine-gun's end and have you cry mercy. We'll yet see that, someday, old boy. Perhaps only in the next World-war, we'll find out our true calling.

But, honestly, I don't care a damn about the whole lot of it. I would soften a little, however, thinking about the 11 millions, should I not have learnt in my old school-books that world history is only a great shambles and never was something resembling fairness and humanity brought out to actuality among our gallant fathers. And thinking that 11 millions of to-day are the result of a ten years of boasted 'prosperity' I can't help grinning. Our literatures here in Europe are quoting merrily your unemployment figures and do you know what they find to say about? They hold you are damned lucky to have been granted the calamity, hold that your national pluck and boldness through suffering will come to perfection; that nothing America was in need of but this wholesome crash and wreck in misery and exposure; to make a long story short, that you'll profit immensely by the unheard-of depression. How do you like it? Ain't we the gallant undertakers? But let's drop it in the dung-hill, where it belongs.

So you also are looking out for books? Thanks be to God that my opportunity has at last arrived! You want something to translate into *American* which I think is a little hard to find in our libraries, as our writers are slumbering since two hundred years. However, the most obvious name is here useless, as all your stage-men have already rifled it. I mean S. E. Pirandello. But perhaps over there a novel by him remains unknown: you could reveal it to an eager public: *Il fu Mattia Pascal* ... Naturally it's now out of printing, but I'll get information immediately whether it is already translated, and where I can find a copy of it to mail you.

Meanwhile, not to let you change your mind, I'm mailing another novel, a masterpiece by our Sicilian novelist Giovanni Verga; the author of the plot of *Cavalleria Rusticana,* perhaps our greatest novelist of the nineteenth century with Alessandro Manzoni. I have inquired about and did not find it has already translated into English. Think about it.

Of course, I'm here ready to help you on whatever points I'll be able, from the meaning of certain Verga's idioms to copyright matters.

Chicago, Illinois, March 8th, 1933
To Cesare Pavese, Turin

Dear Cesare:
I'm answering your letter to-day because I'm taking a one-day holiday! Besides, there is so much excitement around that one really has to take a day off to enjoy it! Cermak is arriving in the city to-day by special funeral train from Miami, Florida – and are the Bohemians ever angry with the Italians![1] You tell 'em! Then, too, the banks all over the country are closed and the States are now issuing temporary money! Even tobacco coupons and soap advertisements can be used for dollars! Are we ever in a helluva fix! And on top of it all Europe's trying to gyp us on our money, and gyp, in current slang, means rob, steal! Anyhow, we are all happy; no work, no banks, no beer and no mayor!

Say, sonny, I've been running my head off trying to find a copy of *In Our Time* of Hemingway, but all I can find is a new copy for two-fifty –

1 Anton Cermak, the Bohemian-born mayor of Chicago, was gravely wounded during an attempted assassination of President Roosevelt on 15 February 1933 in Miami, Florida. He died three weeks later on 6 March. The killer was the Italian-born Giuseppe Zangara, who had become a naturalized citizen of the United States in 1929.

and I know you don't want that. However, just as soon as I find one – if I do – I'll send it along.

I have just finished reading *Ann Vickers* of Sinclair Lewis! Almost 600 pages! And plenty of slang! But it's a great story of the would-be intellectual American Woman around a thesis on prison reform. I shall soon buy me a copy of it, Cesare, and then I shall start to comment all the slang for you. When I have finished I shall send it to you – book and comments – for a reading! Whether you are interested or not, let me know, will you? It is now a best seller, but little is being said about it, because Lewis has suddenly become radical on prison legislation. And he goes after Ann Vickers like he did with Elmer Gantry.

I want to thank you for the novel you sent me, *Mastro Don Gesualdo*! I have translated about a dozen pages so far, only because I have so little time on my hands right now! I have to work at it in spare moments, and that being slow work, you can readily imagine what a task it becomes. However, this summer, when I have six weeks of vacation, I may get a nice run on it. In the meantime, many thanks again for the generosity, which I shall repay you.

A week from Sunday I am appearing in concert at the Conservatory along with others of the Faculty. We get our names in the *Chicago Tribune*, too – another rise to fame! On the 31st I am appearing in a recital for the Woman's Music Club of Barrington, Illinois – and the newspaper (singular, if you please!) is already aflutter with my photograph and write-ups, not to mention that young ladies are having palpitation of the heart in anticipation of seeing and hearing such a handsome artist with the musical name of Chiuminatto – which they cannot even pronounce. And sometime early next month I am to play at the Orrington Hotel in Evanston, Ill. ... so you see what a busy man I am!

Since I wrote you last I have been promoted at the Conservatory! I was appointed to the Board of Examiners in February. When I sat in on the examinations and voted on my fellow-students, I felt like my examiners must have felt on that far away day in June of 1929 when I underwent the agony! Anyhow, I really felt important – and that's saying a lot in these days of depression, depression and more depression!

Our new President is IN now, so look out Europe! All we want from you is OUR money! You can write all the articles you like on the benefits of the depression for us, but give us OUR money! And then if you haven't enough material to write articles with, we'll even be glad to furnish it! Statistics, data, memoranda – anything you like – after you pay your debts! You boys over there are using our money while we have to use wooden nickels and cigar coupons for money! You ought to be ashamed of yourselves! You ought to blush and hang your heads in guilt – but NO, you walk like perfect gentlemen and think up schemes whereby you can gyp us some more!

Well, I don't give a damn about it myself, Cesare, but I'd get heart failure if we ever gave France a break, which means a kind favor! They don't even deserve contempt!

And our little friend (chisto italiano!) Zangara will probably be electrocuted now that Cermak has died.[2] I don't think he's an anarchist or a communist; he's just a spark from the old school of Machiavelli. Opinion has it that the attempt was a direct one on Cermak, and not on Roosevelt – which I am inclined to believe, since Cermak never enjoyed popularity in Chicago – so much as now that he is dead! We have a Bohemian professor at the Conservatory who would like to assassinate me – just as though I were Zangara; the ass! He even made so bold as to speak of the 'wops' in my presence, and though he is an older man, I came right back with 'Bohunks,' which is equally a belittling name for Bohemians! After that he became more respectful – damn his hide!

Only one thing is right as it should be – and possibly so, too, because Man has no control over it; the Weather! We are having beautiful Spring climate, sunshine and cool evenings. I feel like the Neapolitan in the poem who says:

Here een Noo Yorka, where am I
  Seence I am landa las' July,
All grey an' ogly ees da sky,
  An' cold as eet can be.

But steel so long as I maka mon'
  So long ees worka to be done,
I can forgat how shines da sun
  Een Napoli.

But oh, w'en pass da boy dat sal
Da violets, an' I can smal
How sweet dey are, I no can tal
  How seeck my heart ees be.

---

2 Zangara was sentenced to death in the electric chair and executed on 20 March 1933.

I no can work, how mooch I try,
But only seet an' wondra why
I could not justa leeve an' die
  Een Napoli.

Just pronounce it the way it's written, Cesare, and you'll have it!

Just a few days ago I saw the movietone pictures of the Carnival of Viareggio! Talk about the Depression over there! Where is it!? Here we sit like so many gloomy undertakers while you rejoice, drink and be nasty! Anyhow, I wouldn't mind living through one of those carnivals again, at that. We get all the talkies of the current events from Italy – and we see everything but Depression. Most of the time it's just a grand celebration, civil or military! Well, more power to you all!

And with this, Cesare, we shall come to a close with the Papal Benediction! I am always tickled pink to hear from you – so don't keep me waiting too long. In the meantime I'll be working on *Ann Vickers* for you, since I am quite sure you will want to read it, if only in a borrowed copy. Until next time, then, believe me your old pal clean down to the wishbone

Antonio Chiuminatto

APPENDIX
Chiuminatto's Explanations of Slang and Non-Slang Expressions

The first instalment of Chiuminatto's comments on Pavese's list of slang and non-slang phrases from Sherwood Anderson's Dark Laughter.[1]

COMMENTS

I am listing the slang phrases book by book, as you have them, save that those phrases in greater use are first and the others will follow at the end of this list. Get me? (Do you understand?)

First Book

1 A game little kid. – 'Game' è una parola che si usa nel senso della parola 'coraggioso' in italiano, ma che poi in inglese vuol lasciar intendere uno che tenta qualsiasi cosa o atto senza paura! Nell'italiano vi è una frase – ci stai? – che in inglese vien tradotta con 'Are you game?' e che si dice naturalmente dopo che si ha combinato qualchecosa. Ecco degli esempi:

We are going on a twenty-mile walk; are you game?
He is a game fighter, and a game loser!
When it comes to athletics she is game at anything.

2 To let on. – Questa è una frase che si potrebbe spiegare con un'altra in inglese, cioè, 'to make believe' (far credere). Vuol anche dire 'fingere.'

1 Signed in pencil by Chiuminatto with no date.

Let on (that) you know me! (Fingi che mi conosci.)
Make believe (that) you know me. (" " " ")
Don't let on (that) you know about him!
Mr. Mila always lets on that he knows Mr. Pavese! (Ha!)
And Mr. Pavese makes believe (that) he likes Mr. Mila!

3 A cinch. – 'Roba da ridere.' Parola usatissima in America.

As for taking my examinations, it will be a cinch! (Pronuncia – sincc.)
It was a cinch the way Bonaglia beat Muller!
It's a cinch he will do it! (È sicurissimo che lo farà)

4 Bruce, Smart and Feeble – Indubbiamente i nomi dei proprietari! Più ancora che si tratta di 'hardware,' il negozio dove si vende degli articoli di acciaio, ferro, ecc. come quello sotto i portici di Piazza Carlo Felice, poco prima di arrivare in Via Roma! (Bella memoria, eh?)

5 A bum work. – Un lavoro malfatto. 'Bum' si usa come sostantivo parlando di persone, e vuol dire 'vagabondo,' 'uomo di poco buono.'

He did some bum work on my automobile.
A bum is a tramp! (errante.)
It was a bum idea! (Era un'idea che valeva poco!)

'Bum' usato come verbo nello 'slang' vuol dire 'imprestare,' 'farsi imprestare.'

I am going to bum five dollars from Max! (Vado a farmi imprestare – ecc.)
He bummed five dollars from you.
John bums cigarettes! (Giovanni si fa dare delle sigarette gratis)

6 To maul someone. – Non è slang ma puro inglese! Vuol dire 'to beat someone, to handle roughly, to hammer someone.' Si usa quando si vuol intendere il battersi forte.

I shall maul him for this!
He was all mauled up! (Era tutto martellato) (slang).
Meat gets a good mauling before cooking. (senso puro del verbo).

Book Two

1 A loop restaurant. – Un ristorante di centro. Nelle grandi città quali New York, Chicago, ecc. nel centro della città gli 'elevated railways' o cioè, le fer-

rovie al di sopra la via fanno un giro simile ad un otto sdraiato, così '**8.**' Questo si chiama un 'loop,' e si pronuncia come nell'italiano 'lup,' precisamente. Quando si dice 'loop the loop' in inglese, si vuol dire 'il giro della morte degli aviatori!'

While in New York we ate in a loop restaurant. (di centro.)
He is going to loop the loop. (Farà il giro della morte.)

2 The car is a whiz. – Questa parola si usa quando si vuol intendere qualchecosa che ha della vita, che sia in gamba, mi spiego?

I bought a new car and it surely is a whiz!
Mr. Pavese is a whiz at English!

3 The city desk. – L'impiego di editore della gazetta di città. Letteralmente è la 'scrivania di città' ossia la scrivania alla quale si tiene a conto le faccende della città, Quindi le faccende dell'editore del giornale.

He was promoted to the city desk after two years.

4 A hard-boiled guy. – 'Guy' si sa è lo slang per un 'individuo.' 'Hard-boiled' (cotto duro') vuole dire uno che non abbia degli scrupoli, che sia sfacciato, intraprendente. Al contrario 'soft-boiled' (cotto molle) vuol dire l'opposto dell'altro, ossia, un individuo che sia molle di carattere.

For a girl she certainly is hard-boiled!
Don't be so soft-boiled, you hard-boiled egg! (individuo.)

5 You're a darby. (Sei qualchecosa di bello!) Quindi è di uso infinito.

The new hat I bought is a real darby
You ought to see the darby new book I bought.
That show we took in last night was a darby. (dal verbo – to take in – vedere).

6 In my B.V.D.s – Sono delle mutande americane, cioè fatte a buche., ossia, a buchi, a rete, se si può dire. Ne portavo io in Italia se mi è permesso dirlo! Ora il nome 'B.V.D.' viene dal nome della compagnia che per prima ci dava questa forma di mutande comode. Ora dal più al meno le stesse mutande, standardizzate! Ha! Quando si vede una signorina che ha gli abiti stretti adosso, si dice che è in 'B.V.D.s' 'l'esse qui ci dà il plurale dacchè si usa sempre nel plurale.

I bought a new pair of B.V.D.'s! They're a darby!

7 Why she had stood for it to be made to look as the portrait had made her look. – Perché lei aveva tollerato di farsi sembrare come il ritratto l'aveva fatta sembrare.

Anzi tutto 'to stand for' nello slang, vuol dire 'tollerare.' Il pronome neutro 'it' è sempre impersonale se non si vuol sostituire.

I can't stand for it! (Non lo posso tollerare.)
He would not have stood for it. (Non l'avrebbe tollerato.)
I can not stand for your smoking at so young an age. 'qui si sostituisce all'impersonale 'it' con la cosa precisa 'for your smoking.'
I wont stand for your smoking either, Mr. Pavese! Have a Lucky!

8 To sit tight, smiling. – Frase di spirito americano, che vuol dire un individuo che non vuol dare la vinta, ma che allo stesso tempo continua a sorridere. 'tight' vuol dire 'stretto' ma che qui vien inteso come 'rigido' di spirito, deciso, insomma.

Mr. Pavese, in learning his American slang, is sitting tight, but I wonder about the smiling! (persiste non dà la vinta.)
Mr. Mussolini is sitting tight on his principles!

Book Three

1 To get in line – to fall in line. – Mettersi in fila.

Nell'uso dello slang vuol dire di mettersi a fare quello che fanno gli altri.

The soldiers fell in line, two by two. (si son messi in fila.)
The boys got out of line. (si son messi fuori di fila.)
Will you ever fall in line? (Ti metterai mai a fare come gli altri?)
Mr. Pavese is falling in line with us.

2 To give a razzing – to razz. – Leggere la vita, disprezzare con ironia, prendere molto in giro ironicamente.

Mr. Bonaglia was given a razzing all during his fight.
He got badly razzed.
Let's razz him, fellows!

3 A bender – una ciucca – on a drunk. Quando uno va ovunque con l'idea di ubbriaccarsi, si dice che egli va 'on a bender,' 'on a drunk' o 'on a spree.' E in America si va sempre con l'idea di ubbriaccarsi. Dal verbo 'to bend' – 'piegare.'

Well, boys, let's go on a bender!
How about going on a drunk, fellows!
We were on a spree last night!

4 What t'ell. – Abbreviazione di 'What the Hell!' frase esclamativa che detta in americano suona 'What t'ell.' Provi lei, Pavese!

What the Hell! are you studying Greek? (frase di sorpresa.)

5 Mossback. – Contadino, ma proprio delle montagne, sa, l'individuo che è così indietro che sembra primitivo, l'individuo che ha la schiena, 'back,' coperto di muschio 'moss.'

Listen, mossback, don't tell me anything about history!
When it comes to art he's a regular mossback!

6 To go on a grand sneak! – Sa benone, Pavese, che qui è proibito di bere, ma che tutti bevono. Ora per bere certe volte bisogna usar discrezione, andare da soppiatto, mi spiego? Ora quando si va a ubbriaccarsi [*sic*] ma non si sa dove, ma tuttavia si vuol cercare, si dice che si andrà 'on a grand sneak.' È una frase che dà sempre il senso dell'illecito.

Say, fellows, we'll have to go on a grand sneak tonight; I don't know of any particular place.

7 The White Sox. – È una squadra professionale di giuocatori di baseball – giuoco molto amato in America. Ora questa squadra in principio si distingueva dalle altre nel fatto che tutti i giuocatori portavano delle calze bianche 'white socks' che più tardi si trasformava in 'white sox,' ritenendo la pronuncia ma cambiando lo 'spelling' a forma sua. Gli uomini portano dei 'socks' che sono corti, e le donne portano dei 'stockings' che sono lunghi, che spiegherà il caso. (si pronuncia 'sachs.')

The White Sox team will play the Black Sox. (squadra)
The White Sox are [American] League leaders, in the professional game of baseball.

Fourth Book

1 a jelly roll. – È una specie di pane dolce in forma di rotolo intersparso di marmelata, usato molto alla colazione. Altri generi di queste cose sono, – buns, bisquits, cookies, rolls and doughnuts. Per spiegazioni si riferisca alla cuoca!

2 An intellectual jag. – Una sbornia intellettuale. Quelli che si ubbriacconо in un modo 'aristocratico,' cioè non così volgarmente come di solito, hanno 'the intellectual jag.'

He is the fellow for the intellectual jags!
He has a jag on! (Ha una sbornia.)
His jag (on) certainly is not very intellectual!

3 Getting God on Sunday night, etc. – Ebbene, intanto 'getting' è il participio presente, o gerundio, del verbo 'to get' che è un verbo comunissimo per 'ottenere.' 'To get,' poi, è di un uso così vasto che è difficile spiegarlo in poche parole. La frase qui vorrebbe dire così – Si nutriva di Dio alla domenica sera, e poi di Mercoledì (per esempio) di qualchecosa altra, forse di liquore!

Get a little God into you! (Prenditi un po' di religione.)
After years of negligence he got a little God into him!
How much God did you get from that sermon?

4 To cut loose with the colors. – To open up with the colors. – Che vuol dire 'mettere in vista d'improvviso dei colori.' Riferisce forse ai negri che sono usi a mescolare i colori negli abiti e certe volte fan persin male agli occhi! 'To cut loose' viene dalla frase classica che si usa per spiegare l'atto del criminale che d'improvviso scatta dalle mani dei custodi. Nello slang si usa per spiegare un attto d'improvviso che abbia in se qualche cosa di furioso, qualche cosa che urta. 'Tagliarsi libero' è la forma letterale, 'scattare,' direi.

He cut loose on me with a lot of slang. (D'improvviso mi viene a dare 'bea[u]coup' di 'slang.')
After a moment's silence he cut loose and swore!
Don't cut loose with all those reminiscences!

5 To run the show. – Letteralmente (far andare il teatro), ma che da noi vuol dire 'essere il padrone!'

I'm running this show and don't forget it! (Sono padrone io e non dimenticarlo!)
Say, do you think YOU'RE running this show? (solo per enfasi.)
Who's running this show? Who's running this place? (Chi è padrone?)

6 Sweet Mama. – Slang per dire che una signorina è carina! Ne abbiamo ancora come 'Hot mama' (mammina calda) ma già è considerato come cosa volgare l'adoperare parlando di 'girls.' Ad ogni modo-siete più liberi in Italia! Avanti!

7 A roll of bread – Un pane qualunque in forma di rotolo, così formato perchè nei ristoranti da noi sono più comodi a manipolare che non una mica.

8 The coffee is like swill. 'Swill' è un mangiare speciale che si prepara per i porci. È l'avanzo dei cibi vegetali mescolati con dell'acqua. È un mangiare che fa persin vomitare solo a vedere, quindi regolarsi conviene se si parla dei cafe!

9 A lot of pep in his book. 'lot' è comunissimo e si traduce perfettamente con il francese 'beaucoup de' – A lot of. 'Pep' è un americanismo per dire 'della vita.'

Put some pep into you! (Mettiti un po' di vita.)
Work takes the pep out of me! (Il lavoro mi fa fiacco.)
Let's pep up this crowd of fellows. (Mettiamo un po' di vita, ecc.)

10 Over we go! – Facciamo il successo! Ecco per il successo! È una frase che si dice dopo qualche proposta per iniziarla al successo.

Now that we have decided, over we go!
It went over big! (Ha fatto un grande successo!)
Chiuminatto went over big in Green Bay! (Si vede senza spiegare.) Ha!
To go over – Fare successo. To go over big. – Far un grande successo.

11 To mosey. (oppure) To mosey along. – Far la propria strada! 'Move on' oppure – move along.

When he told me that, I told him to mosey along!
I told her she was a sweet mam, and she told me to mosey! (Ha!)

Fifth Book

1 Come on down – Non è altro che un verbo con le preposizioni raddoppiate! 'come on' vuol dire 'venga,' 'Come on down' vuol dire 'venga giù.' In quest' ultimo senso 'on' è superfluo, ma si usa molto nello slang.

Come down to my house tomorrow! ('Venga giù a casa mia domani.)
Come on down to my house. (idem – con 'on' per enfasi.)
Come up – come on up. – (esempio dello stesso con 'up.')

2 Small frame affairs. – 'frame' vuol dire che una cosa è fatta di legno, e si riferisce quasi sempre a delle case, quali quelle americane di solito. 'affairs'

qui è usato come disprezzo, come si direbbe in italiano 'piccolo affair di legno.'

It was an affair of no account. (Era un affare da niente.)
There was a small frame affair by the road. (Vi era un affare di legno daccanto alla strada.) Qui sentiamo che s'intende una costruzione di legno, che ci dà la parola 'frame.'

3 Three-storyed frame hotel. (si riferisca agli esempi sopra.) (Un albergo costrutto di legno.)

4 Ring around the rosy. – È un'espressione che deriva da un giuoco americano dallo stesso nome in cui i bambini si tengono a mano l'uno l'altro in forma di circolo, o rosa, e poi girano saltellando. Oggi si dice pure di certe case moderne in cui la cucina o anche l'entrata, se si vuole, si trova nel centro della casa con le altre camere tutte d'intorno, di modo che chi visita incomincia di qui e a forza di visitare si trova di nuovo al punto di partenza. Questo camminare in circolo si chiama 'ring around the rosy' ossia 'circolare attorno alla rosa.' 'Rosy' è un nomignolo caro di 'rose,' come 'dearie' lo è di 'dear.'

5 that woman's taken a shine to you. – 'Shine' vuol dire 'una cotta.' Se non è così forte si può tradurre con 'a liking.' Un'altra parola usata nello stesso modo è 'crush.'

He has taken a shine to Mary.
He was taken a liking to Mary.
He has a crush on Mary. (Noti le preposizioni a secondo.)

To take a shine to – prendere una cotta per.
To have a crush on – Avere una cotta di.

6 A hallway – Un corridoio – nient'altro. La via d'entrata.

7 Tommyrot – The 'bunk.' Stupidaggini. Roba che non vale la spesa di considerare.

All he told me about Mr. Pavese was tommyrot.
The idea that America is poor is the bunk.

8 To get the most out of someone. – Ottenere tutto quello che si può da qualcuno, materialmente o spiritualmente.

Some people must be beaten to get the most out of them.

We got the most out of him by letting him do what he pleased.

9 To get gay – 'to get fresh' – 'to get flip' (si consulti la lista che ha già. Credo che vi sia una di queste forme. Ebbene è un terzo modo di dire la stessa cosa). Sa come sono 'gay' gli ubbriacchi, ma in compenso come sono noiosi – ebbene – ecco la frase, 'Don't get gay.' 'Non oltrepassare i limiti.'

10 To sit hunched – (classico). Sedersi raggomitolato. Sedersi come il gob[b]o.

He sat hunched in his chair like an old man.
Dalla parola 'hunch-back' – gobbo. 'The Hunch-back of Notre-Dame.'

11 Her mouth fell open. – La mascella inferiore cade d'un tratto, si può dire, quando siamo profondamente sorpresi.

Mr. Pavese's mouth fell open when I told him this, so surprised was he!
'fell' è il passato del verbo 'to fall – falling – fell- fallen.' che vuol dire 'cadere.'
When I told him you were in India his mouth fell open!

12 To be out for. – 'Avere lo scopo di.' È forse un po' difficile a comprendere ma mi stia ad ascoltare – gli esempi.

I'm out for a good time! Ci sono (con lo scopo di) divertirmi.
Mr. Pavese is out for American literature. (Il Signor Pavese ha lo scopo suo nella letteratura Americana.)
Mr. Mussolini is out to re-build Italy.
I'm out to make you understand this.
Some girls are only out for a man's money.

13 To tackle someone for a prescription. – Poche parole. Nell'America della proibizione solo i droghieri ed i medici hanno il diritto di vendere dei liquori, che possono vendere dando un ordine scritto all'individuo che poi quest'ultimo presenta al droghiere che glielo vende. Ora quest'ordine scritto e firmato si chiama 'prescription.' I malati ed anche quelli non ammalati chiedono spesso per dei 'prescriptions.' Se uno ha un amico che è dottore – benone – altrimenti bisogna senz'altro ammalarsi, oppure 'go on the grand sneak.' 'To tackle' in senso classico esprime l'azione di un giuocatore di Rugby che ferma l'opponente pigliando per le gambe mentre che è in corso e portandolo giù a terra. Nel senso di slang, però, vuol dire 'parlare' 'tentare' 'proporre' ecc.

I tackled him for a position. – (Mi sono avvicinato, parlandogli di una posizione.) (per me – s'intende.)
I tackled Mr. Pavese for five dollars. (Ho chiesto $5 a Mr. Pavese.)
He tackled us for a vacation. – (Ci ha chiesto una vacanza.)

Noti bene: si usa sempre con 'for.' To tackle for.

14 To come across – Dare – restituire – concedere. (solo in slang.)

Come across with my book – Dammi il mio libro.
He came across with my five dollars. – (Mi ha restituito i miei $5.)
Are you ever going to come across with a favor? (Mi concederai mai un favore?)

Il verbo è sempre 'to come across with.'

15 To be a jolt. – to get a jolt. – essere (o avere) una sorpresa che fa richiamare lì come di pietra. Mi spiego?

The sudden death of his father was a jolt to him. (colpo secco.)
His action just then was a jolt to all of us. (sorpresa grande)

Il verbo 'to jolt – jolting – jolted – jolted' vuol dire un'azione che viene a scatti, come quando si va, per esempio, in una vettura attraverso un campo di montagne russe. Dico bene? Il sostantivo è 'jolter.'

16 The little cuss. 'Mascalzone' in senso ironico e 'biricchino' in senso vezzeggiativo. Si ha l'idea della parola attraverso l'enfasi che si dà.

The little cuss was playing with his toys. (Biricchino.)
The damned cuss still owes me 10 dollars. (Mascalzone.)

Si usa molto anche nel senso di 'individuo' come l'altra parola 'guy,' che si pronuncia 'gai.' Il verbo, poi, 'to cuss, cussing cussed, cussed' nello slang, vuol dire 'bestemmiare' o meno forte, 'dar dei titoli.'

We cussed him for his action.
He got a good cussing from the fellows.

17 To knock someone off his pins 'Pins' è lo slang per 'le gambe,' forse perché certe gambe sono come 'degli aghi.' 'To knock off' vuol dire 'colpire.'

Bonaglia knocked Miller off his pins in the second round.
We were knocked off our pins by the very strong wind.
Say, if you do that again, I'll knock you clean off your pins.
'clean' usato così, vuol dire 'completamente'

Book Six

1 A banty rooster. – 'Banty' è lo slang che deriva dalla parola classica 'bantam' che alla sua volta deriva dal luogo di Bantam nel Giava, onde viene una razza di galli piccoli. Ora, invece di dire 'a bantam rooster' che è un gallo piccolo di questa razza speciale, si dice 'a banty rooster.' Si dà del 'banty rooster' all'individuo che è quasi sempre di spirito come il gallo lottatore, o quello che noi chiamiamo 'the game rooster,' quelli che si usavan una volta negli spettacoli pubblici di combattimenti fra galli.

For a little man he certainly is a banty rooster! (uno che va nelle furie per poco.)
Say, don't be such a banty rooster; I might pull some feathers off!

2 'To get a hunch.' – to have a hunch. – Avere un'idea (per intuito).

I have a hunch that he is the man! (Ho l'idea che l'uomo sia egli.)
I have a hunch as to who is going to be the winner! (a chi sarà.)
We did not have the wrong hunch as to his decision.
I have a hunch that Mr. Pavese is interested in these comments!

3 To hold onto. – Tenere (Avere nella mente l'idea forte di ritenere.)

Mr. Pavese wants to hold onto his English work!
Mr. Mila is holding (on) to his work, too!

Noti che la preposizione 'on' è superflua, ma volendo si può unire al 'to' per enfasi.

4 Not to work out – (oppure) Not to work – (oppure) Not to pan out.

Vuol dire, tant'uno come l'altro – 'Non verificarsi' 'non venire alla conclusione voluta.'

Prohibition is not working out as the laws originally intended.
It works out well. (Va benone!) (Qualche azione, s'intende.)
The new regulations are panning out well. (Danno dei risultati per bene.)

To pan, panning, panned, panned. – ecco il verbo.

I wonder how Fascism will pan out (oppure) work out? (si concluderà.)

5 To keep an eye peeled. – Viene dal verbo 'to peel, peeling, peeled, peeled' – scortecciare, come si fa con le patate! Nello slang, però ha un uso molto

diverso, e si usa sempre con 'eye' volendo dire che un individuo non fa altro che tenersi l'occhio pronto per qualche affare buono! Continuamente in cerca.

I'm keeping my eye peeled for some more money!
Mr. Pavese is keeping his eye peeled for comments on slang!
I'll keep an eye peeled for some good book to send you, Mr. Pavese!
Mr. Henry Ford always has his eye peeled for more business!

6 Over here. 'Over' è solo un rafforzativo, nient'altro! Noti gli esempi.

Come over here! Venga qui.
Go over there! Vada là.
Look at that man over there! Guardi quell'uomo là!
Come over to my home. Venga a casa mia!

Noti bene quest'esempio – Come over sometime! – che è frequentissimo in America e che vuol dire 'qualche volta venga a trovarmi!' L'esempio si spiega così –'come over (to my house) sometime.' che poi con i soliti tagli americani lascia intesa la frase 'to my house.'

We invited Mr. Pavese over! (Abbiamo invitato M.P. a casa nostra.)
They were over the other night! (Erano a casa (mia) l'altra sera.)
We were over to Mr. Pavese's. (Eravamo dal Signor Pavese.)

7 To offer a lift. (oppure) to give a lift. – Offrire un aiuto, oppure, dare dell'aiuto. Dal verbo 'to lift, lifting, lifted, lifted' – che vuol dire 'rialzare' oppure solo 'alzare.' Nello slang – dare aiuto!

Give me a lift with this work. (Aiutatemi in questo lavoro.)
He gave us a lift in his automobile! (Ci ha dato un 'ride' nella sua automobile. Si usa 'lift' qui, perchè se non ci aveva visti ci toccava andare a casa a piedi, e così è stato un aiuto.
Just now I'm giving you (Mr. Pavese) a lift!
May I offer you a lift again sometime? I shall always be glad to give you a lift with you slang findings!

8 Shack – 'capanna' o una casa che sia mal andata!

The American negroes once lived in shacks. (classico-capanne.)
In our modern times some people still live in shacks! (Slang, per case mal andate.)

9 To hand over. – Dare – Restituire. (slang.)

Hand over that book I just gave you!
Hand over the money first and then I'll talk. (Prima dammi i soldi e poi ne parlerò.)
To hand over – Stendere la mano in atto di dare – restituire.

10 to get someone balled up – Confondere qualcuno.

He got me all balled up. (Mi ha confuso.)
I hope you wont be all balled up on these comments, Mr. Pavese!
Don't get rattled, don't get balled up, just take it easy!

11 Advertising solicitors. – Quelli che sono pagati da un'azienda per andare in giro a sollecitare dei 'reclames.' Specialmente i giornali americani impiegano degli individui a far questo lavoro, cioè, andare da ditta a ditta a proporre dei prezzi di reclames di modo che faranno del reclame nei loro giornali. Business, Mr. Pavese, business!

12 He's a card – Tal quale a 'he's a darby.'

13 On the boat coming over. – È un rafforzativo solo come nell'esempio 'Over there.'

We were coming over to America when it happened. (Venivamo all'America quando successe.
He was going over to France when the war started!
Come over to my house. (Vede?)

14 To keep in with someone. – Tenersi alle buone con qualcuno. Si può anche dire 'to keep in good with someone.'

I hope I'm keeping in good with you.
We are trying to keep in with the school regulations.

15 To be onto someone – Avere capito qualcuno – ma dal lato delle cose malfatte. Si dice specialmente degli individui che sono a doppia-faccia- (two-faced).

I'm onto his tricks now! (Ho capito i suoi brutti scherzi ora.)
I'm onto his ways of doing things now!
We soon got onto his unfair dealings!

Un altro modo di dire la stessa cosa è questo – To have someone's number, oppure, 'to get someone's number.'

After I talked to him only twice I got his number.
I've got your number, Mr. Pavese, but it's a good one!

16 To hit for a raise. – Tentare, o parlare per un aumento di stipendio. Si dice anche 'To strike for a raise.'

After Christmas I am going to hit my employer for a raise.
We hit for a raise last year but we didn't get it!
How many times did you strike for a raise this year?

17 How come? – Come mai? (L'inglese sarebbe 'Come avviene?')
How come that he left school? (Come mai ha lasciato di andare a scuola?)
How come you didn't write to me sooner? (Come mai non stavi bene?)

18 To cramp one's style – 'to cramp' – Il contrarsi dei muscoli –.

Questa frase si dice quando qualcuno fa in modo che un altro non possa più agire liberamente, detto, generalmente, per le cose spirituali. 'Paralizzare lo stile di agire.'

This idea of yours just cramps my style. (Questa tua idea fa sì che non posso fare come voglio.)
I don't like your cramping my style all the time.
I have cramps. (Ho contrazione dei muscoli.) (classico.)
Mr. Pavese got a cramp in his fingers from writing so many phrases, but it didn't cramp my style any; that is, the phrases.

19 To slug. – Dar un colpo con il pugno ma a braccio disteso che poi fa un mezzo circolo prima di raggiungere la meta, come fanno sempre gli inesperti alla boxe. Il sostantivo 'a slugger' si dice di un boxeur che picchia secco!

To slug – slugging – slugged – slugged.

Slugging is not allowed in professional boxing.
Bonaglia is a good slugger! (Picchiatore forte.)

Book Seven

1 to get chesty. – Diventare superbo, orgoglioso. 'Chest' è il 'petto.' Ora si sa quando uno si sente orgoglioso di qualche cosa, come il babbo per il primo figlio, che cosa fa? Espande, senz'altro il petto per darsi dell'importanza!

Now, Mr. Pavese, don't get chesty because you know this!
I still feel chesty over my success! (Ha!)

2 To pass up. – Lasciar passare. – Lasciar andare.

Don't pass up a good opportunity. (Non lasciar andare una buona, ecc.)
Don't pass me up when you meet me! (Non fingere di non vedermi quando m'incontri.)
Never pass up a chance to get some information from me, Mr. Pavese, when you want it and if I can give it to you.
First of all I never pass up a chance to help someone!

3 Drilling – Istruzione militare. (classico.) che poi si dice di qualsiasi cosa in cui bisogna persistere.

To drill – drilling – drilled – drilled.
They are all well drilled men. (Sono tutti ben istruiti militarmente.)
We get plenty of (lot of) drilling in English. (Abbiamo 'beaucoup' di escercizio in inglese.)

Fire drill – Esercizio contro il fuoco.
Hose drill – Esercizio con i tubi dell'acqua (di gomma, eh, m'intendo!)
Leader drill – Esercizio con le scale dei pompieri.

4 Hang on! – È una frase che si usa quando si vuol dire 'resista.' L'idea della frase le verrà più chiara forse pensando ad un individuo che sta aggrapato ad una maniglia di un tramway mentre che è in corsa, ma che ha, poi, un piede, o tutti e due, ancora a terra! Fosse in America si griderà – Hang on!

No matter how hard English may seem, just hang on, Mr. Pavese!
Hang on to your good friends! (Tenete i vostri buon amici.)

5 Shell-shock – (classico) Lo 'scioc' che viene dallo scoppio dei proiettili, malat[t]ia comunissima dopo la guerra. 'Shell' – proiettile. 'Shock' lo 'scioc.'

There were many shell-shocked soldiers after the war.
Shell-shock is a war disease!

6 Buddy. – Compagno in armi. – Siccome di solito dormivano a due a due in tempo di guerra, si dice 'Buddy' di chi è stato il secondo, ossia, il compagno in armi. Come in Italia si potrebbe chiamare 'Buddy' uno dei carabinieri, dacchè vanno sempre in due.

You, Mr. Pavese, were one of my Buddies in Italy.
Mr. Mila was another of my good Buddies.
He's a buddy of mine.
Dopo la guerra si usava la frase per dire 'un buonissimo amico.'

7 To spot someone. – Vi sono due versioni. Una è 'vedere qualcuno d'improvviso' e l'altra è 'di capire qualcuno fin troppo bene' che si esprime così 'To have someone spotted.'

I was in the café when I spotted Mr. Pavese just coming in.
He was very uncivil to me so now I have him spotted.
I spotted him before he spotted me! (l'ho visto prima che mi ha visto.)

'Spotted' si dice di qualcuno che si macchia nell'opinione di un altro. 'a spot' è 'una macchia' in senso puro. 'To have someone spotted' è preciso a 'To have someone's number,' come già ho spiegato.

8 To get a kick out of something. – Trarre un certo godimento di qualchecosa. Usatissimo in America. 'Kick' – calcio – non c'entra qui affatto.

I get a kick out of a good opera.
Mr. Pavese gets a kick out of slang!
I get a kick out of a girl who is really good-looking! Ya!

Book Eight

1 A moron – (solo classico) Un degenerato!

2 To size someone up. – Vedere qualcuno e fare dei calcoli mentali che riguardano la sua persona, il suo indole, il suo valore, ecc. cioè, tentare di farsi un'opinione vera e giusta dell'individuo, che si conosce da poco, appena.

I sized him up to be a wonderful man!
When he spoke to me next I was just sizing him up!
I have him sized up as a good-for-nothing! (Fannullone)

3 To fire someone. – Licenziare qualcuno da un impiego, ecc. (slang)

He was fired from the Fiat!
John only worked two months and then he was fired!
Next month we are going to fire John from our offices!

4 The upkeep. – (classico) Il mantenimento, la manutenzione.

Our upkeep in this school is very great.
Our office upkeep amounts to more than $500 a month!
The upkeeping of this kind of work is excessive.
The upkeep of a personal library is very great.

5 Was kinda nutty. – Forma distorta di 'Was kind of nutty,' che si sente nel parlare in fretta. 'Nuts' oppure 'nutty' vuol dire 'pazzo,' un po' fuori della testa, un po' imbecile.

He is always a little nuts. (È sempre un po' imbecile.)
He's always nutty. (Fa sempre lo stupido – oppure – lo è.)

6 Gee! Espressione esclamativa come 'Diamine' 'Perdinci,' ecc. Altre di queste stesse parole sono 'Gosh!' (di maggior sorpresa) e 'Golly' che è quasi intraducibile.

Book Nine

1 To flee for good. – Fuggire per sempre, fuggire per una volta e per sempre. Usatissimo!

When he left America he left it for good!
I'm in Rome now and here for good.
Mr. Pavese has decided to learn English for good now!
For good – vale – for once and for all. (per una volta e per sempre!)
I shall leave France for good (oppure) for once and for all!

Book Ten

1 To put a banker on the ticket. – Mettere un banchiere sulla lista di uno dei partiti politici. 'Ticket' si dice della lista dei candidati per la presidenza, ecc. politicamente parlando.

Mr. Hoover is on the Republican ticket.
Mr. Smith, instead, was on the Democratic ticket.

The Republican ticket was voted into office. (Si votava la lista dei Repubblicani all'ufficio.)

2 Presy Wilson. – Forma familiare per 'President Wilson.'

Book Eleven

1 Go-getters. – Quelli che si mettono ad ottenere quello che vogliono e quasi sempre riescono.

Mr. Pavese certainly is a go-getter when it comes to English!
Successful business men are mostly all go-getters! (quasi tutti.)

Dai verbi – to go – 'andare' e 'to get' – 'Ottenere.'

Be a go-getter all the time, Mr. Pavese, and you'll have all the success you want!

2 I tell you what, this is a country! – - Ti dico una cosa, questo è un (vero) paese! Frase enfatica che male si spiega! Guardi gli esempi:–

I'll tell you what, Mr. Pavese knows his English! Quel 'what' si potrebbe tradurre con 'quello che è vero.' I'll tell you what, I don't like some of my supposed-to be friends!

Senta, Pavese; provi a leggere quest'esempio con molta enfasi sulle parole sottolineate e sentirà subito tutto il significato!

Listen, I'll tell you what, NOW; he's no friend of mine!

Detto da un vero Americano, non c'è altro a dire poi!

3 a tire – Una gomma da automobile – una pneumatica.

An automobile has four tires – and one spare tire. (Un'automobile ha quattro pneumatici ed uno di ricambio.)
Some cars have balloon tires. (Certe automobili hanno di quelle gomme enormi – gonfiate.)

4 Distraught – Tempo passato del verbo 'to distract' 'distrarre'

To distract, distracting, distracted, distracted.
(oppure) distraught, distraught.

Book Twelve

1 O.K. – Bene, benone. Qualche volta si scrive anche 'O.Kay.' oppure, Oh Kay.

That K.O. certainly was O.K. (Quel 'knock-out' e' andato benone.)
It's O.K. with me! (Per me va benone!)

2 So long! – Addio, arrivederci. (per se intraducibile.)

Well, so long, Max, I'll see you tomorrow at school!
So long, fellows; come over again! (Usatissima questa frase.)
(Arrivederci, compagni, e venite a trovarmi di nuovo.)

3 A corker. – Tal quale 'a darby' 'a dandy' 'a card' ecc.

Antonio Chiuminatto

The second and final installment of Chiuminatto's comments on Dark Laughter.[2]

This is the remainder of the list of phrases you sent me, Mr. Pavese!

Book One

1 To be a rip-terror. (oppure) to be a rip-snorter. – 'to rip' vuol dire 'stracciare' o in inglese 'to tear,' 'to snort' vuol dire fare come fa il toro quando è infuriato. Tant'uno come l'altro vuol dire un individuo che non è disciplinato affatto, che va sempre, che non ha affatto paura di nulla. Quindi 'rip-terror' vuol dire uno che straccia ogni terrore e va sempre avanti indisciplinato ...

2 T'witchedly, t'weedlety, t'wadelty, t'wum. – Sono solo delle parole che derivano forse dalle rime dei bambini, che portatc poi nello slang vogliono dire niente, se non a dare senso di paura ai bambini, ma che poi non dicono proprio niente. E sono sicurissimo di aver incontrato queste parole che mi da Lei adesso, ma se l'autore che le ha usato non ha trovato un modo di farle avere un senso preciso, non posso spiegare nulla dacchè per me son delle parole senza alcun significato. Mi scriva ancora, se mai!

3 To get crusted up. – Diventare sempre piu' intraprendente, più superbo.

Since he was graduated he has become considerably crusted up!
'crust' è la 'crosta' ma non ha alcun valore nello slang!

2 Chiuminatto's accompanying letter on the last page of comments is dated 26 December 1929.

4 Old Harry. – È un modo di dire che si è divertito in modo fantastico, che si ha fatto al diavolo. Un'altra frase piu' comune è 'to raise Hell' – suscitare l'Inferno per dire che non vi era nulla che non hanno fatto per divertirsi.

We had an Old Harry of a time!
We are going to raise Hell Christmas Day!

5 It isn't his lay. – Non è affatto un suo affare! Un suo partito!

Speaking in German is not his lay! (Non è affatto un suo affare, ecc.)
Mr. Pavese's lay is speaking in American slang!

6 A bug – Si dice di un uomo quando è un po' pazzo, un po' imbecile, come si dà del 'nutty.' 'Bug' è 'insetto,' in puro inglese. Si usa molto anche per dire che uno è un po' fanatico su di qualchecosa.

He is a bug on English. (oppure) He is buggy on English! È fanatico.
He is a bug on all sports!

7 Boose-hoister. – Un ubbriaccone! 'Boose' è lo slang per 'liquore,' e 'hoister' viene dal verbo 'to hoist, hoisting, hoisted, hoisted' che vuol dire 'alzare dei pesi forti.'

A derrick is the best hoister. (Macchina da sollevare. senso puro.)
He has always been a booze-hoister. (È sempre stato un ubbriaccone!)

Altre frasi di questo genere sono 'Booze-hound' e 'booze-fighter.'
Il primo si compone di 'booze' – liquore- e di 'hound' Cane da caccia.' Il secondo si compone di 'booze' e di 'fighter' – lottatore, ossia, uno che lotta sempre con delle bottiglie!

In the last few years he has become a booze-fighter! (Ubbriacconi.)
Some people are no more and no less than booze-hounds! (" ")

Book Two

1 There's a note I'd like to strike. Si potrebbe tradurre 'Ecco una cosa della quale mi piacerebbe chiedere.' oppure ' — Ecco una figura che mi piacerebbe fare.' 'Note' – nota (senso puro) – 'to strike 'battere' 'toccare fortemente.'

His is the note I'd like to strike. – La sua è la figura mi piacerebbe fare.
There's a note about him I'd like to strike. Vi è qualchecosa in lui che mi piacerebbe sapere, chiedere.

La frase in sè è un po' ambigua – ecco tutto che posso dare cosi. Spero che serva al suo scopo!

2 How to get the tired fish out from Iowa – Frase completamente sconosciuta a me ed a tutti gli altri. – Si vede che è una frase confinata allo stato di Iowa e che quindi ha un suo valore locale ma non universale. Oppure fu usata dall'autore con una sua intenzione tutta speciale! Dovrei leggere tutto il paragrafo per poter decidermi. Mi spiace!

3 You should see me driving about the joint in the morning in my shift.

'Driving' viene dal verbo 'to drive, driving, drove, driven' che vuol dire 'guidare' (un'automobile) 'Shift' è lo slang appunto per 'l'automobile,' parola che viene dalla maniglia che si chiama 'the shift' e che dà le varie velocità alla macchina! 'Joint' come già saprà è lo slang per un 'luogo frequentatissimo' da qualcuno, e che si riferisce a qualsiasi ambiente o luogo.

The cafe Mugna was our regular joint. (oppure) hang-out. (Si ricorda?)
The Regio Opera House will be a popular joint this winter.
Well, it wont be my hang-out this winter.
I suppose Mr. Mila will make it his regular joint now.

4 To make all men sing small. – Dal verbo 'to sing, singing, sang, sung' che vuol dire 'cantare.' 'to make someone sing small' vuol dire 'far usare della cortesia da qualcuno.' Anche questa frase si usa in sensi diversi – è difficile stabilire un modo solo senza aver letto il punto dal quale fu tolta.

I make him sing small now. (Lo faccio tenere il suo posto ora.)
Some women do make men sing small alright!

5 To go to pot. – Andare a rotoli – andare in aria.

Our proposal went to pot. (La nostra proposta è andata a rotoli.)

6 To get into a jam. – Trovarsi nel grande traffico di veicoli, ecc. senza poter muoversi. (oppure) trovarsi nei fastidi.

The street traffic got jammed! Il traffico della via formava una congestione.
All the automobiles suddenly jammed! (Tutte le automobili d'improvviso si congestionavano.)
I'm in a jam with my English. (Sono nei fastidi con l'inglese.)

Book Four

1 'O ma banjo dog' è una forma negra per 'Oh my banjo dog' ma tutto quello che so di questa frase è qui! Se mai vengo a sapere qualchecosa di piu' Le scrivero.'

2 The gumbo drift. 'Gumbo' è una specie di fango gommos[o] che si trova negli stati del Sud dell'America del Nord. 'Drift' è lo slang per 'l'idea' – ma come mai usano questa combinazione i negri, non saprei neppure. Altro spiacimento!

Do you get the drift. (Capisci?)
Get me?
Did you get it. (L'hai capito?)
No, I don't get the drift. (No, non capisco l'idea.)
No, I don't see the point. ("   ")
To see the point (oppure) to get the drift – capire.

3 A bayou baptizing. – 'baptizing' è un 'battesimo' (baptism). 'Bayou' è un nome indiano, oppure dal francese 'bayouc' che si da alla regione American presso il Golfo del Messico. Forse viene anche dalla parola 'bay' la baia.' Ad ogni modo 'a bayou baptizing' vuol dire 'un battesimo a modo dei popoli nelle terre presso il Golfo di Messico, oppure, degli Stati americani laggiu'!

4 Trimmed – dal verbo 'to trim, trimming, trimed, trimmed' vuol dire 'decorare' come un albero di Natale, 'Aggiustare' come qualchecosa che era mal combinata, ecc. Intanto non capisco la frase che mi dà – They trimmed it for us' – dacchè dovrei leggere di più, a meno che voglia dire 'L'hanno aggiustato per noi.'

Book Five

1 A risen bread – E il pane fatto con lievito. Dal verbo 'to rise, rising, rose, risen 'alzarsi' 'crescere in sù.'

2 A passage between persons. – 'passage' è un 'passaggio' ma altro non posso dire dacchè non sento nulla da questa frase isolata così.

3 A levee-top – La cima di un arginamento fatto contro le inondazioni.

Book Six

1 To be stuck off. – opposto di 'to be stuck on' – 'aver simpatia per.'

I'm stuck on Miss So-And-So! Ho una simpatia per – così – così.
I'm stuck on my English work! Ho una simpatia per il lavoro –
I'm sticking off English now. (Tralascio l'inglese ora.)
I'm sticking off hard work! (Del lavoro stancante non ne faccio!)

Dal verbo 'to stick, sticking, stuck, stuck' – Attaccare – come un francobollo.

It is sticky – È attaccante. – (come della colla.)
Stick around a while yet! (slang.) Stia ancora un poco!

2 To pay out for snubbing. –'to pay out' – Mandare a passeggio – mandare a spasso. – 'a snub' è una persona che si dà delle arie, che si arriccia sempre il naso per tutto e a tutti. Dal verbo 'to snub, snubbing, snubbed, snubbed.' 'to pay out' (senso puro) 'pagare per ogni suo avere' dopo la quale azione si va a spasso, si capisce.

We paid him out in full for snubbing!

3 It ground its way up. – 'dal verbo 'to grind, grinding, ground, ground,' che vuol dire 'Macinare' (senso puro).

Our coffee was ground! (Il nostro café era macinato.)

Nello slang però vuol dire, andare lentamente, come fanno le macchine quando vanno su per le colline, quasi, si potrebbe dire, a stento.

Our automobile just ground its way up Superga!

4 To make a boat. – 'non posso dir altro qui se non che si dà del 'boat' alle automobili. 'Boat' – 'barca' – Nave.

Have you seen our new boat yet? (Hai ancora visto la nostra nuova macchina.) (inteso, più che altro una macchina di lusso.)

5 Comfort-stall – Una sala del 'club' dei 'businessmen. 'le stalle del 'comfort' – Dove si sta bene – all'agio proprio! Puo' anche dirsi di un 'gabinetto.' Mahgia'!

We have some beautiful comfort-stalls in our new building. (Abbiamo delle sale di comfort meravigliose nell'edificio nuovo.)

6 Show 'em up – Forma per 'Show them up.' Dal verbo nello slang 'to show up' che vuol dire 'far vedere,' 'mettere qualcuno ad una dura prova.' 'To show, showing, showed, showed' – (slang.)

Mr. Pavese showed them up on their English! (Mr. Pavese li ha fatto vedere che non sapevano nulla di English.)

The Turinese squad showed up that of Milan. (La squadra di Torino ha vinto da quella di Milano.)

If you think you can do it, show us up! (Se credi di poterlo fare, facci vedere! ci faccia vedere.) In questo caso si vede meglio l'uso di 'to show up.'

7 to slap it home. (oppure) To slap it to someone – ed altre di queste forme con poche variazioni di preposizioni, vogliono dire 'Lasciarlo a qualcuno Darlo a qualcuno' nel senso di 'daglielo'!

When it comes to English, slap it home to Pavese. Quando si tratta d'inglese, lascialo a Pavese! (daglielo a Pavese.)

To slap, slapping, slapped, slapped – 'schiaffeggiare' (classico). Nello slang vuol dire 'gettare ironicamente' come si fa con certe frasi di disprezzo. È di un uso così vasto e diverso che si sa proprio cosa vuol dire solo da come si adopera, e poi si sa, come, che intensità di significato attribuirlo. Ecco diversi esempi:–

Slap it here! Tocchiamoci la mano!
Slap it to them boys! (Dateglielo secco, giovinotti.)
I'll slap your face! (Ti schiaffeggerò la faccia)/(puro verbo.)
Slap it to the women when it comes to being vain. (Daglielo alle donne quando si tratta di essere vane.) (Lasciatelo alle donne.)

In quest'ultimo caso 'Slap it to the women' (oppure) 'Slap it home to the women' equivale la frase classico 'Leave it to the women.'

'Home' qui è solo un rafforzativo per dire che è il luogo proprio in cui si trova bene l'azione della quale si parla. Viene da questi usi americani:–

I'm perfectly at home with English. (Mi trovo al mio agio con l'inglese.)
He's at home in anything that's artistic. (Si trova sempre bene in qualunque cosa che sia artistica.)

8 To give the riz-raz – Equivale 'to give a razzing' che già ho spiegato.
Gush! – Dal verbo 'to gush, gushing, gushed, gushed' – sgorgare 'gettare' come fa il pozzo di petrolio. Nello slang, in forma di imperative come mi sembra

questo caso, vuol dire 'parla.' Poi c'è 'the gush' che è il sostantivo 'Lo sgorgare di qualche cosa.' Si tratterà forse di pozzi di qualche genere! In generale però non si usa nello slang!

9 A lucky fluke. – 'Lucky' vuol dire 'fortunato' 'qualche cosa che sia andata bene per puro caso.' 'Fluke' si dice di qualsiasi azione che sia andata male sul serio, che poi risulta per bene quando aggiungiamo l'aggettivo 'lucky.'

The Turinese squad won from the Milan squad by two or three lucky flukes. (La squadra Torinese ha vinto dalla squadra di Milano solo da due o tre giuochi mal combinati che poi andarono bene lo stesso per puro caso.) Mi spiego?
His life is one continuous lucky fluke! (La sua vita è un continuo andar bene delle cose che dovrebbero andar male.)

10 To get a souvenir fast. – 'Fast' qui si usa per dire 'al sicuro.'

I have that book fast now. (Ora si usa per dire 'al sicuro.')

'Fast' (puro) – Rapido, in fretta – - 'Fast' (slang) – Al sicuro, se è avverbio e se è aggettivo vuol dire 'intrapprendente.'

My watch is fast. – (Il mio orologio è avanti.) (puro.)
Keep this fast for me! (Mettetelo al sicuro per me.)
He is a fast man! (È uomo intrapprendente – uomo svelto.)

Book Seven

1 To find out too much about your fellow-men too fast. – Vuol dire che spesso si impara delle cose che riguardano i nostri amici anche troppo in fretta, cioè, per il puro caso, senza indagare! Generalmente le cose brutte!

2 The jimjams – 'La paura' 'la fifa.' Il tremolo che va sù e giù per la schiena quando si ha paura.

Mystery stories always give me the jimjams. Poe's, for instance.
It gave me the jimjams to see the fight between Bonaglia and Muller!

3 To put a feather in someone's hat – vuol dire, parlare a qualcuno di qualche cosa che non sapeva, ma che gli gioverà. (letteralmente) 'Mettere una piuma nel cappello di qualcuno.' Ora 'To be a feather in someone's hat (oppure) cap. – vuol dire che 'io sono un individuo che posso far molto per un altro.'

I put a feather in his hat about Mr. Pavese. (Ho detto uno di Pavese che non sapeva.)
When it comes to English I'm a feather in Mr. Pavese's hat! (Magari!)

4 To be in a daze. – Essere in uno stato di stupidità, essere così confusi da non capire più nulla.

To daze, dazing, dazed, dazed – Istupidire con un colpo, con una luce forte, con tristezza, ecc.

He was knocked into a daze!
She was so dazed by the strong light that she fell to the ground.

5 Up to the hilt. – 'Hilt' è il manico di una sciabola, o arma qualunque. Questa frase nello slang, allora, vuol dire 'andare al limite.'

We are going up to the hilt in this matter.
When we do anything at all we go up to the hilt!

6 To hang fire between two people. – vuol dire 'far suscitare qualchecosa che poi rimane una macchia sulla loro amicizia.'

Da distinguere i verbi classici 'to hang, hanging, hanged, hanged' che vuol dire 'impiccare' e 'to hang, hanging, hung, hung' che vuol dire 'appendere.'

We hung the picture on the wall. (Abbiamo appeso il quadro al muro.)
We hanged the man on the scaffold. (Abbiamo impiccato l'uomo sul patibolo.)

Ora si vedrà 'to hang fire' – Far pendere 'un fuoco' tra persone! Come un quadro che poi sta lì, solo che 'fire' – 'fuoco' dà il senso di qualche cosa che arde sempre ma che non si spegne.

7 The terrace. – Una terrazzo!

8 To slump – Diminuire il proprio passo nelle cose!

Don't slump in your English, Mr. Pavese!
He has been slumping in school for some time now!
He used to be very active but now he has taken to slumping!

Book Eight

1 To pitch hay – 'raccogliere il fieno' che nello slang vuol dire 'far le cose mentre che si può,' 'lavorare.'

It is about time you were pitching hay! (È ora che tu ti metti a fare le cose mentre che puoi.)

To pitch, pitching, pitched, pitched – (Gettare sù il fieno ai carri dal campo, come fanno colà.)

Pitch – (sostantivo) – la pece.
Pitch-fork – quello usato dai contadini per gettare il fieno.

2 He had seen men in the row. 'Row' – Pronunciata 'rau' vuol dire 'a noisy quarrel, a brawl' (oppure) un litigio, in italiano.

Row – pronunciata – 'Ro' vuol dire una fila.

The men were in a row. – Gli uomini erano in fila.
The men were in a row. – Gli uomini erano in un litigio, litigavano!

3 If the shoe were on the other foot. – Se la cosa fosse all'incontrario, viceversa.

Now if the shoe were on the other foot, I should like to do it ! Ora se le cose fossero all'incontrario, vorrei farlo io! (Letteralmente 'se la scarpa fosse sull'altro piede.')

4 How could you go back of that? La frase è purissima e quindi vi sono diversi modi d'intenderla. Direi che si dovrebbe tradurre 'Come potresti andare dietro le quinte di quella cosa?' Mi spiego? Si dice quando si vorrebbe indagare ma bisognando cercare dei motivi priori. Può anche darsi che voglia dire diversamente, ma dalla frase sola cosi' non posso dir altro.

5 To be a fooler. – Essere un ingannatore, essere uno scherzo, ecc.

This cigarette is a fooler. – Questa sigaretta è uno scherzo. (Forse scoppia mentre che si fuma.)

Dal verbo 'to fool, fooling, fooled, fooled,' 'Ingannare.' 'A fool' – uno stupido, cretino.

Book Eleven

1 When it comes (right) down to the scratch. (oppure) When it comes (right) down to brass tacks. – vuol dire 'quando si tratta di fare qualchecosa proprio sul serio' ecc.

To scratch, scratching, scratched, scratched – Grattare, graffiare. (oppure) scrivere male. 'Brass tacks' sono dei 'chiodini di ottone.'

His hand-writing is all scratching and nothing else!
His hand-writing looks like hen-scratching!
When it comes down to the scratch, he [is] a REAL man!
When it comes right down to brass tacks, he does know his English!

2 The fat would be in the fire. – Ci sarebbe modo di litigare! 'Fat' è 'grasso' (sostantivo e aggettivo) Sa bene come fa il grasso – dà un po' di vita al fuoco! Come fanno certi argomenti, certe discussioni!

Everytime we talk about religion or politics, it's fat for the fire! Ogni volta che ci mettiamo a discutere della religione o della politica, troviamo modo di litigare. (Vi è del grasso per il fuoco.)

Every time I see that man, it's as good as fat for the fire. (Vale)

Book Twelve

1 A pile of brush. – Un mucchio di roveto fitto (brush-wood) oppure, spazzolatura. Dal verbo 'to pile, piling, piled, piled,' Ammucchiare.

Chiuminatto's comments on expressions from Sinclair Lewis's Babbitt.[3]

Babbit[t] — Sinclair Lewis

The New-York Flyer. – È un treno direttissimo che fa servizio fra New York e la città di Chicago. Tutti questi treni di servizi speciali e direttissimi portano un nome di questo genere come l'altro che si chiama 'The 20th Century Limited,' che fa il servizio della posta di valore. Questo si chiama il 'Volatore' e l'altro è il 'Limitato del ventesimo secolo.' Vi sono ancora di questi nomi di treni, ma basta per ora sapere che è un treno.

To crank a Ford. – Dal verbo 'to crank, cranking, cranked cranked,' che vuol dire 'incominciare' ma che poi si riferisce a delle macchine o a dei motori. Sa bene come fanno quando ci mettono una maniglia ad un motore e che poi la fanno girare per incominciarlo! Ebbene, la maniglia si chiama 'crank' ed il verbo viene da sè. Oggi quasi tutti i motori di tutte le marche d'automobili si possono incominciare con un pedale senza muoversi dalla guida, a meno che come da noi in questo freddo il motore si geli ed allora bisogna ricorrere al 'crank.' Il vecchio 'Ford' però si incominciava sempre con il far girare il motore con un 'crank,' davanti, e poi una volta incominciato si sedeva alla guida e, figliuoli miei, avanti!

Our motor was frozen and we had to crank it!
Did you have to crank your car last night?
We have been cranking our auto of late; it's so cold!

Booster. – È una parola che si usa per un indivuduo che fa della propaganda per qualsiasi buona azione in cui vi sono molte persone interessate. Viene dal verbo 'to boost, boosting, boosted, boosted,' che vuol dire 'rialzare' oppure, 'alzare in sù.' 'portare in alto.'

He is a good booster of our Literary Club!
Mr. Pavese is a booster of American Literature!
We boosted him up to the window – and he looked in. (L'abbiamo alzato sù alla finestra, ecc.)
Our actions are either our boosters or our knockers!
He is our leading campaign booster!

3 Pavese includes the list of words and phrases from *Babbitt* in his letter of 12 January 1930. Chiuminatto sends his explanations of this list (chapters 1 to 16), along with his comments from chapter 16 to the end of the novel, on 11 February 1930.

To feel kind of punk. – Vuol dire 'di sentirsi piuttosto male' 'di non stare troppo bene.'

'Punk' in sè una parola classica (? – si ricordi?) che si usa per quella combinazione fiammifera che una volta accesa rimane così di modo che si possa accendere o fiammiferi, le corde della dinamite o anche delle bombe! Ha! È un affare che sembra un lapis e che poi brucia lentamente come una candela. Letteralmente vorrebbe dire 'mi sento, in ispezie, male.' Si vedrà scritto anche 'To feel kinda punk' che poi è la scrittura precisa del modo in cui sembra detto.

I've been feeling kind of punk lately. (Di recente sto poco bene.)
I feel pun[k] to-day. (Oggi sto male.)
I feel rotten to-day (Oggi sto male.) (due modi uguali.)
I feel kind of rotten – (oppure) I feel kind of punk.
After the grand sneak we all felt damned punk!

A Tux. – È l'abbreviazione di 'Tuxedo' che è l'abito che voi Italiani chiamate 'lo smoking.' Noi lo chiamiamo il 'Tuxedo' pronunciato quasi 'Tachsido.'

Ever[y]one must be in Tux for tonight!
We always go to the opera in a Tux.
Out with the Tuxedos – there's a celebration tonight!
To hustle one's head off to get into the soup-and fish.

Bella questa frase! Vuol dire – Fare così in fretta da perdersi persin la testa negl: sforzi a mettere l'abito da sera, ossia, lo smoking ('Tuxedo').

Dal verbo 'to hustle, hustling, hustled, hustled' (fare in fretta' (To hustle one's head off – Da fare così in fretta da fare persin girare la testa.)
Soup-and-fish – lo smoking, ossia, Tuxedo. Così chiamato perché è l'abito da sera, specialmente per le cene formali – di zuppa e di pesce – come fosse, quasi in disprezzo della cena stessa che richiede l'abito speciale. Sono sempre delle cene con poca roba da mangiare, ma tanta formalità, in compenso! Quindi il disprezzo americano per il 'soup-and-fish,' che dà anche il nome all'abito.

Hustle into your soup-and-fish. Mr. Pavese, we're going to the opera! (Metta in fretta i[l] suo smoking (Tux.), ecc.)
My soup-and-fish suit is out of style! (Il mio Tux non è più di moda!)

That new soup-and-fish suit of Mr. Pavese's is a darby! Hustle your head off into that soup-an dfish, otherwise we shall be late for dinner! (Faccia in fretta a mettere il suo smoking, altrimenti saremo in ritardo per la cena.)

To pull something on someone – Far un brutto tiro a qualcuno. Da noi non vuol dire solamente 'fare un brutto tiro' ma fare qualunque cosa che sia una sorpresa, bella, brutta, o qualsivoglia!

Dal verbo 'to pull, pulling, pulled, pulled' (tirare).

I pulled a good one on Mr. Pavese. (Ho fatto un bel tiro a P.)
John pulled a dirty one on me. (Giov. mi ha fatto un brutto tiro.)
Don't you pull anything on me! (Non mi faccia delle stupidaggini.)
I pulled a surprise on Mr. Pavese just yesterday!

A bobtail jacket for a ringtail monkey. – Già, si parla di uno che deve essere o che è già in 'smoking,' ossia, in Tuxedo. 'Bobtail' si dice degli animali che hanno la coda corta come i cavalli, i cani, ecc., anche perché tante volte si tagliano la coda quando sono piccolo. La parola, 'bobtail' quindi, viene da 'bob' che è il taglio a-la-garconne, e 'tail' che è la 'coda.' Ecco che abbiamo una coda a-la-garconne! Ora 'jacket' è una 'giacchetta,' mi spiego. 'Bobtail' qui, si usa per dire che non è il solito abito con la coda di rondine, ma che è una giacchetta con la coda a-la-garconne! (tagliato). 'ringtail' si dice specialmente delle scimmie che hanno la coda ad 'anello,' come pure i porci! Si vede benone che in questa frase si fa un bel complimento a qualcuno dacchè si dice 'che la giacchetta (Tux) senza le code gli va bene come se fosse indosso ad una scimmia con la coda ad anello.' È difficile spiegare, ma in poche parole si direbbe così di un contadino delle montagne se mai dovessi apparire in 'smoking' (Tuxedo). Capisce? Tutto il contrasto della frase, che ci dà il significato, sta nelle parole 'bobtail' e 'ringtail' che ci fanno sentire l'urto. E qui in America vi sono certi tipi di gente ricca che fa proprio questa figura quando si vestono il Tux! Oltre tutto anche il loro contegno è anche da 'monkey.' 'Bobtail jacket' vuol solo dire che è l'abito di sera 'full dress suit' ma che non ha la coda, come appunto lo 'smoking,' il Tux. Quello delle code si chiama il 'swallow-tail suit' ('coda di rondine') come indossano gli artistici uomini di concerti come Chiuminatto! Ya!

Look at that ringtail monkey in that bobtail jacket!
Who is that ringtail monkey in that bobtail jacket?
Look at the soup-and-fish on that ringtail monkey!

Rambunctious – (slang). Si dice di uno che vuol sempre fare, che è sempre in aria circa qualchecosa.

Don't be in a hurry; don't be so damned rambunctious!
He is a rambunctious salesman – always on the go!

A charity-worker. – Uno che è impiegato nelle Società delle Carità!, delle quali società vi sono molte in America. Vi è della gente che va in giro, per esempio, a visitare le famiglie povere per accertarsene dei loro bisogni, e questi si chiamano 'charity-workers.' Ogni anno danno quello che si chiama il 'Charity-Ball' ossia, il gran 'ballo per la Carità' al quale ballo partecipano tutti ed il ricavo va a benefizio delle carità. Qualsiasi individuo, poi, che ha a che fare in qualsiasi modo con delle societa' di carita' si chiama il 'charity worker.'

To plug, plugging, plugged, plugged – dare un colpo, come con il pugno. L'uso di questo verbo è così vasto che non so come incominciare, ad ogni modo, stia attento!

I plugged him on the nose! (Gli ho dato un pugno sul naso).
He thought I was going to plug him!
Don't you plug me, big boy!

To plug along. – andare sempre in avanti ma con fatica, come fa l'uomo stanco.
We had to plug along for ten miles!
He plugged along for three miles before he could get help.
I am still plugging along in my school work!
Mr. Pavese is still plugging along at his English.

To plug the books. – Frase commerciale per il ragioniere che usufruisce della cassa per il suo scopo e poi aggiusta i libri in modo che sembrano perfettamente a posto. 'Plug' qui si riferisce ad una cosa che vien tolta e sostituita con un['] altra, come appunto con dei numeri o delle somme!

The government men caught him plugging the books!
He had been plugging the books for two years!

To plug. (classico) vuol dire 'turare.'

Plug that hole! (Turi quel buco.)

Da questo si vede la forma 'to plug the books.'

To read thrillers. – Leggere delle cose che danno delle grandi emozioni, o sensazioni. viene dal verbo 'to thrill' 'far fremere,' 'emozionare.' 'a thriller,' allora, si dà ad un volume di Nick Carter, per esempio, o a quei volumi di amore che fanno andare in visibilio le signorine! Una volta li chiamavano 'dime novel' (novella da dieci soldi) ma oggi per non essere così volgari, li chiamiamo 'thrillers,' ed il prezzo non c'entra per disprezzarci! Oggi, però, si dice 'Thriller' per qualsiasi volume, pellicola, ecc. che ci piace.

I'll bet *Nigger Heaven* was a thriller, Mr. Pavese!
I hope you'll find a thriller in Hemingway, too!
No history book is ever a thriller in America, Cesare!

To thrill, thrilling, thrilled, thrilled. (far fremere)

I was thrilled clean through when I saw that film!
It was a thrilling fight between Bonaglia and Miller!
It was a thrilling surprise to me.
Do you ever read thrillers like Conan Doyle?

To nag – Star sempre in dietro a qualcuno, dire continuamente, e generalmente sempre la stessa cosa!
To nag, nagging, nagged, nagged.

He has been nagging (at) me for a week now about studying!
My mother always nags (at) me for being late for meals!
He is the biggest nagger I ever met! He's always nagging!

Don't start nagging now about my English or I'll plug you!

To nag at – oppure – to nag.

hon. – E' l'abbreviazione di 'Honorable' (Onorevole).

He is the hon. John Smith.
The hon. Mussolini.

Quando si scrive, come qui, con lettera minuscola, è sempre la forma di disprezzo, benchè vi sia la tendenza oggi di scriverlo sempre con minuscola.

A filing-clerk – L'imp[i]egato di qualsiasi ufficio, il qual impiego è quello di tener a conto tutte le lettere e tutte le carte di formalità della ditta! Vi sono negli uffici dei grandi cassettoni a tiretti numerevoli nelle quali si tengono le carte, le lettere, ecc. in ordine alfabetico, e questi si chiamano 'files' di modo che li custodisce si chiama un 'filing-clerk.' Dal verbo 'to file, filing, filed' (mettere via in ordine alfabetico.) 'Clerk' è un impiegato qualsiasi, d'ufficio, di negozio, ecc.

Store-clerk – impiegato di negozio.
Lady-clerk – L'impiegata.
Receiving-clerk – Chi riceve la merce per la ditta.
Shipping-clerk – Chi spedisce la merce per la ditta.

Filing-clerk – Chi tiene in ordine tutte le carte.
Freight-clerk – Chi tiene a conto la merce che va per ferrovia.

Ecc. Ecc.

A talkfest – È l'abbreviazione, se si vuole, di 'Talk-festival' ossia, 'festa di chiacchiere.' Quando le donne s'incontrano diciamo che stanno facendo un 'talkfest.' Si dice anche dei Clubs quando convengono, specialmente quelli dei viaggiatori delle ditte.

When women get together there is always a talkfest.
She is president of the Ladies talkfest! (Club)
The Salesmen's Club will hold their talkfest tonight!

Free grub. – (slang) per 'del mangiare gratis.' Quando si è invitato a cena da qualcuno si dice che si ha avuto del 'free grub.' La parola 'grub' (classica) è un vermo bianco, grassoccio, che abita nelle piante morte e che è gustatissimo dagli uccelli e che per loro e veramente del 'free grub.' Una volta si diceva 'free grub' per quel poco di mangiare che si dava gratuitamente, naturalmente, ai mendicanti, ma oggi si dice di qualsiasi mangiare che ci viene gratis. 'Grub' si dice pure di mangiare.

The Hotel Ligure has good grub on their meals!

We had some good grub at the Café Mugna yesterday!
We had some free grub at Mr. Pavese's last night!
Mother, is the grub ready, it's noon!?
We had an invitation to some free grub over at Mila's!

A highbrow – (un aristocratico) da 'brow' (fronte) e da 'high' (alta). Quindi, quelli che sono aristocratici o che lo vogliono essere, date le loro arie, si chiamano 'highbrows.' Altro slang per 'la gente aristocratica' è 'ritzy people.' E 'lowbrow' (uomo da poco) è opposto di 'highbrow.'

Can you imagine that lowbrow trying to be a highbrow!
He's trying to be ritzy, you know, a highbrow!
We went to a ritzy dance last night with the highbrows!
Look at the ritzy ones in the soup-and-fish!

Blueprints – sono dei disegni di architetture, i quali disegni sono su della carta 'blu,' Con i disegni in inchiostro bianco. Da 'to print' (stampare) printing, printed, printed, – e 'blue' il colore della carta spessa usata.

This is corking! Ah, questo è magnifico! – come si dice in italiano per qualsiasi sorpresa, Ecc. Meglio di così a tradurre si muore!

It's beyond me – per dire che 'non si capise' che 'va oltre l'individuo.'

It's beyond me how he can do those things!
It's beyond my comprehension! (Si vede bene qui, vero?)
It was beyond all of us why he died so suddenly!
It just went beyond me when I heard he married!

Department-store. – Sono i grandi 'negozi a reparti.' Citerò il famoso 'Montgomery & Ward' di Chicago, il quale negozio conta dei piani e dei piani e che vende della 'mercanzia generale' (general merchandize) in un reparto, per esempio, degli abiti, in un altro, dei cappelli con un 'p' solo, in un altro, delle scarpe, in un altro delle stoffe, in un altro, dei sigari e delle sigarette, ecc. ecc. così via in tutti i piani. 'La Rinascente' da noi, si chiamerebbe un 'department-store' benchè non sia così completo come quelli da noi.

Buck (oppure) Plunk – si dice di un 'dollaro.' 'Buck' si dice di quella a carta, e 'plunk' di quello d'argento, dacchè fa un rumore tale quando vien gettato a terra! Plunk! Tant'uno come l'altro si usano per il dollaro in generale.

This book cost me a perfectly good plunk!
This article will cost you an even two bucks! ($2.00)
Give me a plunk and you may have it!

The curb. – è quella parte del marciapiede rialzato che scende alla strada, ed alla quale si fermano le automobili, come, per esempio, davanti a Porta Nuova. Insomma è quella parte del marciapiede che fa angolo retto con la strada! Va bene così!

The policeman told me to drive to the curb!
The automobiles were all lined up at the curb in front of the theater!
I could find no room at the curb so I stopped in the square!
We stopped at the curb in front of Porta Nuova!

The running-board. – È quel pezzo lungo sull'automobile sul quale si scende e discende, e che corre lungo l'automobile da tutti due i lati. Insomma, è lo scaglione dell'automobile. Buon Dio, quante parole ci vogliono prima che io possa spiegarmi – ma pazienza! It's the running-board just the same!

Blizzard – È la tormenta di neve che da noi a Green Bay non è sconosciuta! Direi che è il superlativo di 'snow-storm.'

A flivver. – Si dice di una Ford (automobile) oppure di qualsiasi macchina che sia malandata!

My car is a regular flivver now!
Where did you buy that damned flivver?
Let's buy a flivver, fellows, and have a good time!

Fill'er up! – Abbreviazione di 'fill her up' (riempitelo). Scritto al modo di dire e non al modo giusto!

Here's my glass, Mr. Pavese, fill'er up again!
Don't be afraid; fill'er up to the top!
Fill'er up with coffee and milk – here's the cup!

Noti che si usa il femminile – 'her' per l'astratto!

To root for – Dal verbo 'to root, rooting, rooted, rooted,' che vuol dire 'Prendere le parti d'uno' come si fa, per esempio ad un 'match' di boxing, di football, ecc. Vi sono di quelli che gridano per questi e di quelli che gridano per gli altri. Questo gridare si chiama 'rooting.'

I rooted for Bonaglia!
The crowd was rooting for Juventus but Milan won!
I rooted as much as I could for him!

Stolen. – dal verbo 'to steal, stealing, stole, stolen' – che vuol dire 'rubare.'

The bumper (of a car) – È quella sbarra di ferro pesante che ha davanti all'automobile per non rovinare l'automobile se si dovesse urtarsi con un'altra. Vi sono pure di queste sbarre dietro all'automobile per pure proteggere la macchina da chi non sa cosa fa e vien a cozzarsi di dietro. Di queste sbarre vi sono di tutte le forme, ma si chiamano 'bumpers' quando servono a questo scopo.

Viene dal verbo 'to bump, bumping, bumped, bumped' e spesso con la preposizione 'into' che vuol dire 'urtarsi con' come fa un vagone della ferrovia quando cozza contro un altro.

He <u>bumped into</u> me on the street! (Si è cozzato con me, ecc.)

I bumped into him as I rounded the corner! But I excused myself!
I bumped my head on the table as I fell asleep!

Utility-man (oppure) handy-man. – L'individuo che fa di tutto nell'azienda in cui lavora. Ma di lavoro manuale. Il portinaio delle vostre case sarebbe un 'utility-man' oppure un 'handy-man,' uno che viene all'utile.

Four freelance, part-time, commission salesmen. – Spiegherò così – e Lei mi capirà. – Four – quattro. – Va bene? Freelance (di lancia libera) che vuol dire in slang che si fa il comodo proprio. 'Part-time' vuol dire solo 'parte del tempo' 'tempo perso.' 'Commission' vuol dirsi di quelli che lavorano per una 'percentuale.' 'Salesman' è un viaggiatore commesso. Quindi, qui vi sono 'Quattro commessi viaggiatori,' che lavorano per una ditta solo a tempo perso, o anche solo di mattina oppure di pomeriggio, o solo a tempo perso, o anche solo di mattina oppure di pomeriggio, o solo di sera (part-time) per una percentuale sulle loro vendite (commission) ed in più non hanno nessuna preoccupazione per queste vendite (freelance) dacchè possono occuparsi o non siccome la ditta li paga solo per quello che fanno e non li obbliga nemmeno di vendere se non vogliono, dacchè è puro interesse loro! Benone Chiuminatto! Bello l'inglese, eh? Quattro parole e tutto è detto!

To pro-rate. – Dare una 'qualifica professionale.' La forma giusta sarebbe 'a professional rating' (qualifica professionale) ed il verbo e' 'to pro-rate.'

A form-letter (oppure) a circular letter. – sono di quelle lettere mandate a centinaia dalle ditte ai loro commessi viaggiatori, con le quali li tengono al corrente dei prezzi, le condizioni di manifattura, di vendita, ecc.

To kid – (oppure) to kid along. – Scherzare con qualcuno, contare delle frottole, prendere in giro. 'to kid, kidding, kidded, kidded.'

Don't kid me like that! (Non si scherzi con me cosi.)
We were just kidding him along when he became angry with us!
Don't kid me about that incident, I know all about it.

A spud garden. – Un giardino di patate. – 'spuds' sono 'patate' nello slang.

Bring me some meat and spuds, please.
How are your spuds to-day?
Look at our spud garden; a darby, eh?

A gas log. – Si dice di un focolare che ha l'apparenza di avere un tronco d'albero disteso, ma che invece di bruciare, ha dei getti del gas per riscaldare. Vi sono tanti in America. 'log' è il tronco d'albero, che una volta si bruciava nel focolare. Oggi, vice-versa, si fa uso del gas ma si conserva l'apparenza. Mi spiego?

Junk. – Sono tutti i pezzi di scarto di qualsiasi genere; si dice pure dell'ammondizia [*sic*].
Dal verbo, to junk, junking, junked, junked (gettare allo scarto).

Our automobile was so old we had to junk it!
After that accident both automobiles looked like junk!
Yes, they both went to the junk pile!
In all this book-store there is nothing but junk! Not even one classic!

A shyster. – Si dice di un ebreo, o di uno che cerca di approfittarsene commer cialmente. Viene forse del nome di 'Shylock' del *Mercante di Venezia* che da noi viene chiamato 'Shy' e che poi dopo si trasforma in 'shyster.' Uno che sembra Shylock, quindi.

A piker. – Uno che promette di fare e poi non fa niente o non si fa nemmeno vedere. Si direbbe di uno che dà un appuntamento ad una signorina, per esempio, e poi la lascia lì ad attendere all'angolo. Uno che non fa mai come fanno gli amici, e chi sa perché.

Don't be a piker – we are going to ask for a vacation!
When I found out what kind of a fellow he was, I piked on him!
He piked on me twice, so I cut his acquaintance!
to pike, piking, piked, piked – dar il giro, piantare.

To jew down. – Dal nome 'Jew' (ebreo) che contratta sempre e non importa che prezzo vien chiesto. Quindi si dice di uno che sta per comperare e che fa delle questioni per il prezzo, uso ebreo.

It was worth $5 alright, but I had to jew him down to $3.
Don't try to jew me down; it wont do you any good!
To jew down, jewing, jewed, jewed. (far ribassare il prezzo.)

A selling spiel. – 'spiel' è il tedesco per 'a talk' e che si usa da noi nello slang, per dire il parlare di uno che lo fa come una macchina, come fanno i viaggiatori commessi – tutto a memoria. 'selling' viene dal verbo 'to sell, selling, sold, sold' (vendere). Quindi, un 'selling spiel' vuol dire 'una lunga parlata per vendere qualchecosa.'

He gave me a selling spiel on his article ladies' gloves.
As a salesman he has a good selling spiel!

A poor dub. – Un povero fesso! Eccolo in poche parole!

To bully – bullying, bullied, bullied – si dice di un individuo di 30 anni che si mette a litigare con uno di appena 14, diciamo. Anche del boxeur di professione che si mette a litigare per far vedere nei risultati la sua bravura. In fine, si dice di qualunque individuo che ha un vantaggio netto su di un altro e che si approffitta.

He is a bully. – (un individuo che cerca i suoi inferiori per far saltar fuori la sua superiorità) (si dice generalmente di forza fisica.)
He tried to bully me, but I stopped him!
He was bullying a little fellow when I met him!

The cash-and carry chain stores. – Ecco! 'Store' come già saprà, è il negozio. 'Cash-and-carry' vuol dire che in questo negozio si pagherà 'in contanti e poi si porterà la roba a casa da sè.' 'Chain' ('catena' vuol dire che è un genere di negozio che si troverà in tutte le città d'America, e sotto la stessa direzione). Con questo sistema 'cash-and-carry' si eliminano le spese di consegna della merce e delle perdite che avverrebbero forse nel fare del credito alla clientele. Quindi si paga in contanti, e poi si porta via la roba da se. Chi ha trovato questo sistema economico – la roba così costa di meno dato che le spese non ci sono – ha fatto mettere di questi negozi in tutte le città d'importanza, con lo stesso nome e lo stesso sistema ed ecco che diventano 'chain' stores, ossia, 'negozi a catena.' Sono quasi tutti di negozi di commestibili, però.

'Chain stations' si dice delle stazioni radiofoniche che trasmettono l'una all'altra per poi diffondere lo stesso programma agli ascoltatori. La ragione – business!

Cash – contanti. Carry – portare.

A good mixer. – Uno che sa star bene in qualsiasi compagnia. Dal verbo 'to mix, mixing, mixed, mixed' – Mescolare, mescolarsi.

Let's invite Mr. Pavese; he's a good mixer!
He's not a good mixer at all!

A josher. – Uno che scherza, che conta delle frottole. Un buontempone! Dal verbo, to josh, joshing, joshed, joshed – scherzare.

He's quite a josher with the women!
He is always joshing someone!

The missus. – Come si pronuncia l'abbreviazione 'Mrs.' che è 'Signora.'

Meet Mrs. Pavese. – (Detto da un americano sembra che dica – Meet missus Pavese! (Mi spiego?)
The missus will not let me go out! (Mia signora non mi lascia uscire.)
I'll talk to the missus about it (Ne parlerò alla signora)

A tightwad. – Un avaro, uno che ha paura di spendere benchè ne abbia. Da 'tight' (stretto) e 'wad' 'rotolo di carta-moneta.' Guardi quest'esempio:–

He has a big wad nevertheless he's tight! (stingy)
I'll tell the world he's a tightwad; he's so damned tight his knee-caps squeak! (Ha!)
Don't be a tightwad; buy me some cigarettes!

Nut-center chocolates. – I dolci di cioccolato che hanno l'interno (center) riempito di noci o mandorle. I 'liquor center chocolates' son quelli che avete voi in Italia, tipo Perugina, che a me piacciono, e che hanno del liquore nell'interno, Strega, Vermouth, Benedictine, ecc. Gosh!

A simp. – Abbreviazione di 'simpleton' che vuol dire uno che è 'semplice' di spirito, quasi cretino. Quindi, 'simp' è 'cretino' bell'è buono.

A rep. – Abbreviazione di 'reputation' (reputazione).

If we go on a grand sneak we'll lose our rep!
She doesn't care about her rep at all!
You have a good rep in English, Mr. Pavese!
You'll have a better rep when I finish with you!

Wooden money – Moneta di legno – che significa della moneta che non vale – o come si direbbe da noi – a rubber nickel – ossia, una moneta da cinque soldi fatta di gomma!

Ha! Moneta illegale si chiama – Wooden money – perché non serve!

Are you still carrying wooden money around with you?
Put that wooden money in your pocket; I'll pay for this cup of coffee myself!
The cafe Mugna doesn't want your wooden money! I'll treat!

Gee whiz – Esclamazione di sorpresa o di sdegno!

Gee whiz! I thought you were going to tell me, too!
Gee whiz! Let's ask Mr. Mila too!
Gee whiz! We surely had a good time!

The davenport. – È il sofà – dove si passa la serata con la fanciulla. Nel Canadà li chiamano 'Chesterfield.' Sono così chiamati da noi, pero,' perché la fabbrica che per prima li faceva si trova nella città di 'Davenport' nello stato di 'Iowa.'

We are going to buy a new davenport soon.
Kindly be seated there on the davenport; I'll call Mr. Pavese.
Wont you have a seat on the davenport?

A hasbeen. – Uno che è stato qualche cosa ma che ora non lo è piu.' Si dice di uno che nella vita dà segni di farsi una bella strada ma che poi finisce male! Ecco perché si usa solo il passato del verbo – has been'
Da –has – e – been.' Bella questa parola, perché dice molto!

He's only a hasbeen now! Too many women!
Here's another hasbeen on account of drinking!
She's just another hasbeen, too!

A hockey-stick. – È il bastone caratteristico che si usa nel giuoco di 'hockey' che si fa d'inverno sul ghiaccio e sui pattini. Danno la corsa ad un pezzo di legno che deve attraversare il 'goal' per il punto. Questo bastone ha la forma pressapoco della lettera 'J,' di fatti, rassomiglia molto. Se va bene Lei ne ha già visto giuocare almeno nelle pellicole prese a St. Moritz!

A chessy cat – Viene da 'a Chesshire cat' che è un tipo speciale di gatto. Sembra che rida ironicamente e che non cessa mai - di modo che oggi quando vediamo un individuo che ha una ghigna da cretino gli diamo del 'chessy cat.'

Podgy – Aggettivo per descrivere la condizione del corpo che ingrassa solo in certi punti – l'obesità mal distribuita. Ha mai visto una bambola di stracci dopo essere stata nelle mani di un bambino? Testa gonfia, collo quasi non più, pancia sproporzionata – ecco il 'podgy' risultato.

A G.A.R. veteran. – Un combattente nella Guerra della Ribellione dal 1860–1865. Le iniziali vanno per 'Grand Army of the Republic.' 'La Grande Armata della Repubblica.'

'veteran' – (veterano) vuol dire 'combattente.'
'A World War Veteran' è 'un combattente della Grande Guerra Mondiale.'

A slob. – Uno sporcaccione nel senso che tutto quello che fa rimane sporco, le mani, gli abiti, la carta sulla quale scrive, ecc. Individuo molto, ma molto negligente con sè e nelle sue cose.

He's a slob. (Trascuratore di tutto).

A never wuzzer. – Dall'avverbio 'never' (mai) e dal verbo al passato 'was' (pronunciato all'americano – wuz) che vuol dire 'era.' Si dà del 'never-wuzzer' all'individuo che non solo non è di buono ora ma che non lo era giammai!

Yes, he's just a never-wuzzer; he never was any good and never will be! (Veda dalla pronuncia l'origine.)

To hog. – hogging, hogged, hogged –Voler tutto per sè. Viene dal sostantivo 'hog' che è il maiale, il porco, che vuol tutto e ne prenda di tutto.

Say, don't hog that book, let me have it a few days, too!
He wants to hog everything he gets!
Quit hogging the chairs, give me one so I can be seated!
Don't be so damned hoggish! (hogish) (specialmente detto a certi individui quando mangiano, o quando hanno qualche cosa di nuovo.)

A hick. – Slang per quello che è 'contadinesco.'

A hick. – Un contadino.
A hick laugh. – Un ridere da contadino.
A hick walk. – Un camminare da paesano.
Listen to the hick talk!

Hot-air artist. – Detto dell'individuo che è artista a fare lo spaccone. Quello che dice lo chiamiamo 'hot-air' 'aria calda' dacchè fa nausea. Questa frase è una, caro Pavese, che non bisogna usare troppo se si vuol tenere la pelle!

Listen to him give us the hot-air, will you!
He's always blowing hot-air about something!
He's so good at hot-airing somebody, he ought to be a stove salesmen!

A yegg. – Un criminale della professione dei 'safe-blowers' ossia, di quelli che 'fanno scoppiare le casse-forti.' Chi si dà al furto di casse-forti, e che data l'occasione pure ammazzerebbe!

Live-stock. – Bestiame. L'insieme di porci, mucche, vitelli, ecc. si chiama – live-stock. Da 'live' – vivo.'

Live-stock market. – Market del bestiame.

A stunt. – Un trucco. Si dice anche dei gesti dei saltimbanchi, contorsionisti, ecc.

That was a good stunt. – (Era un bel trucco.)
To walk on your hands is a good stunt!
To walk into a theater backwards so that the usher thinks that you are coming out, is another good stunt!

Hootch. – slang per 'liquore.'

We want some hootch for tonight!
Where did you get that hootch?

A rube burg. (Una borgata contadinesca). Si dice di certe nostre città piccole che non hanno gran chè di divertimenti o dei passa tempi. Da 'rube' (contadino) e 'burg' (borgata)

This city is rapidly becoming a rube burg!
This is a regular hick town, a rube burg!
This is such a rube burg that they blow out the street lamps at nine o'clock and bring in the sidewalks! (marciapiedi.)

A pal. – Un carissimo compagno, uno che lo è stato da molto tempo. Espressione di Grande affetto per un amico!

You are a good pal of mine, Mr. Pavese.

Mr. Mila is another pal of ours!
He's almost everybody's pal!
He's my Buddy, my pal!

Soda-fountain – sono i 'bars' americani dove vendono delle bibite dolci (soft drinks), perché hanno delle macchine (fountains) che danno le bibite mescolate di 'soda-water' che è un po' come 'l'a[c]qua selz.' Qui si vende dei gelati, delle bibite che non ubbriaccono, dei dolci, ecc.

Dante, the Wop poet. – Wop – è il più grande insulto che si possa dare all'Italiano in America, e che purtroppo spesso fanno gli americani. È un po' come in Francia che si dà del 'maccaroni.' In America danno del 'Wop' oppure del 'Dago' (pronunciato – 'dego') all'Italiano. Qui voleva solo dire – Dante, il poeta italiano – ma lo ho detto con l'insulto americano!

He's a Wop fighter – that Bonaglia!
Michelangelo was a Wop painter!
In America the Italians are Wops!
Call me a Wop again and I'll kill you!

Out-and-out (oppure) down and out – vuol dire che uno non ha più nulla, che è rimasto senza un soldo, o senza un po' di salute (se è dopo una malattia) o che è sfinito se è dopo un lavoro massacrante.

After my day's work I feel down-and-out.
After ten years in America he returned to Italy down-and-out! (senza un soldo.)
He felt down-and-out about his mother's death!
He was rich once but now he's down-and-out!

An old grouch. Dal verbo 'to grouch, grouching, grouched, grouched' (lagnarsi continuamente). Come fa l'individuo che è di mal umore, o come fanno quelli che ce l'hanno per natura di lagnare sempre di qualchecosa o di qualcuno. 'old' qui vuol solo dire che è 'inveterato lagnatore.'

Don't be so grouchy. (Non essere così lagnoso).
John is nothing but an old grouch!
He's always grouching!

To know the ropes. – Vuol dire 'sapere a fondo'
Qualsiasi cosa, luogo, ambiente, ecc. 'Conoscere le corde' diciamo noi.

He is a boxer who knows the ropes in the profession!
I know the ropes in that ritzy cafe!
When it comes to the highbrows I know the ropes alright!

Rigamajig. – Si dice di qualunque cosa della quale non sappiamo il nome, o la parola giusta, perché ci manca il vocabolo, la quale cosa avviene spessissimamente in America, ed è allora che la gente la chiama un 'rigamajig.' (L'accento cade sul 'rig') (si pronuncia 'rigamagig.')

What's this rigamajig? Oh, that's a hammer!
Where did you buy that rigamajig? You mean this long pencil? Oh, I bought it at Winter's store!

A bell-hop ... – Sono i giovinotti in uniforme che fanno servizio degli alberghi, hotels, ecc. Sono quelli che 'saltellano al suono della campana o campanello,' perché il loro nome viene da 'bell' (campanello) e dal verbo 'to hop, hopping, hopped, hopped' '– Saltellare.' Quando lei suona il campanello, ecco che le salta davanti uno di questi inservienti! Se non dormono! Ed allora le fanno il servizio voluto!

Tell the bell-hop to call a taxi!
I rang the bell twice, where's the hop? (bello, eh?)
Oh, the bell-hop must be busy just now!

That's the i. – That's the idea! Siccome 'idea' si pronuncia 'aidia' diciamo solo 'Do you get the i'? (oppure) 'That is the i alright' (È proprio l'idea, eh già.)

Do you get the i (ai) on this phrase, Mr. Pavese?
Ask the fellows if they get the i on this proposition!

Cuspidor. – È la sputacchiera! Che si chaima anche 'spittoon' da noi, con l'accento alla francese. 'Cuspidor' è vero inglese, e 'spittoon' e slang. Da 'spit' – sputo.' Cuspidor – viene dal francese 'cuspir' – sputare. Dico bene?

To whittle, whittling, whittled, whittled. – aguzzare, raffilare, come si fa quando si passa il tempo come un pezzo di legno ed un coltello, o coltellino, o come si fa con un lapis quando si vuol fare una punta. Si taglia solo un pezzettino alla volta – ebbene, questo si chiama 'to whittle.'

To whittle time away – Sprecare il tempo poco a poco!

Attaboy! Espressione sportistica per dire 'That's the boy' e che se detta in fretta all'americana sembra che si dica 'attaboy' come di fatti si scrive per dare l'effetto sulla pronuncia. 'Attagirl' – 'That's the girl' quando si vuol lodare una fanciulla in un giuoco qualsiasi.

As he made another goal the crowd cried out 'Attaboy, Henry!'

È una frase che esprime la contentezza degli spettatori per un bel giuoco del momento, giuoco che la folla, o l'individuo vuol riconoscere al giuocatore. Ora quando si è contenti di qualsiasi azione che fa un uomo, giovinotto, fanciulla o donna, diciamo, a secondo, 'Attaboy' oppure 'Attagirl.' Sarebbe come dire 'Bravo!' oppure 'Brava!'

Attaboy, Pavese, keep up the good work!
Attaboy, Cesare, you'll learn slang yet!

Chubby – grassoccio – come sono i bambini!

To wiggle, wiggling, wiggled, wiggled – Torcersi.

The snake was wiggling in the grass.
I held the eel in my hands but it wiggled out!

Questo verbo esprime l'azione che fa un pesce vivo quando lo si tiene per la coda. – it wiggles! Mi spiego? Caro Pavese, in un modo o in un altro bisogna esprimermi!

A tot – Un bambino, un piccolino.

He is only a one-year old tot!
He's just a tot yet – don't let him drink wine!

Highball glasses – sono i bicchieri nei quali fanno il 'highball' che è una bibita fatta di diversi liquori, e proibita in America; ecco perché si fa! 'Glass' – 'vetro' oppure 'bicchiere.'

We had two highballs last night at the dance!

Grillroom – Una specie di 'bar' e 'ristorante.' Se Lei può pensare per un momento a quelle sale al Regio, dove si va durante l'intermissione per prendere una bibita, o in piedi oppure da seduto, ecco che capirà cosa è il 'Grillroom.' È una sala, insomma, adibita al pronto servizio di mangiare o di bere, per quelli che non hanno del tempo a sprecare. Ora al Regio non si mangia, ma Lei avrà l'idea (you'll get the i) se penserà ai nostri teatri che danno da mangiare oppure da bere fra un atto e l'altro! Grillroom Service!

After the first act we went to the Grillroom for a sandwich.
The grillroom is on the ground floor in this theater!

Kind of all in after that spiel. – Essere piuttosto sfinito dopo quella parlata. To be all in – essere sfinito.

After a hard day's work, I'm all in. (Sono sfinito.)
When he comes out of class he's all in, poor fellow!
He was all in at the end of the first round!
He has such a long salesman's spiel that he's all in when he recites it once!
If we go on that hike we'll be all in when we get back!

To pull off a banquet (oppure) to throw a banquet. – Vuol dire 'dare un banchetto.'

We are going to throw a dinner in Mr. Pavese's honor!
Let's pull off a banquet for Mr. Mila, boys!

Caboodle. – slang per 'il tutto' 'l'intiero.'

We played cards for money and I took the caboodle!

A knocker. – Uno che dà sempre incontro alle cose o alle persone. Dal verbo 'to knock, knocking, knocked, knocked' 'Battere.'

He's a Fascist knocker!
Not only, but he's a Church knocker, too!
He never will be a booster because he always was a knocker.
He's always knocking someone! (Dà sempre incontro a qualcuno.) (Sparla sempre, ecc.)

Roustabout – Uno che è sempre al suo agio ovunque, come fa il vagabondo, o l'individuo che vive a forza del piccolo lavoro che trova qui e la, e dorme anche di qui e di la! Si pronuncia 'raustabout.'

The pants-pressing sign. – Da 'pants' (pantaloni), 'pressing,' dal verbo, to press, pressing, pressed, pressed (stirare) e 'sign' – 'cartello.' Quindi si vede che era 'un cartello da sarto' per dire che si stirava dei pantaloni. Ne abbiamo appunto di queste sartorie dove stirano gli abiti mentre che si attende in una camera attigua! Il cartello leggerà cosi' 'PANTS PRESSED WHILE U WAIT.' (Pants pressed while you wait.) (Si stirano i pantaloni mentre chè si attende.)

Ouch! – Espressione di dolore come quando qualcuno pesta i piedi! Si pronuncia – aucc!

A Voodooistic power. – Da 'Voodoo' ch'è il nome del mago negro. 'Voodooism' è la forma di superstizione e di magia degenerata che si trova fra i negri degli Stati Uniti e che è l'eco della barbaria Africana. Quindi qui vuol dire 'avere la potenza, il potere del mago negro.' Si pronuncia – vudu – con l'accento sulla prima!

Conditions (in school). – vuol dirsi di uno che è promosso sulla condizione che raggiungerà una certa percentuale entro un certo tempo altrimenti gli toccherà tornare indietro alla classe che ora sta per lasciare. Ammettiamo che uno studente si trova in prima liceo, e che bisogna avere la qualifica di 80% alla fine dell'anno prima di poter essere promosso alla seconda classe liceo. Ebbene alla fine dell'anno si trova con la percentuale di 75 e la condizione di quattro mesi. Entrerà senz'altro in seconda classe, ma entro quattro mesi deve portare la sua percentuale almeno a 80 per il suo lavoro nella nuova classe altrimenti gli si verrà a dire che bisogna tornare alla classe inferiore! È il sistema americano nelle scuole alte o 'high schools.' Per non bocciare addirittura danno una 'condizione,' che è vantaggiosa, per chi vuol far bene.

The feature film. – È il film, la pellicola, principale.

'The Big Parade' will be the feature film at the Palazzo this week. Other films will be the LUCE and a comedy!

Feature film – pellicola di spettacolo principale. Dal verbo, to feature, featuring, featured, featured – che vuol dire – Presentare in precedenza.

Next week we shall feature Al Jolson in the 'Jazz Singer.' After that we shall feature Charlot (Charlie Chaplin.)

A Union Club Hop. 'Hop' si chiama un 'ballo' dacchè si saltella. Invece di dire 'Are you going to the dance?' si dice anche 'Are you going to the hop?'

'Union Club' è il 'Club' del Sindacato. Ho spiegato il verbo nel caso della parola – 'bell-hop' – si ricordi?

Poky – essere molto lento nelle cose.

He is poky in everything.
He is a poky fellow. (Fa tutto da mezzo morto.)

Every other day. – Pavese, Pavese, dimentica il suo inglese puro, ora? Questa frase vuol dire 'un giorno sì, ed un giorno no.'

We go to church every other Sunday
We have English class every other day.
We have our vacation only every other year!

A grafter. – Uno che si dà alla camorra! Dal verbo, to graft, grafting, grafted, grafted. – Fare le cose ingiuste.

He is a political grafter!
There is a lot of grafting in politics.

A bad give-away. – 'Give-away' si dice di una cosa che vien detta, diciamo, da una persona circa un'altra e quale cosa ci cambia addirittura la nostra opinione della persona. Suppponiamo che Mila mi avesse detto che una tale Domenica era andato a Milano. Benone! Quando trovo lei ci mettiamo a parlare di Mila e senza pensarci o senza volerlo lei mi dice che in quella tale Domenica è stato a casa di Mila a studiare, supponiamo. Questa sua frase che mi dice questo si chiama il 'give-away' perché vengo a sapere che Mila mi ha contato una bugia! Povero Max! Cosa mai diciamo?

It was a dead give-away. (Era un rendersi palpitante.)
I gave him away. (Ho fatto, o detto, la cosa che lo ha messo nella sua vera luce.)
To give away (mettere alla vera luce).
He said he could speak English, but when I spoke to him in English it was a give-away!

To give the once-over. – Dare un'occhiata ad una persona in sù ed in giù come si fa quando si studia un tipo nuovo! Diciamo pure 'to give the double-O' (guardare uno con due occhi) dacchè gli occhi sembrano a un doppio O. Guardare in fretta per rendersi un certo conto di una cosa o di una persona.

I gave her the once-over and decided I should never like her!

She gave me the double-O and smiled, so I followed her!
I only gave this book the once-over so I don't know much about it!
Give this essay the once-over and then give me your opinion of it!

To hit the hay. – Andare a letto. Dal verbo, to hit, hitting, hit, hit (colpire, andare a colpire) e 'hay' che è il 'fieno' e che vuol dire 'letto' nello slang.

I hit the hay at ten o'clock every night.
We hit the hay at midnight last night.
At what time are you going to hit the hay to-night?

Hubby. – è il nomignolo di 'husband' – (marito)

My hubby was out last night on a grand sneak!
He's a darling hubby, alright, he only gets drunk once a week!
Oh, missus, where's the hubby to-night?

Chop suey. – È un piatto cinese, gustatissimo, fatto con dei cavoli, cipolle, ecc. e ne mangio ben volontieri. Si dà solo nei ristoranti cinesi. Si pronuncia – ciap-sue-.

Top o' the morning! È il saluto irlandese per 'good morning' solo che loro vi augurano persin il 'principio' del mattino, ossia 'Top' (cima). È facile tuttora negli ambienti irlandesi sentirsi salutare al mattino con 'Top o' the morning to you, sir!' L'O con apostrophe [*sic*] è solo l'abbreviazione di 'of,' come in 'o'clock.'

An A 1 lo diciamo 'An A Number One.' e, si pronuncia precisamente come l'ho scritto. La lettera A è la prima dell'alfabeto ed il numero 1 è il primo dei numeri quindi si sa ora che 'A-1 vuol dire di primissimo ordine, o per lo meno, di primo ordine.

He is an A 1 fellow (He's an A number one fellow.)
Mr. Pavese is an A-1 slang slinger!
She's an A-1 girl!
That's an A-1 job for an A-1 fellow! (lavoro) op. (posizione)

Gavel-wielder. – Dal verbo, 'to wield, wielding, wielded, wielded' – maneggiare. 'Gavel' è quel piccolo Martello di legno che tiene il presidente di qualsiasi seduta per tenere l'ordine. Il giudice del tribunale ne ha uno e di tanto in tanto se lo vede a battere per un po' di silenzio, o per dire qualchecosa pure egli. Questo si chiama, perciò, il 'gavel-wielder' ossia 'il maneggiatore del Martello di legno,' che non so come si chiamo in italiano.

He's the gavel-wielder in our Club! (Presidente.)
We are going to elect a new gavel-wielder!

Doodad. – Si dice del superfluo!

There are too many doodads in this architecture!
I can see a lot of doodads in this picture.

The dashboard (of a car) – È quel pezzo di legno di fronte alla guida, internamente, sul quale c'è il tassometro, l'orologio, la mano che indica la quantità della benzina nel serbatoio, la mano che indica la quantità dell'olio, ecc. Sa dove si mette quella chiavetta per incominciare il motore; ebbene, quella parte lì si chiama il 'dashboard.'

A dingus. – Sinonomo di 'rigamajig,' che si usa quando non si sa il vocabolo giusto, o quando si vuol disprezzare qualchecosa!

I don't want to put this Tux on!
I don't want to put this dingus on!

Truck (in eating). È sinonimo di 'junk' (ammondizia [*sic*], scarto).

That coffee is regular truck!
That was real truck they gave to eat last night!
Why don't they get some good truck once in a while?

A plug. – Abbiam già visto il verbo 'to plug' ed ora guardiamo questo sostantivo che si usa per gli attacchi elettrici, dove si mette la spina elettrica, sia per il respire- polvere, per il ferro da stirare. È un attacco che si mette dove è più comodo.

The electric-iron plug is just behind the door!
The vacuum-cleaner plug is down near the floor!

Kittiedoolie. – È un termine d'affetto, come sarebbe la parola 'darling.' Vi sono diversi di questi termini stravaganti nello slang.

hon. – È pure l'abbreviazione di 'honey' (miele) e che si dà alle persone femminili da noi molto amate, come la moglie, la sorella – o la suocera!

Listen, hon., bring me my book!
Oh, kittiedoolie, where's my pen!?

Flipflop. – Sinonomo di 'doodad' (superfluo) chè si usa per descrivere un'azione che ha il moto di un pezzo di carta che sia in balia del vento, per esempio. L'uso è vario!

He is a flipflop in business! (Niente di buono.) e quindi, superfluo!

to blurt. – blurting, blurted, blurted – seguito generalmente dalla preposizione 'out' e che vuol dire 'parlare senza pensarci su'' come fa l'individuo che deve risponder subito e che non sa cosa dire e quindi dice basta che sia, interrottamente!

He blurted something about my being wrong!
He merely blurted out that he was right and I was wrong!

Aw punk! – Espressione di sdegno, che è quasi sinonomo di 'Oh, darn it!' 'Oh, damn it!' solo che non è una frase così robusta di volgarità come le ultime due!

Aw punk! Why not stay home to-day and rest?

To gas. – Parlare così tanto da asfissiare la gente! E parlare solo per il gusto di parlare, senza dire qualchecosa che valga un centesimo! È pure usato come sinonomo di 'to Kid' (prendere in giro, scherzare').

He has been gassing me all afternoon!
Don't gas me like that!

Stuck-up, gabby, four-flushers. – 'Stuck-up' (superbo) 'gabby' che viene dallo slang 'gab' (bocca) e che vuol dire fanno buon uso della bocca. 'four-flushers' sono degli individui che fanno l'amico quando conviene e poi, poi fanno l'indifferente oppure anche l'inimico, a secondo come conviene.

Quindi qui si parla 'di questi bei tipi che sono dei superbi chiacchieroni.' Va bene così?

Shut your <u>gab</u>! (Chiudi la bocca!)
Don't be so damned <u>gabby</u> – give me a chance!

A baalamb. – Si dice di un individuo che è umile come la pecora, o per lo meno sembra esserlo, e si dà a quegli individui che sono sempre tranquilli, come

Max! Viene, appunto da 'lamb' (pecora) e 'bass' che è quel misero grido della pecora! Quindi in questa parola si sente il tipo dell'individuo (lamb) e pure la sua vocetta (baa).

Sassiety stunt. – Society stunt. (Trucco di società) che qui vorrà dire 'costume di Società,' uso di società 'Sassiety' è qui così scritto per far vedere come gli americani in generale pronunciano la parola 'society,' quando vogliono disprezzare questa società. Il dover metter l'abito da sera sarebbe un 'society stunt'! E 'stunt' appunto si dice di quelle cose fuori del comune che si fanno in categorie speciali, come già credo di aver detto, per i saltimbanchi, i contorsionisti, i prestidigitatori, e quegli usi di società. Ha!

High-binder. – Dal verbo 'to bind, binding, bound, bound' che vuol dire 'legare' 'High' (alto). Quindi 'high-binder' si dà all'individuo che è legato ai costumi di società, o a quelli che lo vogliono essere.

Tin-horn (tromba da latta) si dice di un contadino, paesano, o qualsiasi tipo che vale poco. La tromba d'argento dà un suono vibrante, chiaro, rotondo e bello, e quindi fa sì che lo strumento sia di valore musicalmente ed anche commercialmente. 'Tin- horn' invece non avrebbe nessun valore. Quindi l'individuo 'tin-horn' è quello che non ha un valore, se non quello che se ne prende da sè.

Parleyvoo – Dal francese 'parlez-vous' che si usa da noi per dire una 'conversazione' 'a talk' come fra amici! Per esempio, se lei vedesse ad un angolo della via dei suoi amici che stanno parlando fra loro potrebbe intromettersi e dire 'Hello, fellows; what's all the parleyvoo about?' That was some parleyvoo we had yesterday at your home! Oh we were just parleyvooing! (We were just talking.)

A whaleuva favour. – È il modo parlato di 'whale of a favor.'

'Whale' è la 'balena' e 'favour' è un 'piacere.'
Quindi, qui vuol dire' un grandissimo favore, piacere.'

A hell of a good time (A helluva good time).
Please do me a whale of a favor (whaleuva favor).

A peach of a thing. (slang) 'Peach' vuol dire 'bellissimo esempio.'

He is a peach of a fellow. (È un bellissimo esempio di amico, compagno.)

It was a peach of a thing to do for me!
She's a peach when it comes to dancing!
'Peach' è la 'pesca' (frutta).

To give a whale of a run. – Spieghiamo così. 'to give a run' vuol dire 'fare, oppure, dare della concorrenza, della competizione.' To give a whale of a run vuol dire dare della grandissima concorrenza, come fa l'America nel campo commerciale.

To give – (dare) a run – (una corsa)

I gave him a run for his money. (slang) (Gli ho dato della concorrenza per i suoi sforzi.) Per quanto abbia fatto gli ho dato della concorrenza.
I'll give you a whale of run in slang, Mr. Pavese. Ready?
Mr. Ford will give the Fiat a whaleuva run!

Yuh! – È il modo americano di pigrizia per dire 'yes.'
Forma distorta di 'ya' tedesco! Tutti i vagabondi, ed i pigri in generale parlano così.

How's old socks – Slang per 'Come stai?' quando rivolto all'amico.

Well, Pavese, how's old socks!
Ask old socks Mila how he is!

A bull-pen. – La prigione. – Da 'bull' (toro) il nome che si dà ai 'policemen' e 'pen' che è il nome di quelle recinte dove si tengono le bestie, specialmente i porci (pig-pen). Quindi 'bull-pen' è la Questura più che altro!

Tough nuts, raise cain. – 'To raise cain' (fare del chiasso, essere indisciplinati, disordinati).

'tough-nuts' – individui senza scrupoli, morali e disordinati, indisciplinati, che cercano sempre di fare le cose che non si dovrebbe fare. Da 'tough' (duro) e 'nut' (nocciolo).

You fellows must not raise cain in this cafe!
Go somewhere else, you tough nuts, if you want to raise cain!

Old hoss. – Americano famigliare per 'old horse' che si dà ad un amico caro e che forse rispecchia l'amore per i cavalli che ha tanta gente!

How's the old hoss this morning?

A slew. – che vuol dire una ('infinità')

I have a slew of things to do yet!
We were given a slew of work at school yesterday.
You sent me a slew of slang phrases! Si pronuncia slu.

Yep. – Altro modo pigro di dire 'Yes.'
Nope – Lo stesso modo per dire 'NO.' Oppure 'Nup.'

Hunk of cheese. – 'Hunk' (slang) per 'un pezzo.' Si dà del 'pezzo di formaggio' a qualcuno tanto per cambiare il solito saluto. Bene, eh?

Listen, hunk of cheese, what are you going to do to-day?
Well, Well, how's old socks, old hunk of cheese, old hoss?!

Si direbbe così dopo un pezzo che non si è visti! Quel 'old' è sempre nel senso di 'vecchio amico' e non dà il senso di 'vecchiaia.'

A slick actor. – Un attore molto in gamba.

He's a slick business-man.
He's as slick as a Jew!

To beef – (lagnarsi). Beefing, beefed, beefed.

You are always beefing about something (complaining).
Say, quit beefing, will you?
Everytime we are assigned our school work, he beefs!

All-fired successful. – Il superlative di 'successo.' 'tutto infuocato di successo.'
'Una sola fiamma di successo.'

The poor skate. – 'skate' è sinonomo di 'slump' ma che in più vorrebbe dire ('il miserabile,' insignificante, ecc.)
'a poor skate' – 'un povero miserabile' 'un povero insignificante.' L'uso di questa parola è anche vario!

A blow-hard. – Da 'to blow, blowing, blew, blown' (soffiare) e 'hard' (forte) – in questo caso. Vuol dirsi di un individuo che parla sempre di sè ed a voce alta senza timori di qualsiasi cosa, che fa tutti gli sforzi, insomma, per far intendere il suo valore.

He is always blowing hard about himself!

Therefore, he's a blow hard!

A stinker. – Uno che fa tutto sotto mano! Chi sà perché ma viene dal verbo 'to stink, stinking, stank, stunk' (puzzare).

A good two-for – Si dice delle cose che si possono comperare a due per poi pagar di meno, come dei sigari, dei pacchi di sigarette, dove vi è sempre il prezzo per uno ed il prezzo ribassato per due; per esempio, un sigaro Havana costa 15 soldi americani ma si possono comperare due per 25 soldi. Il prezzo a due è standarizzato a 25 soldi, quindi si dirà 'I bought some Havanas, two-for' ('25 soldi' – inteso).

This is a good two-for Havana (È un buonissimo sigaro Havanna che si vende a a due per il prezzo o corrente).

Viene dalle frasi come questa 'These books are <u>two for</u> $1.' 'Questi libri sono in vendita a due per un dollaro.' 'Quando poi si passa al tempo in cui questo prezzo si standardizza' allora dicono solo 'These books are two-for.' Mi spiego?

Mollycoddle. – Un deboluccio, senza carattere, senza vita!

To chuck, chucking, chucked, chucked – Metter via, mettere da parte.

I am going to chuck my books for the day!
He tried to chuck his wife, but the law forbade him!

Wire-glass – Si dice di quei vetri di vetrina che internamente hanno una rete di ferro per rinforzare, e che, se pure spezzato il vetro, rimane ancora tal quale nella protezione della proprietà. A wire-glass window!

To mooch – elemosinare, come chi fa che va in giro cercando dei piaceri dagli amici, dei soldi, ecc. 'to mooch, mooching, mooched, mooched.'

I'm going to bum a cigarette from Pavese.
I'm going to mooch a cigarette from Pavese. (Vede?)

To haul folks over the coals. – Leggere la vita alla gente!

To haul, hauling, hauled, hauled – Strascinare.
'Over the coals' – Sopra le ceneri roventi – se posso dire così. (Ha!)

The next time I meet Mr. Pavese I'm going to haul him over the coals!

To prod. – Spingere in avanti, come si fa con le bestie!

To prod, prodding, prodded, prodded – Spingere in avanti. Si usa anche con 'along' (in avanti).

The teachers are continually prodding us in our work!

A streamline body. – La linea della carozzeria d'automobile! Il taglio di carozzeria, ecc. Si direbbe che 'The Fiat has a beautiful streamline body while the Ford has not.'

To live in a compound. – Abitare in un albergo, hotel! Si dice così per questi alberghi, ecc. sono 'composti' di diversi individui, famiglie, ecc. 'Compound' da il senso di 'una cosa sull'altra, come negli alberghi, le camere, le suites,' ecc.

Compound interest – per esempio – il termine commerciale è 'l'interesse sull'interesse' dei soldi investiti. L'interesse dei soldi che dopo un certo tempo fa parte del capitale e frutta pure esso l'interesse.

The dump where we lunched! Il luogo dove abbiamo mangiato!

'Dump' si dice di un luogo qualsiasi malandato. 'To lunch, lunching, lunched, lunched' – Fare merenda, mangiare, desinare.

Last night we went to the same old dump, the Mugna!

Qui ne faccio uso per far vedere come si può anche usare il termine 'dump' per dimostrare il disprezzo o la noia di dover trovarsi sempre nello stesso luogo.

A tony fee. – Un mangiare da primissimo ordine! To feed, feeding, fed, fed. – (dar da mangiare) A feed – un mangiare.

This is good feed. (È del buon mangiare questo!)

We had a good feed at Pavese's last night. (Pavese ci ha dato un buon pranzo ieri sera.)

To cover the ground. – Fare tutto quello che si deve.

Da 'to cover, covering, covered, covered' – coprire. 'ground' e' 'terra.' Per esempio, ora – se un corso di studio è di due anni, ammettiamo, e un individuo riesce a completare questo corso in un solo anno, diciamo che 'he has covered the ground in a year.' (lo ha fatto in un anno).

It is going to take me two years yet to cover the ground! (passare la materia).

How long is it going to take you to cover the ground in slang?
You will cover the ground soon, Mr. Pavese!

To duck. – Schivare dei colpi delle boxe! Giù con la testa!

Duck your head! (Giù con la testa!)

To whale the daylights out of someone (oppure) to lambaste someone. – Battere qualcuno sino a che non vi sia che un filo di vita. 'Daylight' è 'il luce di giorno' ma altra spiegazione non si può dare. 'to whale, whaleing, whaled, whaled' (slang) – battere secco!

That wins the fire-brick necklace. – O Dio, Pavese, come si fa a spiegare certe nostre stupidaggini! Questa, per esempio, è una frase cretina che esprime la cretineria che avrà detto un altro, o la cosa cretina che abbia fatto.

Ammettiamo che Lei mi venga a dire che Massimo, pur sapendolo, era andato a mettersi la mano nel fuoco! Io rispondo, 'Well, that wins the glass tooth-brush' – Ebbene, perdinci, un atto tale vince una spazzola di vetro per i denti.' Vede ora le due cretinerie? Ne abbiamo tante di queste frasi. Guardi le frasi d'esempio:

I offered him $10 for that book but he sold it to Mr. Pavese for $5. Well, damned it, that wins the rubber dollar!

He threw a match into the gasoline tank! Yes? Well, well, he wins the asbestos cigar!

He had the nerve to tell me that he bought that car! You don't say so! Well, he wins the leather medal!

Nel primo esempio abbiamo un 'dollaro di gomma,' nel secondo un 'sigaro di asbestos' e nel terzo una 'medaglia di cuoio.' Cretineria che servono lo scopo di sdegno!

Il suo 'fire-brick necklace' sarebbe una 'collana fatta i mattoni.'

Bezuzus. – Un nome qualsiasi come si direbbe 'Tizio, Caio,' ecc.

a rag rug. – Un tappeto fatto di stracci, artisticamente! 'Rag' è 'straccio' e 'rug' è 'tappeto.' Si fanno molti da noi con i frammenti di stoffe, come pure i famosi 'patch-quilts' americani che sono le coperte da letto fatto nello stesso modo.

to yip. – Lagnarsi come fa un cane quando si fa male! Yipping, yipped, yipped. È quasi dell'armonia imitativa – dei cani, pero.'

My culture is not-yet. – La mia cultura non è ancora completata, la mia educazione non è ancora terminata.

The slum – Quartiere dei poveri, o della mala-vita! Come al 'balon' a Torino!

He lives in the slums. (abita nel quartiere della mala-vita.)
He goes slumming. (Andare in giro come quelli della mala-vita.)

cut-glass. – È un vetro fino, artistico, di un taglio 'al brillante.' Vi sono dei servizi di bicchieri, ecc. che sono fatti di questo vetro. Costa pure caro!

An up-and-coming fellow. – Un individuo che sia già sulla strada e che sta per andare ancora più in sù.

Mr. Pavese is an-up-and-coming fellow in slang!

a garnet. – È una preziosa pietra di color rosso! Più non so! Cerchi lei l'Italiano!

The con. – Ah, qui, devo commentare un po' se voglio farle capire! È quasi senza dubbio che è una sillaba da qualche parola, la quale sillaba si usa per dire 'la sostanza' della cosa stessa. Guardi gli esempi:

He puts the con in economica! (È egli mette, o che sa mettere la sostanza nelle materie commerciali.)
He puts the math in mathematica! (È egli che mette, o che sa mettere della sostanza, della vita, dell'intelligenza nelle matematiche.)

Mr. Pavese is the fellow who can put the ish on English! (È il signor Pavese che sa mettere, o che sa fare, come si deve nell'inglese, di slang, e di tutto. Insomma è un vero maestro, perfetto, l'individuo che può dare del suo, che può accrescere la materia.) Già, caro Pavese, spero di spiegarmi almeno per questa forma che è comune da noi.
Mr. Alfano is the fellow who puts the com in composition! (È Alfano, per Dio, che sa comporre, che ci dà qualche cosa di buono, che vale, ecc.)

A monkey-wrench. – è un implemento di meccanico, con il quale lavorano attorno gli accessori d'automobili, motori, machine, ecc. È un implemento che si apre e chiude alla grandezza voluta per girare questa o quella, cosa. Non so l'italiano!

Fluff. – Qualsiasi cosa che dia l'apparenza della schiuma di mare, per esempio, che poi in fondo non vi è della sostanza ma solo l'apparenza. Si dice 'fluffy' di una capigliatura dopo che si è fatta lavare! Mi spiego!

A fly chicken. – Le galline che non si contentano di mangiare quello che si trova a terra ma che vanno piuttosto dietro alle mosche e così nella loro più grande preoccupazione mangiano anche di meno. Si dice 'fly- chicken' delle nostre signorine delle classi medie, borghesia, che non si contentano di rimanere nel loro ambiente, sposarsi così ed accontentarsi, ma vanno piuttosto alla ricerca di qualche millionario, ecc. per poi magari finir male! Ed aver meno ancora di quello che avrebbero potuto avere.

Mr. Pavese:[4] At this point of my commenting I have succeeded in getting *Babbitt* from the public library in order to read it and thusly give you a far better explanation of slang than I otherwise could have. From what I have read of it so far, I consider it a marvelous piece of work, insofar as the portrayal of our American type, is concerned. Lewis, too, is most efficacious in his descriptions and is beyond praise in his personages, their talk and manner of living. I am surprised, though, that you were able to delve into him for he not only makes an almost 100% use of slang in his personages but has them speaking the most every-day common English, and he writes it just as they speak it and not as it should be written! I do hope, though, that you understood him at all times; at any rate, I shall read along, and every time I come across a word or phrase which I think you might not understand I shall explain it, whether your chosen list arrives or not. I have the book now so am fully prepared 'to make you understand it better.'

Tony

Babbitt – Sinclair Lewis – Edizione Harcourt, Brace & Co. Tutte le frasi e parole che si trovano di qui in avanti sono tratte cominciando da 'Chapter XVI.' Segua, ora, il suo testo ed avrà tutto sotto mano!

Lodge – È il nome che si dà ad un Club, una Società, ecc. L'insieme di tutte queste società si chiama 'lodge.'

What lodge do you belong to? The Elks and the Rotarians.

4 At this point Chiuminatto opts for a larger paper format to continue his comments on *Babbitt*.

Prosperity-boosting lunch-clubs – Dei clubs o delle società che danno delle cene, feste, ecc. Alle quali portano in sù la prosperità, cercano sempre insomma di progredire commercialmente per l'ambiente in cui vivono.

Joiner – Dal verbo, to join, joining, joined, joined – Far parte, entrare, come di una società.

Pep and punch. – Aver della vita, e della forza da fare, in sè.

A bang – Un ciuffo (parlando di capigliatura) come si fa qui.

The real cheap skate – Il vero, povero avaro – è l'uomo che non impresterà al Signore! (dal testo)

Nursery – Camera adibita per i bambini con gioccatoli [*sic*], cavallucci, ecc. Vi sono tanti in America per le madri che lavorano, così possono lasciare i loro bambini nelle cure delle infermiere municipali! Si paga un tantino al mese, al giorno, ecc.

pants. – Pantaloncini per i ragazzi; ma pantaloncini in generale.

grubby. – miseri, angusti. (Si parla di cappelle.)

Can you wait a jiffy? – Puoi aspettare un momento?

Smart Set. – La Colonia degli Aristocratici! La Combriccola Aristocratica.

To need bucking up. Dal verbo 'to buck up, bucking, bucked, bucked' – che è slang per 'farsi animo, farsi coraggio, ecc.'

I need bucking up. – Ho bisogno di farmi coraggio!
I need to be bucked up. (Ho bisogno di essere spinto in animo.)

To take somebody's dust. – Prendere la polvere da qualcuno. Se Lei sa cosa vuol dire una gita in automobile nella campagna aperta per la polverosa strada e poi avere un'altra automobile che le passa a 60 chilometri all'ora lasciando lei e la sua automobile in una spessa nuvola di polvere, allora capirà l'uso di questa frase. Qui si usa perché il ministro non vuol che un'altra chiesa gli sia prima nell'elenco delle classi di religione. Fatto si è che dice subito –'We ought to be first.' (Dobbiamo essere i primi.)

To get nicked – (To be caught) (essere preso) Dal verbo slang 'to nick, nicked, nicked, nicking' – Pigliare, prendere – 'catch.'

To get off by one's self – Mettersi da solo.

a kiddy. – Nomignolo di 'giovinotto.'

Fidgety. – nervoso.

To get a glad hand. – Ricevere il benvenuto. (Avere la mano felice.)

To have get-up-and-go in you. – Vuol dire 'avere dell'ambizione che le spinge di andare sempre in avanti.' 'La volontà di andare sempre in avanti.'

Bunch. – È il titolo familiare che si dà al 'gruppo,' alla 'combriccola.'

To sweep the country – Prendere la nazione come fa il ciclone, far furore!

Depleted nerve tissue – La fibra dei nervi che è sfinita.

Sunday School journals. – Riviste religiose. Tutte le riviste e gazette o stampe si chiamano 'journals.'

skunk. – È una bestia selvatica che puzza terribilmente e che si difende a forza di spruzzare l'individuo con 'la sua acqua.' Mi spiego? Si dà dello 'skunk' all'individuo che lavora sotto mano.

To spring a thing. – Fare qualchecosa d'improvviso! Dal verbo 'to spring, springing, sprang, sprung' – Scatenare.

To hand it to someone. – Dar credito a qualcuno!

How's tricks, ole socks. – Come vanno le cose, vecchio amico? (How are tricks che l'Americano dice 'How's tricks'.) 'Tricks' 'Giuochetti' della vita.

Toddy – bibita speciale di liquore.

To throw fits. – Aver degli spasimi per qualche cosa! 'Fit!' la malattia degli epilettici!

Folderols and doodads. – Cose insignificanti, superflue.

Wieniewurst. – Una salsiccia, uso tedesco – Wienerwurst, che Babbit dice, 'wieniewurst.'

Frinstance – Americano per 'for instance.' (per esempio)

To bring home the bacon. – Portare i risultati. ('Portare in casa proprio i risultati voluti.') 'Bacon' è una specie di carne gustatissima da noi.

Pussy – Nomignolo per 'gatto.'

oldsters. – vecchietti.

part-time press-agent ... Agente di stampa che lavora a tempo perso!

Babbitt did not drive home. – Non è andato a casa nell'automobile.
To drive a car – Guidare un'automobile.

Drug-stores – Drogherie ma che da noi vendono di tutto e quasi tutti hanno il 'soda-fountain' per le bibite dolci ('soft drinks'). Ecco perché dice che gli amici si radunavano di sera a chiacchierare, nella drogheria.

Patrol-wagon. – L'automobile di Questura per trasportare i delinquenti.

The wallop in the velvet mitt. – Il pugno nella mano di velour. – Dice così di Eathorne che è uomo raffinato eppure commerciale a differenza degli altri suoi amici. 'Slip me the glove' è sinonimo di 'slip me the mitt.'

Hooptedoole stuff. – Roba cretina, stupida.

a boom. – Un rialzamento spirituale, commerciale, ecc.

Cocksure young men. – Giovinotti convintissimi, positivissimi, ecc. 'sicuri come un galluccio' fiducissimi in sè.

Gee whillikins. – Espressione di contento o di scontento, che esprime bene all'immaginazione ma che in sè non dice nulla!

Wholesaler. – Colui che vende all'ingrosso. Wholesale company – in contrasto con 'retailer' colui che vende al minuto.

Doc. – nomignolo di 'Dottore' (Doctor)

To ring up the paper. – Telefonare al giornale. 'to ring up' (telefonare).
To ring up a sale – Metter giù il tasto alla cassa, che suona, mentre che si annota una vendita. Mi seguita, Pavese?

To chase a reporter – Mandare sù un giornalista.

publicity-grabber. – Raccoglitore di pubblicità. Dal verbo 'to grab, grabbing, grabbed, grabbed' – Raccogliere tutto.

Blackjack. – È un'arma che usano i delinquenti, un bastoncino piccolo con il quale danno il colpo alla testa. 'To blackjack' vuol dire qui 'tradire.' 'blackjacking, blackjacked, blackjacked.

Zip. zipping, zipped, zipped – Andare benone, Andare a gonfie vele.

So nice of you. – Così gentile di you (voi)!

It's so nice of you to do this for me!

To put a thing over. – Fare successo di una cosa. Far valere la propria idea, proposta, articolo, ecc.

I put that business proposition over nicely!

It's up to the dominis to blow the three of us to a dinner. (Ora resta al ministro (da -Dominus) da pagare una cena per noi tre.) 'To blow one's self to' vuol dire 'incomodarsi nel fare' ecc.

I'm going to blow myself to a new hat (Voglio scomodarmi a comperarmi un capello nuovo.)

A loan. – Un imprestito.

A deal. – Un affare – commerciale.

Motoring. – Girando nell'automobile. To motor, motoring, motored, motored – Fare delle gite in automobile, andare in automobile.

Senior year. – Il quarto ed ultimo anno della Scuola Alta (High School) dalla quale si va al Collegio privato o all'Università. Vi sono quattro anni e gli studenti si chiamano 'Freshmen' (I.° anno) Sophomores (2.° anno) Juniors (3.° anno) e 'Seniors' (4.° anno)

Tut-tutting – si dice di uno che vuol sempre interrompere il discorso che a lui non piace. To tut-tut – tut-tutting - tut-tutted – tut-tutted. –

Don't keep tuttutting me; let me finish what I was saying!

Shiftlessness – Trascuratezza, mancanza d'interesse, pigrizia.

Fact-mill – Si usa qui per dire che Howard Littlefield era uno che si dava alle statistiche – ossia 'la fabbrica dei fatti.' Era un vero mulino quando si trattava di dover compilare delle statistiche.

Racer-body – carozzeria da automobile da corsa!

went skidding around corners – girare agli angoli magari su due ruote solo scivolando.

eerily – timorosamente. Da 'eerie' che dà il senso di spettro, di quello che fa rabbrividire con la paura.

Rumble-seat – È quel sediolino sul di dietro della motocicletta.

Ted's mother spoils him. (Lo guasta, lo rovina, gli dà dei vizi.)

To tell one what's what. Dire a qualcuno come sono le cose. Fargli vedere dove ha torto. What is what! La cosa come lo è.

I'm elected the goat. – Sono io scelto a far la brutta parte. (Sono io scelto a fare la capra) andare contro un altro.

To bring up – in questo caso vuol dire – Allevare.

Sapheads and lounge-lizards. – Teste di solo sugo e plundroni [*sic*]. Da 'lounge' ('poltrona') e 'Lizard' una bestia che rassomiglia al piccolo coccodrillo – lento nel muoversi!

Charade – dei giuochi nei quali gli individui prendono la parte di un sostantivo, di un verbo, un avverbio, ecc, e che poi gli altri devono indovinare attraversare la mimica in via di spiegazione. Si sa che più è difficile la parte che si prende e più difficile sarà poi far capire all'altro cos'è attraverso la sola mimica.

Dumb-bells – cretini – che sono poi i nostri birilli di ginnastica. Viene dal tedesco 'dumb' che vuol dire 'stupido.'

more'n half the time – Americano parlato per (More than half the time.)

Juh hear what I said? – Ancora dell'americano parlato per (Did you hear what I I said?) Nella nostra fretta e fur[i]a pure nel parlare – pronunciamo anche così.

going-ons – (oppure) goings-on – avvenimenti – quello che si sta facendo.

'parking' – depositare – lasciare. Quando lasciamo l'automobile per andare in qualche posto per poi tornare dopo un certo tempo, diciamo che l'automobile è 'parked.' Quando l'uomo d'affare lascia la sua automobile davanti all'ufficio per poi prendersela per tornare a casa a mezzogiorno, diciamo che 'he has parked his car 'till noon.'

We parked our car in front of the Regio. (Abbiamo lasciato la macchina davanti al Regio.) (Sino dopo lo spettacolo). To park, parking, parked, parked – lasciare, depositare temporaneamente.

Qui le signorine 'lasciavano in deposito' – i loro busti!

Cuddling and petting – si dice degli amanti quando si trovano da soli, come quelli in Parco Valentino da notte. 'cuddling' raggomitolarsi nelle braccia di un altro – come fa un gatto al caldo sotto la stufa – e 'petting' 'carezzando.' Mi spiego? A word to the wise is sufficient!

pup – pups (plurale) si dice dei cagnolini. Un cagnolino – a pup.

To pass out. – (slang) Morire.

Naw. – Americano parlato per 'No.' Pigrizia! Il 'No' di sdegno!

To suit – Far piacere – andar benone.

Your idea suits me. (La vostra idea mi piace, s'accorda con la mia, mi va benone.)

To be under foot. – Essere pestato da qualcuno, con parole, con delle azioni ecc. Every time we talk about English, I'm under foot! (Se la pigliano con me.)

Discouraged celery. – Sa bene che figura misera fa il sedano quando non è più fresco – ebbene lo chiamiano 'sedano scoraggiato,' dacchè ha proprio l'aria di esserlo.

bootees – nomignolo di 'boots' – (stivaloni).

Buggy – una vettura a cavallo.

Congress. – Corpo governativo composto dei Rappresentativi del Popolo. A Washington, la sede del governo, vi sono 'The Senate' (Senatori) e 'Congress' per i Rappresentanti.

To make it hot – Dar dei fastidi a qualcuno. (Farlo caldo)

To stick by – Oppure – to stand by – prendere le parti di, essere leali a – sticking, stuck, stuck. – To stick to-gether (Star insieme).

To hint – insinuare – dar segno – far capire a poco a poco. hinting, hinted, hinted.

Yankee – si dice del vero Americano – sangue di Boston.

Quel paragrafo che incominc[i]a – 'I think this baby's a bum' ecc. è una ripetizione della stessa cosa, tanto bella però, per dipingere l'individuo che sta parlando ad un bambino, un infante. Con ogni toccarlo con il dito dice la stessa cosa – come facciamo tutti, solo che Babbitt forse si vendicava sul padre e la madre del bambino.

Bum – vagabondo – che qui però vuol dire 'biricchino.'

I'm sick of it. – Sono stanco di questo!!

Whole damn bunch lean on me. – Tutta la 'damn' combriccola s'appoggiano [*sic*] su di me!'

Pick on someone – Prendersela con qualcuno! Picking, picked, picked.

To give way. – Spezzarsi di salute, rendersi alla malattia.

Back-slapping – Salutare un individuo col dargli un colpo di mano sulla schiena! Uso americano! To slap, slapping, slapped, slapped – Schiaffeggiare. 'Back' – schiena.

Zenith Street Traction Co. – Compagnia di Zenith dei Tramways! Tramvie.

Suburb. – subborgo.

Options. – Sono dei privilegi a base di contratti nei quali un individuo può o non può comperare qualsiasi cosa. Per esempio, faccio un contratto con un padrone di casa, nel quale contratto gli pago una tale somma per poter avere il diritto di comperare la sua casa quando voglio io entro due anni, diciamo, e poi, terminati i due anni, la compero se voglio o non la compero, secondo come stanno le cose. Intanto il padrone non può vendere senza il mio per messo, nè prima della scadenza del 'option' che tengo io. Se mi decido di non comperare la casa, ci guadagna sù il padrone tenendosi la som[m]a pagatagli da me e riacquista la sua libertà di libera azione. Se mi decido di comperare, quella som[m]a pagateli fa parte della som[m]a chiestomi [*sic*] da lui – sarebbe come una caparra. Qui Babbitt teneva appunto un privilegio di questo genere sul terreno che voleva comperare la Compagnia dei Tramways e naturalmente stava a Babbitt a chiedere il suo prezzo che poi dopo gli permetteva di comperare addirittura da chi gli aveva dato l''option,' e gli rimaneva certo il proffitto, già previsto quando aveva chiesto l''option.'

Stockholders. – azionisti. – Tenitori di azioni.

Swag. – si dice di una somma grande di denaro, e generalmente di quelle somme che sono rubate.

Think I'm going to see that bunch, ecc. – Credi che io starò a vedere quella combriccola di santi truffatori chc sc nc vanno con le grandi somme e che noi non c'entriamo?

To double-cross. – Tradire sfacciatamente! (doppia-croce.)

After I told him what to do, he double-crossed me!

To have someone pinched. – Far arrestare qualcuno. To pinch, pinching, pinched, pinched (monosillabo) ... arrestare.

Buzzer. – Campanello con il quale il capo-ufficio chiama le impiegate. Non suona da campanello ma bensì fa un rumore come un'erre prolungata, come un trillo, una volta per una certa impiegata, 2 volte per un'altra e così via. Dal verbo 'to buzz, buzzing, buzzed, buzzed' – il rumore che fa la mosca, l'ape ecc. nel volare.

The bee buzzed right past me! It buzzed by my ears.

To fire someone ... Licenziare qualcuno.

To lay things on thick. – Mettere sù spesso, contare grandemente, contare delle frottole – come nel commercio.

To spread it on thick. – Far grande.
To spread butter. – come si fa a mettere del burro sul pane.
To lay on thick. – metterci più che non ci voleva.

Pinching ... In questo caso vuol dire 'rubare.'

trucks. – Dei camion. Automobili da trasporto.

Slush. – 'pacciocco' – benone, eh? (Ha!)

jail. – prigione.

Discharge. – scaricare, licenziare.

Dapper, eye-glassed, with a foppish mustache. – Allegro, con degli occhiali, e con dei baffi disordinati, mal tenuti.

He sticks out – Ci sta!

To sign up – firmare.

To get rid of someone. – Disfarsene di qualcuno.

I skun up there – Mi sono affrettato fin là. (and got back the lease) (e ho riottenuto il rilascio)

To pull something crooked. – Combinare qualche cosa di illegale.

A good lesson that'll jog you up a little – 'Una buona lezione che vi scuoterà un poco.'

I'm tickled to death ... Sono solletticato sino a morire. – Si dice così per esprimere la grande soddisfazione che si prova, benchè qui sia detto ironicamente! Per dire 'sono contentissimo' 'diciamo' 'I'm tickled to death.' To tickle, tickled, tickled, tickling. – solleticare.

To get away with something. – Farla franca.

To pull some raw stuff. – (Combinare di quelle crude) (roba cruda – raw stuff).

Tut, tut! – Zitto, zitto!

To holler – (slang) gridare. Hollering, hollered, hollered.

crooked. – storto. – Nella slang vuol dire 'dishonesto' senza l''h.'

skinflint. – Chi pela la gente, da 'skin' – la pelle.

flat broke. – senza un soldino. I'm broke! (non ho dei soldi.)

wishywashy – di poco valore, senza carattere, senza volontà, senza qualsiasi qualità o virtù umana.

To bellow – Fare come fa il toro quando è arrabbiato. Bellowing, bellowed, bellowed. 'Bellows' sostantivo al plurale, è lo st[r]umento con il quale si soffia sul fuoco, per accendere.

Attorney – procuratore – avvocato.

District Attorney – procuratore del Distretto – Parte Civile.

high-up traction guns. – Gli individui che sono di alto locato presso la compagnia delle tranvie. (slang – naturalmente, come lo dice.)

As I gather it – Come l'intendo io – I'm fired – Sono licenziato.

Knocking me to any other firm – Parlar male di me presso altre ditte.

I'll squeal – ne parlerò io (detto da chi ne avrebbe dei segreti spiacevoli).

Paint that lil ole town red. (Paint that little old town red.) Si dice così per dire che ne faranno di tutto per divertirsi.

a shove. – Uno spinto [*sic*].

I'll bet you didn't miss many tricks! (Scommetto che non hai lasciato passare troppe occasioni!)

To put someone over the jumps – Dargli delle cose alle quali dovrà rispondere. Farli saltare da una domanda all'altra.

No, not till next fall. (no, non sino al processo autunno.) Fall – Autunno.

A platter of French fried potatoes (spuds). (Un piattone di patate fritte alla francese.)

Young fella. – Young fellow! (Pronuncia americano – ormai di moda.)

I'll hold the wire! (Terrò la linea) Si dice così quando si sta telefonando è l'altro deve lasciare il telefono per cercare qualchecosa – che insomma deve assentarsi un momento. 'Wire' – filo.

ash-tray – porta cenere.

To toss – gettare – come si fanno con le cose piccole, le sigarette, i lapis, della carta, e che so io! Tossing, tossed, tossed. Sa quel 'gettare' che non è a lunga distanza.

To call up – telefonare.

Arms. – qui vuol dire 'Lo stemma.'

pop eyes. – occhi saltellanti.

tie. – per (neck-tie) – cravatta.

'Member – per – remember? (Ormai le interrogazioni dello slang non incominciano più con 'Do you' ma incominciano subito con il verbo.)

Trip – viaggio, gita.

doggone – si usa come 'darn' oppure 'damn' perchè è piu' gentile, più fine – per la finezza americana. Ovunque si usa come aggettivo sta bene.

That's a darn shame. – That's a doggone shame – Eccoci! (È un vero peccato.)

Shindig. – celebrazione, festa, divertimento, ecc. (Molto slang – questo. Fatto si è che Sir Gerald Doak si stupisce che il Babbitt lo adopera.) Shindig – divertimenti tutt'altro che spirituali.

Tchicahgo – L'inglese, Sir Gerald, che pronuncia 'Chicago.' Peccato che non ci sia io per pronunciarla, Pavese.

A raft of dames – una infinità di donne. A raft (oppure) a slew – infinità.

six-shooters and broncos. – Pistole a sei cartucci e cavalli, non troppo domestici. Pellicole uso Tom Mix!

Who run the whole show. (Che se ne curano di tutto.)

Lookit. – Americano per 'Look at it.' (oppure) solo 'Look.' 'Lookit' in questo caso vuol dire 'Mi stia ad ascoltare' dacchè Babbitt sta per fare una proposta.

The latch-string is always out. – (La cordicella della porta di casa sta sempre di fuori) – così gli dà il benvenuto.

Pleasmeech – per – Pleased to meet (you)! (Piacere di conoscervi.) Detto da arrabbiato ed ancora all'americano. Pronunci – plismicc.

If you wanna – per – if you want to! Sempre la stessa storia!

that dried-up hag. – Quella vecchiaccia seccata, sciupata!
What are you sore about? (Di che cosa sei arrabbiato?)

To butt into – intromettersi senza permesso. Butting, butted, butted.

phiz. – per – physiognomy. (fisionomia).

To say howdy – to say 'how do you do!' (Come stai?)

To boss. – commandare.

snooty – da 'snoot' (slang) per 'il naso.' 'Snooty' allora, si dice di chi parla con il naso in aria, da arrabbiato, o da superbo.

buttinsky – uno che si intromette senza permesso – dal verbo – to butt in, e che qui vien detto all'americano con l'appendice russo 'sky.' Il vero sostantivo sarebbe ' a butter-in.' Detto con disprezzo qui! E riferisco a 'buttinsky' non a 'butter-in.'

cranky – irritabile – lagnoso.

To have someone shadowed. – Far pettinare qualcuno (dalla questura) o che è 'pedinato' – Damned if I know, Pavese! Dev'essere – pedinare.

To bust into a place – Entrare un luogo da furioso.

Hallelujah's sake. – per amore dell'Alleluia. Americano di nuovo, benchè sia corretto di scrittura! Si scrive anche 'Alleluia.'

Fancy fixings on a story. – Di contare una frottola con un contorno elegante. Ritoccare la bugia con delle appendici d'eleganza.

a good loaf. – Un buon far-nulla – riposo da pigro. Da 'to loaf, loafing, loafed, loafed' – far nulla – far il plundrone.

want to take some coffee mit – per – want to take some coffee with - Babbitt ricorre al tedesco 'mit' per ischerzo. (Voglio portare del caffè con (noi).)

to run into someone – Imbattersi con qualcuno, per caso.

Chasing skirts. – Dar dietro alle donne. – 'skirts' – 'le veste' and 'to chase' dar dietro

Make me out a liar? – Farmi passare per buggiardo?

That's what get's me! – È quello che mi fa incazzare! Arrabbiare!

To cuss – bestemmiare, dare dei titoli, come in questo caso!

But zize saying – per –But as I was saying. (Ma, come dicevo ...) Lo dica in fretta e vedrà che quasi, quasi dirà 'zize'; si sente solo 'L'esse' del – 'as,' 'L'"i" dell'"I" e l'esse finale del 'was.' Vede? 'as I was' – zize.

critter. – per – creature (creatura).

The way you pan him. – Il modo in cui tu gli dai addosso.

Till I bust out and say a lot of things I don't mean. – sino a che scoppio e dico tante cose che non voglio dire, non intendo dire.

weeping drably – piangendo miseramente, solo poco, niente da spaventarsi! To weep, weeping, wept, wept – piangere.

There was agitation abroad. – Vi era dell'agitazione in giro.

oneness – unità

To pump someone. – Far dire qualchecosa da qualcuno senza lasciarlo accorgersene. Da 'to pump, pumping, pumped, pumped' – 'pompare.'

Dancing-pumps. – sono 'pantaloncini da ballo' per le signorine. Qui si scherza in un modo difficile da spiegare. Giuoco di parole!

fambly – slang per – family – (famiglia)

a present – un regalo.

To draw up (in un'automobile). Avvicinarsi al luogo voluto e poi fermarsi lentamente!
We drew up to the Station of Porta Nuova.

To yank out of – Trascinare fuori di –

We yanked him out of the café – (L'abbiam strascinato dal caffè.) yanking, yanked, yanked. 'to pull away from.'

Hizzonor – per – His Honor ('Suo Onore'). Parla di 'Hon. Lucas Prout, il sindaco!' City Hall – Municipio.

The undertaker. – Il becchino.

Coupla – per – couple of. (un paio of).

traffic cops. – I polizziotti addetti al traffico!

I don't care a rap – che vale – Non m'importa un fico secco!

musickers. – slang per – musicians – (musicisti).

Swell conductor – direttore in gamba!

moneyed people – gente di denaro.

to crab this orchestra proposition – Mettere il bastone nelle ruote di questa proposta per l'orchestra. 'To crab a thing' – crabbing, crabbed, crabbed – far andar male, metterci il bastone nelle ruote.

to whoop it up. – Gridare forte. 'Whoop' è il grido di guerra dei pellirossi! The war-whoop!

a blur – un misto – come al cinematografo quando la pellicola gira ben male! Come fa la vista quando gli occhi sono stanchi!

fussiness – quello stato d'animo che dà delle preoccupazioni per ogni cosa sia pure piccolo. Da to fuss, fussing, fussed, fussed – Toccare le cose, o andare in giro come fa l'individuo molto, ma molto nervoso.

The poor guy is off his nut – Il povero diavolo è pazzo, probabilmente! to be off one's nut – Essere demente, pazzo.

whatever you call um – whatever you call him (Quello che lo chiama).

Fuzzy – che si riferisce alla pelle di pelliccie (furs). Quando passiamo la mano sulla schiena di un gatto, di un orso, ecc. diciamo che è 'fuzzy.' È quel pelo speciale, specialmente al tocco della mano.

Lecturing murderers – Far la predica agli assassini.

a shot. – un'iniezione. A hypodermic!

drip-pan – è quel recettacolo in cui cola l'olio superfluo dell'automobile. To drip, dripping, dripped, dripped – colare. 'Pan' – casseruola.

gritty kitchen soap – del sapone di cucina che morde nella sporcizia!

foreman – capo-squadra.

To sneak up on someone, or something. – Avvicinare qualcuno cautamente, in punta dei piedi e senza far rumore. Sneaking, sneaked, sneaked.

wire screen – la retata che si usa nelle vece di finestre d'estate.

Jailbird. – Slang per 'prigioniero' ma che si usa piuttosto per dire il tipo che è abituè delle carceri – vi è quasi sempre e sovente!

Lissen – per – Listen (ascolta – imperativo.)

Just made it up – L'ho composto solo ora.

Whadi write – per – What did he write? – detto da un ubbriaco – ma non solo sino a che vi sono degli americani non ubbriachi.

Cheer-up poems. – Poemi per far coraggio ai poveri diavoli!

Poor boob. – Povero imbecile!

Hooks – ganci – che qui vuol dire 'mani.'

They had something on him. – Avevano qualchecosa, nella loro mente, di Babbitt, che sapevano che una volta detta gli darebbe fastidio, eppure davano solo segno si saperla senza dire.

to have something on someone – Sapere qualchecosa di uno che saprà o che non saprà quest'uno e della conoscenza della quale cosa diamo segno o con atti o con certe parole magari sconnesse.

To take somebody on – impiegare.

Spring it! Spring it! (Ditelo! Ditelo!) Vede qui che 'they had something on Babbitt' – Sono venuti a sapere della sua famosa serata con Sir Gerald Doak, ma intimavano che forse aveva incontrato qualche signorina, ecc. Da 'to spring' – Scatenare.

Boneheads. – Teste di osso.

guffaws – scherzucchi buffoneschi.

spun. – Da 'to spin, spinning, spun, spun' – per – girare su sè stesso.

To steer careful – guidarsi cautamente. Steering, steered, steered

Got to get back. – Devo tornare.

giggling – Da 'to giggle, giggling, giggled, giggled' – Ridere sotto voce, come fanno le signorine.

towel – asciugamano. – Attic window – Finestra di soffitto.

Do you honestly like it? – Ti piace, sul serio? (Honestly!) in questi casi vuol dire 'sul serio.'

Honestly now, tell me the truth!
Did you do it, honestly?

To throw over someone – Dar il giro a qualcuno.

wiz – per – wizard. – (mago).

To be through – Aver finito. I'm through with him! (Ho finito con lui).

howitzer – Tipo di cannone usato durante la guerra.

a real gent. – a real gentleman – Un vero signore.

wisenheimers – per – gli aristocratici.

To give someone the north and south – Vale – to give someone the up-and-down che vuol dire – guardare qualcuno in sù ed in giù da sdegnato.

I just gave him the north and south and continued walking!
She gave me the up-and-down as though I had insulted her!

Kike – Ebreo. (slang) (Pronunci – chaich)

Ko. – La pronuncia di 'Co.' che è l'abbreviazione di 'Company.'

Hoof-paring. – Da 'to pare, paring, pared, pared' – Come si fa con delle patate per togliere la pelle, e 'hoof' – zampa.'

To rubber at someone. – Fissare qualcuno, dacchè sembra che uno abbia il collo di gomma, così elastico da vedere tutto, anche dietro gli angoli. Rubbering, rubbered, rubbered. – Cercare di vedere e di intendere.

To say nighty-night – To say good-night!

gutter-pup – Cagnolina da strada! 'Gutter' è quella parte della strada ai fianchi dove corre l'acqua, e dove si getta la sporcizia, e dove la gente ubbriaca va a finire naturalmente quando non s'accorgono che vi è il marciapiede rialzato.

To kick one'self. – Il senso d'animo che ci viene quando abbiam fatto qualche cretineria della quale siam consci. (Darai dei calci.)

ragamuffin – Scugnizzo – Straccione da strada.

And yet – Eppure.

chuffer – chauffeur.

Backwoods – Foresta vergine, fitta.

Four-flushes – Quattro carte dello stesso genere – 4-dieci – 4-tre – ecc.

Well, jus' soon! – per – Just as soon. – Ebbene, tanto vale! (Slang idiomatico)

To hit the trail. – Darsi per i sentieri dei boschi!

summerites – villeggiatori – Da 'summer' (estate).

To camp out – come fanno i soldati in tempo delle manovre!

Bust up the quiet with a chugging motor? – Disturbare, rovinare il quiete con un motore scoppiante? 'To chug, chugging, chugged, chugged' – Quasi armoni imitativi di come fa un motore quando funziona.

The pack – lo zaino.

Couple o' old birds – due vecchioni.

Trolleys grinding – Le Tramvie che scricchiono [*sic*].

guest-shack – rifugio – Capanna degli ospiti.

Take a claim – Prendersi un tratto di terreno secondo le leggi dei terreni fertili, le così chiamate 'Homestead Acts.' 'Homestead Act' è quella legge che dà gratis un pezzo di terreno all'individuo che lo lavora per un certo tempo, dopo il quale tempo rimane automaticamente proprietà sua. 'to claim' – Far domanda di possesso.

He chewed his cud – Masticava il suo tobacco.
A plug of tobacco – a cud of tobacco – Un pezzo.
To chew a cud – si dice delle mucche quando stanno facendo il latte! Ha!

carbon paper – carta copiativa.

hello – Cerea – oppure – ciau, nel salutare qualcuno.

Going to run for mayor again? – Concorri per il posto di Sindaco di nuovo?

My bucking you – 'il mio darvi incontro.' 'buck up – incoraggiare'

To go on the stump. – Da 'stump-speaker' quelli che si mettono anche su di una scatola di legno, o su di un tronco d'albero tagliato per fare dei discorsi, come facevano gli antichi americani nella campagna aperta.

To go on the stump for someone – Far propaganda per qualcuno.

upholder – sostenitore.

I.W.W. – International Workers of the World, che noi chiamiamo viceversa, The I Wont Work Association. ('Non lavorero') È organismo dei comunisti.

tam o'shanter – Un abito da donna – uso irlandese.

To go in for something – Occuparsene di qualchecosa!

To make the football team. – Farsi entrare la squadra di Rugby.

Light half-back – Leggiero 'half-back' che' è una posizione dietro alla linea principale.

chumps – Maccaco! Ha!

a walk-out – uno sciopero. Oppure. – a Strike.

Industry was tied up. – L'industria fu in un nodo!

Strike-beater – Quelli che rimpiazzano gli scioperanti.

a scab. – Uno che non sia iscritto al Sindacato.

pug-dog. – Un 'bull-dog.'

Get onto de tin soldier! – Guarda il soldato di latta! (Ironicamente.)

A condensed milk plant – Una Fabbrica di latte-condensato.

All lies and fake figures! (Tutte bugie e dei numeri falsi!)

pew – banco – di chiesa.

To give someone hell. – Leggere la vita a più non posso!

poo-bahs. – fischiatore – Quando si fischia qualcuno si fa il 'poo-bah!'

cooked-up wage scales. – Basi di stipendi che sono combinati a modo di sfruttare! 'Stipendi già cotti.'

poppycock. – Mascalzoneria.

News-stands – I giornalai – Come davanti al Mugna.

mud. – Fango.

It doesn't mean a darn thing. – Non vuol dir proprio nulla.

Court House – Il Tribunale.

'bo – chi si dà nelle veci di 'fellow.' È l'abbreviazione di 'hobo' 'vagabondo' nel senso proprio.

Billy – nomignolo di 'William' (Guglielmo)

Posters. – Cartelloni.

a swell like him. – Un aristocratico come lui.

thugs. – delinquenti.

a club. – un bastone, un manganello.

hell-hounds. – cani da caccia dall'Inferno. Individui di questa attitudine.

Hoodlums. – della malavita.

to hold out. – resistere.

hulking. – robusti.

stuffin's – per – stuffings. – Quello che si usa per imbottire, come quando si fa cuocere una gallina, ecc.

savvy – da 'savez-vous' – per 'Understand – get me? ecc.

I savvy what I'm doing. – I know what I'm doing. (So cosa faccio.)

Leak. – buco – perdita. A leak in a pipe – (Una perdita in un tubo.)

crooning. – Dal verbo 'to croon, crooning, crooned, crooned' – cantare sotto voce, come fanno appunto i negri sulle piantaggioni del cotone mentre che lavorano o che tornano dal lavoro. Fanno un canto melanconico, nostalgico.

fencing. – Dal verbo 'to fence, fencing, fenced, fenced' – parare, come si fa nella scherma, una volta ad uno e poi all'altro.

So I up and said. – Così incominciai io e dissi – I up – è il modo americano per dire che poi io ho incominciato, sia pure per un'azione, per parlare o per cantare.

When Mr. Pavese had finished, then I up and sang a song!
Then he up and told me all about it.

old fogies – vecchi rimbambiti ... (old fogy) singolare.

To get pickled – Ubbriaccarsi. –

I got pickled last night. – Mi sono ubbriaccato ieri sera.
Let's get pickled fellows – Ubbriacchiamoci, compagni!

pee-rading – Americano enfatico per – parading – in parata.

all dolled up fit to kill – Tutto così ben vestito da ammazzare. Si dice così dell'individuo come si direbbe della gallina che è ben curata prima della festa! 'all dolled up' vuol dire 'tutto ben vestito.' Da 'doll' – bambola.

lil cap'n's uniform – little Captain's uniform – Uniforme di Capitanuccio!

Busting the strike? – Stai interrompendo lo sciopero? Da 'to bust, busting, busted, busted' – che è lo slang

per 'to burst, bursting, burst, burst,' che vuol dire 'rompere, spezzare, interrompere, far scoppiare.'

To tell someone where to get off (at) – Mettere i puntini sui 'i,' porgere i limiti nelle cose.

To keep an eye skinned – vale – to keep an eye peeled – che vuol dire 'tener l'occhio aperto,' da 'skin' (la pelle, il pelo).

To have fat nerve – Avere la faccia tosta – dei nervi grassi.

to have a date – Avere un appuntamento. Americano schietto!

I have a date at eight o'clock tomorrow night!
I have a date with Mr. Pavese at the Cafe Mugna!

We will proambulate in to the magnolious feed. – Cammineremo al pranzo squisito – Detto con la gioia infantile americano! 'Proambulate' viene ancora dal latino 'ambulare' ma 'magnolious' non dice niente se non nella radice di 'magnus' (grande, squisito.)

like all get-out – Come il peggio che si potesse avere! Se si parla delle cose belle allora vuol dire, come il migliore che si potesse avere.

It was as good an opera as any get-out!
It was as poor an opera as any get-out!
Era un'opera (peggio) meglio non si poteva!

To get out – creare, mettere in mercato, fare – (che bisogna essere americano per usar bene.) Ora a Lei, Pavese! Mi faccia degli esempi!

motor-tires – gomme da automobile.

freigh t train. – treni-merci.

to be cocky – Essere un po' superbo.

to lug in – portar dentro, far entrare. Lugging, lugged, lugged.

I lugged my trunk into the room!
We always lug the same discussions into our conversations.

to tout, touting, touted, touted – leggere la vita.

high-muchamucks – Aristocratici – sinonomo di 'highbrows.'

two bucks apiece – due dollari caduno!

drift – andamento – in questo caso!

Shake a leg – Faccia in fretta!

flat! – apartamentino.

To make a getaway. – Scappare.
road-house. – Tabarin – che si trova lungo le vie d'automobili nella campagna aperta; ecco perché si chiamano 'road-houses' da 'road' (strada) e 'house' (casa). Vendono dei liquori proibiti, ballano al ritmo delle orchestre da jazz e vi sono delle signorine – non so se mi spiego!

To be stewed – Essere ubbriaco. Sinonimo di (pickled).

ossified. – Incretinito – instupidito. (Di nessuna origine – se non da 'ass' (asino) che poco alla volta si fa 'oss'; allora si potrebbe tradurre 'asinificato.' – mi spiego.

Crabs, pikers and poor fish. – lagnatori, faccie-doppie e poveri cretini.

Yump. – Americano per – 'Yes.' Detto da chi non è interessato.

cash-girl – la cassiera.

'to jolly someone along.' – Dire della roba da ridere a qualcuno, tanto per farli di buon umore.

Leggo, quit crushing me cootie-garage. – (Dio – che tipo!) Anzi tutto, 'leggo' – per 'let go' – (Lascia andare); poi viene quello che dovrebbe essere 'quit crushing my cootie-garage' che vuol dire 'smettila col schiacciare il mio capello.' 'cootie-garage' (il garage – rimessa – dei pidocchi) bellissima espressione per il 'capello.' 'to quit – quitting, quit, quit – smettere, e 'to crush, crushing, crushed, crushed' – Schiacciare. 'Cootie' è una parola che ci veniva dopo la guerra per dire quei 'pidocchi' che i soldati se ne prendevono in trincea! 'Garage' è la 'rimessa' delle automobili. Quel 'Hey' sarebbe come l'italiano 'Oila.'

To lap up – succhiare – o far come fanno il gatto o il cane quando bevono! Lapping, lapped, lapped!

To munch, munching, munched, munched – mangiare a poco a poco, come fa la mucca che poi da un boccone all'altro dà delle occhiate a sinistra e a destra e poi va in giù con la testa per mangiare un po' ancora!

Skating-rink – Il quadrato grande per il pattinaggio.

Fender – è quella parte dell'automobile che corre attorno alla ruota e che non lascia andare in lungo ed in largo il fango!

Hard to get along with someone. – Difficile di andare d'accordo con qualcuno.

Shoot! – Americano – imperativo – per. – Dica! Avanti! (Tira!) = 'Spring!'

cranks. – qui vuol dire – gli scontenti.

Kibosh. – il freno. (si pronuncia – caibasc – dal più al meno!)

To put the kibosh on someone or something. – Mettere i freni a qualcuno o a qualchecosa.

To shoot off one's mouth. – sparlare.

All he does is shoot off his mouth! (Tutto quello che fa è sparlare.)

To light on someone – cadere su qualcuno – come si cade su di una discussione, per esempio; fissure su un punto!

totties – giovinette.

tattling – andare poi a raccontare le cose – to tattle, tattling, tattled, tattled – raccontare dietro la schiena! Far la spia!

Telephone-booth – Una 'separè' con il telefono! Una stanzuccia con il telefono solo.

cubeb cigarettes – sigarette che si danno per certe malattie – come quelle che fumava Lei, Pavese, con delle preparazioni speciali. Si pronuncia – chiùbeb.

brat – birichinaccio.

To tote – portare – che si dice generalmente delle armi, pistole, ecc. toteing, toted-toted.

lovey dovey conferences – conversazioni d'amore – Da 'love' – amore – e da 'dove' – 'colomba.'

To show up – qui vuol dire – farsi vedere. He didn't show up – Non si è fatto vedere.

A good line of guff. – Una buona chiaccieratina quando si tratta di parlare.

Walkover. – passo da ballo.

Oh, punk! – Oh, no good! (Niente di buono)

A toss up. – Sa come si fa quando si tratta di fare due cose, ma che si deve fare solo una di due – ebbene, si getta in aria un pezzo di moneta e poi, a secondo come cade il pezzo, si decide di fare o l'una delle cose o l'altra. Quest'atto di gettare in aria il soldino – si chiama 'toss-up' (da 'to toss up') ('gettare in su').

all that blaa – Tutto quel niente!

dive – ritrovo di dubbia fama! (si pronuncia – daiv)

mix-ups – pasticcio.

to be bulldozed – Preso in giro.

The first crack out of the box – La primissima cosa!

to be huffy – alzare la voce, alzare il becco, come si dice.

a rubber eraser – Una gomma da cancellare.

Stick-in-the-mud – Uno che non si muove mai – (Legato al fango – da non poter muoversi.)

git – per – (get) che qui vuol dire – della vita.
To have some get – avere della vita!

agin – per – against. (contro)

the block – Il marciapiede da un angolo all'altro.

to peter out – to die out – Morire – sparire.

to bullyrag – Quando tutti vogliono avere il loro dire, e quindi si mettono tutti quanti su di un individuo. Bullyragging, bullyragged, bullyragged.

scatter-brained – testa leggera. – da 'scatter, scattering, scattered, scattered' – spargere – 'brains' – le cervella – il senno.

in a month of Sundays. – in un mese composto di domeniche – ossia – 30 o 31 domeniche. Si dice così per stabilire un tempo discretamente lungo.

leery – irritato – arrabbiato.

die-hard – (uno che muore lottando) Si dice degli individui che non danno mai la vinta – o per lo meno la danno a duri stenti!

Mr. Pavese is certainly a die-hard when it comes to English.

powder-puff – quello che usano le donne per incipriarsi! Powder – cipria.

hash. – Piatto fatto con gli avanzi di carne dai pasti da due o tre giorni.

to have a hunch. – Avere l'intuizione – Aver un presentimento.

slights. – trascuratezze.

To eat dirt – dover digerire lo sparlare degli altri, il mal parlare di sè.

I'll not eat your dirt! – Non tollererò il vostro mal dire – le vostre brutte azioni. 'to eat' – mangiare, 'dirt' sporcizia.' 'polvere da strada.'

to rifle the ice-box. – Perquisire il rifrigorifero. To rifle, rifling, rifled, rifled – perquisire disordinatamente.

dodging the issue – schivare la discussione, argomento, o il fatto che fra poco verrà. 'issue' da 'exire' (latino). 'to dodge, dodging, dodged, dodged' – Schivare.

bicarb – Bicarbonate – Bicarbonato.

ousted – licenziato. Da 'to oust, ousting, ousted, ousted' – Kicked out, licenziato – lasciato andare.

pill-pedler – slang per – dottore. 'Pill' (pillola e 'Pedler' da 'to peddle, peddling, peddled, peddled') – Distribuire, vendere, come colui che va da casa a casa.

hunky-dory – benone. – I feel hunky-dory this morning!

Mob – la folla.

to slacken up – Andare più adagio nelle cose. Slackening, slackened, slackened – che si usa per descrivere la corda, per esempio, che da tesa molto vien rilasciata pendere – si dice che è 'slackened.' Quando si corre e che poi si cammina – si dice che è l'individuo 'has slackened his pace.' (Adagiato il suo passo.)

To take a chance – rischiare.

Does it score against him in the long run? – Gli va, gli dà incontro, nel lungo andare?

joy-rides – gite di piacere, inteso però, con delle donne!

Squeezing girls – abbracciando delle signorine. Come si fa con dei limoni!

A knight of the grip – Un viaggiatore – un commesso viaggiatore. Letteralmente – Un cavaliere della valigia. Sa che i viaggiatori portano una valigia, naturalmente – ebbene, hanno il titolo gentile di 'knight' come gli antichi cercatori di bellissime donne – titolo che non è sprecato!

up-state – down-state – su' nello stato – giù nello stato!

packed an awful wallop – Aveva un pugno duro – Qui siccome si tratta di un giuoco di dama vuol dire che aveva una mano educatissima al giuoco.

to dicker – far affair. Dickering, dickered, dickered.

to lick. – abbattere, battere. – licking, licked, licked!

Pinochle – giuoco di carte.

lots. – Quadrati di terreno.

wireless telephone set. – Apparecchio telefonico senza fili.

to skip – far un salto, come si direbbe di chi vuol fare una scappatina e poi tornarsene quasi subito.

to be packed off – to be sent off – Essere mandati a (scuola) Da 'packed' o meglio da 'to pack, packing, packed, packed' – preparare i bauli.

Spanking – Da 'to spank, spanking, spanked, spanked' – Battere, come si fa ai bambini – prendendoli attraverso i ginocchi e poi – giù secco!

Flippancy – (slang che viene da 'flip' – avere del becco.) Avere, sa quell'aria che dice – Io me ne infischio.

To sting someone. – stinging, stung, stung – rubare – nel senso di chi crede di dover pagare solo 30 lire per una cosa, diciamo, e che poi viene chiesto di pagare 45 magari!

six dollars and two bits. (Sei dollari e venticinque soldi.) Slang americano per la moneta. (Two bits – 25 soldi) (dime-(daim) – 10 soldi) (nickel – 5 soldi) (buck-plunk – un dollaro.) (green-back (indietro verde) la moneta di carta che ha appunto un lato color verde.)

putting in their oar – Mettendoci i loro remi – Vuol dire che troppa gente ci metteva le mani nella discussione, nel leggere la vita a Ted!

To dry up – (seccarsi) – slang – Chiudere la bocca, star ziti.

The way the cars are stacked – Si dice così per dire – nel modo in cui sono le cose oggi – La frase origina – ha la sua origine dai famosi giuocatori di carte che sapevano combinare tutte le carte al piacere loro di modo che guadagnavano sempre. 'stacked cards' allora, si dice di cose che si può cambiare – ormai sono così e così ci vengono.

college degree – Una laurea – dal colleggio o Università.

rods. – sono delle misure lineali – .

To tame down – domesticare.

To back someone – sostenere qualcuno, spalleggiare qualcuno.

To be scared. – Aver paura.

Swooping family – da 'to swoop, swooping, swooped, swooped' – quando tutti vengono insieme attorno ad una cosa, come fanno gli uccelli quando vengono dall'aria in massa per mangiare qualcosa a'terra!

End of *Babbitt.*

Chiuminatto's explanations of expressions from Sinclair Lewis's Arrowsmith.[5]

COMMENTS ON — ARROWSMITH — by Sinclair Lewis
By Antonio Chiuminatto

Female fixings – Delle cose delle femmine. Da 'fixings' – abbellimenti.

cot – lettino, uso militare.

Fishing-tackle – tutti gli accessori per andare alla pesca. Da 'tackle' quello palo lungo con l'amo o con l'apparecchio americano.

sawdust-box cuspidor – Una sputtachiera fatta da una scatola di legno e riempito di segatura. Da 'saw' (sega) e 'dust' (polvere).

dead-beats – quelli che non pagano i debiti. (slang).

cigar-butt. – pezzo di sigaro già fumato. Un givo di sigaro.

got chick nor child – Non ho nè casa e nè bambini – slang modo di dire.
Da 'chick' – vezzeggiativo di 'chicken' (gallina).

Road's damn disgrace. – La strada è una vergogna! 'Sgrace – per 'disgrace.'
Ditto da ubbriaco – e che vuol dire 'vergogna.'

culvert – Un tubo dell'acqua sotto la strada.

I'll splain – per – I'll explain – (spiegherò).

pom-pom-pullaway – giuoco di bambini in cui uno trascina gli altri.

nap – sonnellino.

slick – bellissimo!

basket-ball center – posizione di giuoco nel palo a cesto.

5 The date '24 Febr. 1930' is handwritten in pencil on the left margin. This first installment of comments on *Arrowsmith* covers chapters I through IX.

co-eds – studentesse. Da 'co-educational.'

collie – razza bellissima di cani.

At Home's. – Festa di casa, radunanza a casa propria.

crapehanger. – Si dice di uno che vuol rovinare qualsiasi discreto godimento – che vuol smorzare il divertimento. Da 'crape' che è un pezzo di stoffa (crepe) e da 'to hand, hanging, hung, hung' – Appendere. Da noi il becchino è il 'crapehanger' dacchè mette sempre questo pezzo di crepe color purpureo alla porta delle case in cui vi è un morto. In Italia si mette quella tela larga alla porta; qui viceversa si mette il crepe purpureo con dei fiori. Costume!

Don't be a crapehanger! (Non essere così da voler mettere il bastone nelle ruote.)

doughnuts – delle paste dolci con un buco solo nel centro – come ruota!

Boarding-house – pensione. Da 'to board, boarding, boarded, boarded' – pensionare. 'Room and board' (Camera e pensione).

campus – il campo di giuoco.

top-coat – soprabito.

janitor – custode – portinaio.

dumb-waiter – l'ascensore come si ha negli alberghi per trasportare i piatti da un piano all'altro – ascensore nel muro, piccolo. (Il servitore muto.)

gawk – cretino che va, come tanti, con la bocca aperta, e che fissa con gli occhi di qui e di là.

cubbyhole – un buco – cameretta piccolissima.

liddle – per – little – da Tedesco.

banana-split – piatto di gelato mescolato con fettine di banana.

bar of almond chocolate – pezzo di cioccolato con mandorle.

smart – intelligente.

barb – una spina – si dice così di quelli che non appartengono nemmeno ad una società scolastica – come si dice 'scab' di quelli che non appartengono al Sindacato degli operai.

rushed – qui vuol dire che era stato avvicinato circa la sua entrata in una di queste società universitarie.

brand – marca.

breeches – pantaloncini, di quelli che vanno solo ai ginocchi.

I could bawl – potrei piangere! 'to bawl bawling, bawled, bawled' – piangere. (slang).

football-practice – le prove del giuoco – football.

spooks – spettri – spiriti.

stubs – givo di cigarette.

instalment plan – a rate.

manure-pile – lo sterco delle bestie.

galoots – sapientoni.

hell-raisers –riotosi.

derby hat – tubolino.

frat-brother – fraternity – brother (socio della Società universitaria).

lager – birra.

dough-face – faccia di pasta.

Shake you for it – Giuochiamo ai dadi per questo (la bibita).

innards – per – inwards – intestine.

studes – per – students (studenti).

to cash-in – qui vuol dire – far dei soldi.

to take an awful fall out of something – Disfare qualchecosa.

grad – per – graduated – diplomata – licenziato.

to stand a haircut – aver bisogno di un taglio di capelli.

narrow upper bunk – lettino stretto di sopra – come usano nei vapori.

marshmallows – dolci americani.

Quiz-Book – Libro delle Domande.

quiz – inter[r]ogatorio.

crib – degli appunti preparati per copiare agli esami.

lulu – vale – it's a whiz!

to get through – riuscire.

hams of profs – macachi di professori.

lab – per – laboratory.

racket – chiasso.

that's a cinch – Quello è certo!

guinea pig – porchetto d'India.

shirt-sleeves – maniche di camicia.

pogrom – massacre degli Ebrei in Russia.

to swamp – innondare – coprire completamente.

Dew Drop Inn – che viene da 'Do drop in.' (Venga a trovarci.) È giuoco di parole.

tiny – piccolo.

Prince Albert – Lo Smoking – Il Tuxedo.

Feeding one's face – darsi da mangiare. – mangiare.

hidey-place – Luogo da nascondersi. – Da 'to hide, hiding, hid, hidden' – Nascondere.

old tables – le vecchie – da 'tabby' – gatta.

humbugs – stupidaggini.

undertaker – becchino di professione medica.

shanties – capanne.

patentleather – cuoio come si usa nelle scarpe a vernice, luccicante.

batch – una certa quantità di qualsiasi cosa – come la pasta per fare il pane, ecc.

comfy –.comfortable – all'agio.

to rustle something – far saltar fuori qualcosa, rustling, rustled, rustled.

laddy – nomignolo di 'lad' – fanciullo, compagno, ecc.

pool-room – sala da billiardi.

blind-pig. – luogo in cui si può avere da bere, ma che in apparenza dà negli occhi alla gente. (porco-cieco).

pop – bibita dolce di tutti i gusti.

swell line of jaw-music – la lingua di persuasione!

gents – gentlemen.

I couldn't make out – non potevo capire.

interurban – tramway intercomunale.

Or did the Giants win in the ninth? – I Giants sono la famosa squadra di 'baseball' e 'ninth' qui si riferisce alla 'nona' ripresa che è la ripresa finale del giuoco professionale. Una vittoria nella nona ripresa è sempre sensazionale!

mess – pasticcio – impaccio.

To feel down in the mouth – star male di spirito – d'umore.

Have 'nother shot! – Have another shot! – Prendi un altro bicchiere, un'altra bibita!

to sidetrack – mettere a parte. – Da 'side' (lato) e 'track' – binario, sentiero, ecc. Si dice di vagoni delle ferrovie che son presi dal binario principale e messi sul binario a fianco a disposizione ulteriore. Parlando di persone vuol dire che uno vien messo da arte intenzionalmente – o parlando di discorsi, come si fa qui nel testo, vuol dire che non si riusciva a far cambiare di soggetto – di dis cussione. Sidetracking, sidetracked, sidetracked.

lucky dog – individuo fortunato.

to fall to something – incominciare.

We fell to eating – Incominciammo a mangiare!
We fell to. (Incominciavamo.)

to give up – rendere – lasciar andare.

hussy – una che borbotta sempre!

to tag after something or someone – andar dietro – seguire tenacemente. tagging, tagged, tagged.

dress-suits – abiti da sera – Tuxedo – lo 'smoking.'

spiffy – chic – elegante.

Modom – Madame – . Americano che parla il francese. Ha!

vurry – per – very.

hobbledehoy – di nessuna importanza – insignificante.

U. – University.

the go-by. – Quel passer sempre davanti e indietro senza riconoscersi come fanno appunto quelli che si trovano in pubblico con un nemico – cioè passano davanti per forza ma non salutano e nè si curano.

a stag. – Uno, donna o uomo, che va alle feste senza il compagno o la compagna, specialmente quando si tratta di feste dove è inteso che bisogna venire a coppie.

wallflowers. – donne o uomini che vanno, sì, alle feste, ma che poi sono sempre da soli, isolati, come se non si divertissero, anche perché tante volte sono dei tipi spiacevoli. Quindi stanno al muro a godersi lo spettacolo degli altri che si divertono. 'Wall' (muro) 'flowers' (fiori) – come la tappezzeria! Ha!

boob – stupido – cretino.

owl trolley – tramway che va, o meglio, che è ancora in servizio dopo l'una di notte.
Da 'owl' (gufo) che è sveglio di notte.

all night lunch – ristorante aperto tutta la notte.

white mule – marca di brand – whisky.

catsup – salsa piccante.

closed motors – automobile di lusso! Così detti – closed motors – dacchè i motori sono chiusi e per qualsiasi guasto bisogna portare la macchina alla succursale per un meccanico adetto a tali automobili. Non sono come le automobili solite che si possono riparare personalmente.

to kick – lagnarsi.

every man jack of you – Ogni Giacomo di voi – come si direbbe in italiano 'Ogni tizio di voi' (ogni individuo). 'Jack' è un nome – forse nomignolo di 'Giacomo' (James).

good hard cash – denaro buono, solido –

to lay away – mettere da parte – come si fa con dei soldi – risparmiare, in so[m]ma.

University of Hard Knocks – La vita, l'esperienza – ossia – l'università dei Colpi Secchi – le peripezie della vita.

hand-me-down chairs – sedie comperate ad occasione – oppure che siano venute da una generazione all'altra della famiglia.

second-hand – a occasione – come libri, ecc.

to put over – imporre.

interns – giovani dottori che fanno la pratica presso i dottori già legalmente sta biliti.

lobby – sala da riposo presso gli alberghi e luoghi pubblici in generale.

soggy – come uno straccio che sia ben bagnato!

surgeon – chirurgo.

Unpressed – non stirati.

Charley and Will – I famosissimi chiru[r]gi americani – Charles e William Mayo. – Qui detto da amicissimo – spirito americano.

dean – rettore.

Whoopee! Il grido che si dà per iniziare qualche diavoleria! 'To make whoopee' vuol dire – far di tutte le diavolerie.

football tackle – posizione nel giuoco di football – qui dicesi dell'individuo che accompagnava Carr.

I might of known – americano per – I might have known – Avrei dovuto sapere. Nel parlare in fretta il verbo ausiliario 'have' vien spesso pronunciato solo come 'of' ed ecco che l'autore qui lo scrive così!

to spill the beans – far andar a rotoli le cose già combinate.

catgut – budello – come si usa nelle corde del violino.

to pump someone – trovare il modo di far parlare qualcuno.

M.D. – la laurea (degree) di Medical Doctor.

So long. – Arrivederci – Addio.

billboard – muro fatto di legno sul quale appiccicano dei reclames.

roadster – automobile – con un sedile solo – tipo piccolo.

Headlights – fanali.

the boat – slang – per – automobile.

brakes – i freni.

'Sweetie' – carina!

mucho famoso majordomoso – americano (slang) spagnuolizzato – per – much famous majordomo. Detto da chi scherza spenzieratamente.

if he's broke – se è senza denaro.

Charge it to me – mettilo a conto mio.

Watch my smoke – noti il mio andamento! (Da vanitoso – prepotente.)

hoch-gecelebrated – distorto americano a-la-tedesca per – highly-celebrated – di alta celebrità.

benzine buggy – vettura a benzina – quindi un'automobile.

yours truly – che è il modo di firmarsi in una lettera – e che si dice parlando di noi stessi, o anche degli altri.

Let <u>yours truly</u> tell you about it (Let <u>me</u> tell you about it.)

between me and you and the gatepost – si dice per dire 'inter nos' – mettendo una terza persona che poi è sempre qualcosa inanimata.

Between me and you and the lamp-post.
Between me and you and Julius Cesar.

alderman – delegato civico nel governo della città.

It's the first time I ever fell down – È la prima volta che mi sono sbagliato.

to get out – andarsene.

Haf – per – have – e 'wretchet' per 'wretched' – detto da tedesco.

dive – ritrovo basso.

Founder – Fondatore.

to tattle – andar a raccontare.

to let someone down – mandar a passeggio.

hearse – automobile da funerale, quella che porta la bara.

catchum little drink – per – catch a little drink – (pigliarsi una bibita) – detto da pellerosso che metto spesso un 'um' su tutte le parole nostre, come l'italiano ne mette sempre la vocale 'a' quale degno finale per le parole nostre.

footlessness – il non essere in gamba.

to bring someone to – far rinvenire.

Wanderlust – il forte desiderio di girare.

section-gang – I lavoratori delle ferrovie – quelli che mettono giù i binari, ecc.

blind baggages – i vagoni del bagaglio. 'blind baggages' si dice dell'individuo che viaggia sotto il vagone sui ferri massicci che lo possono reggere – come fanno appunto i vagabondi americani, gli avventurieri che non hanno dei soldi, e che non devono lasciarsi vedere o pescare. 'To ride the blinds' vuol dire – viaggiare in questo modo su qualsiasi vagone di qualsiasi treno. (i ciechi).

Slim – nomignolo che vuol dire 'Magro' e che si dà appunto agli individui che sono magri e alti.

hobo – vagabondo, girovago.

I was pretty-high strung. Blew up. (Ero ben teso di nervi. Scoppiai.)

buckwheat cakes – un mangiare di colazione, fatto di grano.

wheat-elevators – i serbatoi di grano – come dei grat[t]acieli in America.

cattle-pen – recinto per la bestiame.

Oil-tank – serbatoio dell'olio (petrolio).

slushy – di neve mezza sciolta e mezza da sciogliersi.

row – discussione infuriata.

scrap – la lotta.

block – isolato.

feed and implement store – Ferri da contadino e mangiare per il bestiame. Negozio di rifornimento per il contadino.

Sort of. – un poco – piuttosto.

wire – telegramma

creamery – dove si fanno i prodotti di latte.

a lay-off – vacanza.

to chew the rag – chiacchierare. (masticare lo straccio.)

scrapping – litigare.

(Continued) **ARROWSMITH – Sinclair Lewis** (From Chapter X)[6]

dese merry vedding or jail bells – Tedesco – per 'these merry wedding bells, or jail bells.' (Queste gaie campane di nozze, oppure di galera.)

to be dropped from something – Farai togliere da qualcosa. Da 'to drop, dropping, dropped, dropped' – lasciar cadere.

shorthand – dattilografia – lo scrivere a segni.

bath-tub – vasca da bagno.

Coaches – i vagoni lunghi dei treni americani.

plumb crazy – addirittura pazzo.

waste land – campagna aperta – quasi deserta.

brewers – Quelli che fanno la birra.

two-reel films – pellicole a due parti.

up-hill and down-gully – Su per le collinette e giù per le ripe.

owl-car – tramway di sevizio notturno – dopo l'una di notte.

to buckle down to something – mettersi sul serio a far qualchecosa. Da 'buckle' fermaglia della cintura) – buckling, buckled, buckled seguite da 'down' – mettersi sul serio.

6 No date is found on this second installment of comments on *Arrowsmith* (chapters X–XXII).

Hot Dogs – sono dei sandwiches fatti con delle salsiccie, cipolle e della salsa piccante – e che si vendono ovunque tanto per togliere l'immediato appetito. È stata una innovazione greca – ed ora è attacattissimo! Siccome nel fare le salsiccie – si dice – che i macellai usano della carne di terza classe ed anche di quella carne di cavallo, asino e qualsivoglia – l'americano è andato oltre ed ha detto che usavano persin carne di cane – quindi i 'dogs' di oggi! 'hot dogs' perché vengono caldi caldi dal fuoco. Oggi quando qualcuno perde un cane o che il cane va a perdersi, dicono che è diventato un 'hot dog.' Ha! E non si cerca più.

motor-salesmanship – l'arte di vendere delle automobili.

muffler – di un'automobile – è lo smorzatore del romore! 'The muffler always cut out' – vuol dire che lo smorzatore era sempre aperto come chi va a piena velocità – ventre a terre – e quindi fa un romorone!

I'll buy you a feed – Vi comprerò! una cena!

to penalize – multare – penalizing, penalized, penalized. – dar la multa.

case-histories – quando si prendono tutta l'informazione dei casi degli ammalati, il nome, altre malattie sofferenze in generale, delle operazioni in generale già fatte, ecc.

charity patients – i poveri che sono negli ospedali a carico della città.

Main Medical – Ospedale Medicale Centrale. La Clinica.

curtain-call – la chiamata al sipario alzato.

baby-snatcher – Prenditori di bambini – l'ostetrico. Da 'to snatch, snatching, snatched, snatched' – prendere al volo.

midwife – levatrice. (La moglie di mezzo).

duck-hunting – caccia all'anitra.

Chapter XI

Get back there – indietro – là!

factory-hand – imp[i]egato operaio della fabbrica.

tools – ferri.

That don't make no never-minds. – Nobody can't get through here! (Non importa – nessuno può passare da qui') Inglese – Americano proprio da tipo che non è mai andato a scuola – eppure a forza d'abitudine quasi tutti parlano così.

to get through – passare, riuscire.

shed – stanzuccia sola fatta a casuccia, specie di capanna, di quelle che costruiscono gli operai temporaneamente quando lavorano lontani da casa per ris parmiare l'alloggio.

to keel over – cadere faccia in giù – keeling, keeling, keeled, keeled.

goner! (già andato.) nel senso di 'morire.'

I'm a goner. – Sono perso – sono morto (da terrorizzato).

to come around – rinvenire.

getum – get him into an ambulance. – hustle – Mettilo in una ambulanza – svelti!

to pull through – riuscire – come dopo una malattia – o qualche disastro nella salute. – rimettersi.

hood – la parte che contiene il motore sull'automobile. (Capuccio).

Midnight Express – Direttissimo di Mezzanotte.

backing motors – motori che indietreggiavano – automobile che si ritiravano dal traffico – regolamento civile quando è in servizio un'ambulanza.

Shooting case – un caso di qualcuno che si è tirato una schiopettata o a sè o a qualcun altro.

<u>to sneak in</u> something – far qualche cosa di mezzo – in fretta.

undarned socks – delle calze non ricucite.

on their nights off – sulle loro notti di libertà, di uscita.

This is my day off – È il mio giorno di uscita – di libertà.

slum – quartiere dei poveri, della malavita, ecc.

His black bag was a pass. – La sua valigia nera era il suo passaporto, la parola d'ordine, ecc.

hold-up men – Furfanti di quelli che ti mettono la rivoltella alla faccia e ti chiedono i denari – benone, eh?

saloon-keepers – tenitori di bars – liquori, ecc.

revived would-be suicides. – Quelli che vorrebbero essere dei suicidi ma che furono rinvenuti.

foolhardy – da spenzierato – da non-curante.

bobbing church pew – Una panca da chiesa che galleggiava.

headlines – Le intestazioni dei giornali – le prime linee di stampa.

I better cut this out – È meglio che io smetta.

chop-house – ristorante di cotellette di carne. tutti i generi.

whitewash – le calce.

I'd black his shoes – Luciderei le sue scarpe. 'to black, blacking, blackened, blackened' – oppure – to blacken, blackening – dare il (nero) lucido.

Horseless Carriages – Vetture senza Cavalli – ossia – treni e Automobili.

ragtime – tempo di ballo dal quale è nato il 'jazz.'

tightwad – avaro.

nincompoopery – infanzia ridicola – stato di bambino.

golf-links – campi dove giuocano al golf.

fish-hook – amo da pesca.

Delivery – consegna.

Live Wire – filo vivo – che si dice degli individui che sono sempre in gamba. Sempre all'erta per gli affari. Trafficone.

baseball coach. – allenatore del giuoco di baseball.

boned up on it – se si studiasse – rifarai un po'.

Chapter XIII

Well, I guess you're the party. 'Hola wire, Long distance wants you.' Dovrebbe Essere (Hold the wire. Long distance wants you). Traduca – Ebbene, mi pare che Lei sia quello voluto. Tenga in linea. L'intercomunale (long distance – telefono a lunga distanza –) vi vuole.

Firm – Ditta – Azienda.

counter-jumper – imp[i]egato di negozio – chi vende e quin[d]i salta da un banco all'altro.

Livery stable – scuderia.

dough – il denaro. – (slang) Pronunci – do.

spell – periodo di tempo – piuttosto corto.

combination on the safe. – i numeri della cassaforte. Sa che bisogna girare a certi numeri ed in certi modi prima di poter aprire la porta di una cassaforte – ebbene questo girare a cercare i numeri combinati si chiama 'combinazione' – combination. 'safe' è 'cassaforte'

vamoose – scappare.

plank walk – marciapiede di legno.

the whole shooting-match – tutto completo.

phony – illegale – a modo d'un trucco.

Auger – ferro da bucare.

Chapter XV

eye-glassed – con occhiali.

to be buffaloed – essere perplesso

Dubs – quelli che sanno a fare – i disgraziati delle professioni.

up-to-the-jiffy – che vale – up-to-date – modernissimo – ultima moda.

Outfit – Apparecchio.

kiddies – bambini.

vale of sorrow – valle di lagrime – tristezza.

by jiminy – una delle tantissime frasi di contentezza – solo esclamazioni che appagano l'immaginazione ma che in sè non dicono nulla, come 'by golly' by heck 'by gingo,' ecc.

caboose – vagone ferroviario sempre ultimo nel treno in cui vi sta il personale del treno merci che è in viaggio.

swole – per – swollen – gonfio.

she killed the engine. – Ha fermato il motore – involontariamente. Si dice 'ammazzare il motore' da noi – dacchè in questi casi dove vi è una mano inesperta a guidare – di un tratto il motore dà un soffio ed un suo da cannone e poi si ferma – là. Questo fermarsi così è prodotto da mal funzionamento dovuto alla mano inesperta.

yoost – per – just – da Scandinavo.

fireman – fuochista.

fifty-seven – il numero del paziente – o della sua camera.

fee-splitter – uno che divide la tariffa.

pluck – coraggio

slews – paludi.

sleigh-rides – gite in slitta.

sociables – intrattenimenti.

kit – pronto soccorso – first aid kit – come quelli che portano gli esploratori per casi imprevvisti.

lizzie – automobile dilapidata, mal andata.

to make up something – fare il 'deficit' – fare delle riparazioni. Fare la contra azione.

to ante – mettere giù il prezzo stabilito prima di incominciare il giuoco delle carte – poker – per esempio.

a big game on – un grandissimo giuoco incominc[i]asi. Si usa 'big' qui nel senso che chi giuocava aveva dei soldoni – e non perché vi fossero tanti individui nel giuoco. Gran denaro – big name – naturalmente.

to go to the dogs – andare in malora. – finire male.

megaphoned – detto attraverso il megafono.

Big Guns – gente di alto rango nella professione medica. (Cannoni grandi).

truck-driver – guidatore di camion.

to boss – bossing, bossed, bossed – commandare.

The con. – la tisi. – (consumption) (consunzione.)

T.B. – la tisi, di nuovo, da 'tuberculosis.'

Two-by-twice. – altro modo per – two-by-two – che vuol dire '2X2' come una multiplicazione che ci dà poco – che vale poco, che è piccolissimo. Qualsiasi cosa che sia 'two-by-two' è insignificante, vale ben poco.

scads – molti.

a plug hat – capello alto – uso società, di quelli che chiamiamo pure 'stove-pipe hat' – (canna da stufa) dacchè la somiglia nel colore nero lucido e nella forma.

pickaback – sulla schiena a quattro gambe.

diapers – stracci che si mette sui bambini prima che possono indossare pantaloncini, ecc.

N.D. – North Dakota – lo stato.

'Excuse our Dust' – cartelloni che tanti americani sfacciati mettono sulla loro automobile, più ancora se è una macchina potente, di modo che passano tutte le automobili sulla strada a grande velocità lasciando una nuvola di polvere in dietro e dentro a questa nuvola il disgraziato che andava più pianino – e che si consola nella sua meno potente macchina con il leggere il cartellone dell'altro che 'chiede scusa della polvere.' Ironico, eh? Eppure!

A.M.A. – American Medical Association.

half-cocked – mezzo-sicuro.

to chin with someone – parlare con qualcuno. Da 'chin' (mentone).

to let on to something – fingere qualchecosa.

a nip – una piccola bibita.

Tooth-picks – stecchi per i denti – come si usa a tavola.

quack – si dice degli uomini che sono nella professione di medicina senza avere il titolo – o di quelli che trovano una cura – che non segue le norme della medicina.

to have a bat – divertirsi.

Fat chance! – Poca possibilità! (Idioma speciale.)

poster[7] – Cartellone di reclame.

singsong – andamento musicale nel parlare – cadenzare.

zinc-lined – foderato di zinco. Stomaco potente.

VAI-ter – per 'Waiter' – Cameriere! Come si grida da noi (Ha.) Detto da Svedese.

Seventh Day Adventist – setta religiosa in cui osservano il Sabato e non già la Domenica come quasi tutte le altre sette.

ash-barrels – i barili delle ceneri – che vengono poi raccolti da appositi impiegati di municipio.

manure – sterco di mucca.

schoolboard – La commissione della scuola.

garbage – ammondizia [*sic*].

squatters – vagabondi – viandanti.

Bohunks – gente di nessun conto.

poor-farm – casa dei vecchi – che quando possono lavorano la terra.

jail-delivery – una forzata consegna dalla prigione.

7 Next to this term an 'x' has been marked in pencil.

butt of the land. – lo scherzo della terra (vicinanza).

I'm licked. – Sono battuto.

I guess you aint any too popular – ecc. – Paragrafo senza 'punctuation' appunto Per dare l'idea di una donna chiacchierona che fila sempre in avanti, Bellissimo!

If you just stuck to it. – Se voi solo rimareste a ciò. (il lavoro). Da 'to stick to something' – resistere – durare – rimanerci tenacemente.

Buick agency. agenzia della Buick, automobile.

Bull – (slang) sbaglio, errore.

We panned you? – L'abbiamo contrastato? – To pan someone – dar incontro, contrastare. – panning, panned, panned.

to roast someone – tener dietro a qualcuno – sgradevolmente – leggere la vita a qualcuno sempre per delle piccolezze. Roasting, roasted, roasted

unlicked cub – cagnolino non battuto – oppure – cagnolino non ancora leccato dalla madre – stato di infanzia prima.

guff – stupidità – roba da poco.

agin you – per – against you (centro di voi) detto da contadino.

Chapter XIX

lumber-wagons – vagoni per il trasporto dei tronchi d'albero.

overalled farmers – contadini in 'toni' – abiti da lavoro.

horse-shoe pitcher – gettitore del ferro di cavallo – un giuoco piacevolissimo da noi – in cui a un[a] certa distanza si cerca di infilare il ferro da cavallo ad un palo piccolo piantato lì in terra.

Alley – vicolo – strada corta – cieca. Come quelle vie in Vecchia Torino.

to bank on something – dipendere – aver la certezza su qualcosa.

Bowling Club – i club che si dedicano al giuoco dei birilli.

cheer-leader – quelli che intonano i gridi di corpo durante le manifestazioni.

Grown-ups – adulti.

A-tall – americano enfatico per – at all – affatto.

rocker – sedia dondolante.

Uneedarest – cartellone di un solo nome che poi vo[r]rebbe dire – You need a rest (Hai bisogno di riposo). Manie.

pump-handling – Come si fa alla pompa – in su ed in giù con la maniglia. Qui dicesi di Pickerbaugh e di Martin – toccandosi la mano. Ha!

chickabiddies – gallinuccie.

poem-slogan – motto a forma di poema.

popsywopsies – nomignolo di tenerezza – carini.

Upsy – per – up (sù) detto da chi parla con dei bambini.

paw – per mano – altrimenti è la zampa di gatto, cane, ecc.
Or does he pull the bunk, too? – O che egli pure faccia delle cretinerie?

jever – per – did you ever? – Americano affrettato.

into their noodles – into their heads (nelle loro teste.)

to soft-soap someone – parlare gentilmente per ottenere un piacere. Raccontare delle pene per ottenere lo scopo.

Chapter XX

local slants – conoscenze locali.

a straight tip – un consiglio franco.

the right dope – le cose come sono.

to tie up with someone – fare dell'amicizia.

cheer – un grido di corpo.

bidding at bridge – scommettere sui punti al g[i]uoco di bridge – giuoco di carte. Si dichiara i punti, insomma, che si vuol fare.

a cold snack – a cold meal – un pasto freddo – una cena fredda.

bob-sled – una specie di slitta.

tags – specie di bigliettini con una cordicella che si mette all['](occhiello) dopo aver pagato una certa somma durante una campagna qualsiasi – per i tubercolotici, per i poveri, o per i mutilati, ecc. Quando si fa di queste campagne in America, le signorine apposite si mettono agli angoli delle vie e raccolgono i soldi, in cambia per i quali vi danno questo bigliettino sul quale sarà scritta 'I gave' (Ho contribuito) ed il quale bigliettino si mette all'occhiello per non essere più seccato. Delle campagne poi vi sono sempre qui – come appunto leggerà in questo paragrafo o due.

bonniest – dallo scozzese – che vuol dire – più belle.

You must come across – Deve contribuire – enfatico.

Your Money Creates 'Appiness (happiness). Il vostro denaro crea della felicità.

Banish the Booze Week – La Settimana per la campagna di 'Scartare il Liquore.'

Tougher Teeth Week – La settimana per 'I Denti più Duri.'

Stop the Spitter – Fermate lo Sputatore.

Clean-up – Pulizia Generale.

Part – per – partner – socio, compagno.

Swat the Fly – Abbattete la Mosca.

Fly-Swatter – quello con il quale si ammazzano le mosche.

you gotter – per – you got to – e qui è inteso il verbo principale (swat the fly). C'è il – gotter – per far rima con 'swatter.'

Can the Cat – Licenziate il Gatto.

Doctor the Dog – Curate (di salute) il Cane.

She-males – per – Females – Femmine.

Bee – Convegno.

Hop-to-it – Avanti – Al lavoro! Ecc.

men as kin talk – per – men that can talk – Uomini che possono parlare.

So we can lug a think or two home wid us – per – so we can lug a thought or two home with us – Di modo che possiamo portare a casa con noi un pensiero o due.

[**Chapter XXI**][8]

To lug – lugging-lugged-lugged – portare, trascinare come chi trascina un peso sul pavimento per trasportarlo – come un baule, per esempio.

Wim and wigor – per – V.M. and Vigor – Vita e Vigore

(Caro Pavese – questo è inglese terribile – commerciale – e slangizzato – come spero lo possa capire.)

neverything – per – and everything.

nall – per – and all. (e tutto)

8 The comments from chapters XXI and XXII are found on a loose sheet of paper found in the 'Fondo Sini' at the Pavese archives.

Part your hair Jack and look cute, the ladies sure love you – (Fatti la riga nei capelli, Giacomo, e fatti la faccia da carino – le donne ti vogliono proprio bene.)

On your tootsies, fellers, thar she blows – per On your tootsies, fellows, thar she blows!

Che vuol dire – Su! – ai vostri treni – compagni – ecco che fischia (per la partenza). Da 'to toot, tooting, tooted, tooted' – fischiare come fa il treno.

Hie ourselluƒs – per – hie ourselves – portar – ci.

Wild Wittles – per – Wild Vittles – che nello slang vuol dire – del buon mangiare.

somepun – per – something – da americano

[hobby] passatempo – avocazione.

Pasteurized – data la cura di Pasteur – il francese.

slaughter-houses – gli ammazzatoi. Da 'to slaughter, slaughtering, slaughtered, slaughtered' – Ammazzare. (in quantità)

quarantined – isolato – come si fa con certe malattie infettose. Proibito l'ingresso a tutti meno il dottore.

winkulus pinkulus – giovinotto che dice così per arrivare al suono di certe malattie di Latino! Ha!

ta, ta – good-bye. Addio – cerea [?]

a chat – piccola conversazione.

Do Jewen – per – Don Juan (Don Giovanni).

milline – cappellai – chi fa dei cappelli, insomma – da donna.

punk – non buono.

glum – di mal umore.

Chapter XXII

Chatauqua tour – Una compagnia che gira da una città all'altra – una compagnia composta di musicisti, letterati, scienziati, ecc. che hanno il loro programma da fare sulle sere stabilite. Compagnia mista d'artisti.

Stonewall Jackson – Generale Americano

manhood-rotting – quello che fa marcire lo stato di uomo.

quippish – corto – sarcastico.

tin-cans – scattole di latta.

cobbler – calzolaio

smart-aleck cracks – osservazioni da impudente, da chi vuol darsi delle arie.

to ram home – far vedere, far capire

outskirts – i dintorni.

plant – fabbrica – manifattura.

strep – per – streptococcus.

to be hard-up – mancare dei soldi – non avere che pochissimo denaro

to catch up – rifare il tempo perso.

heathen – irreligioso – pagano.

shower baths – doccie.

knap-sacks – gli zaini.

porker – grassoccio – come il porco.

depot – stazione. Pronunci – di-po.

to be up against something – Trovarsi d'avanti a degli ostacoli.

To lay down – venire meno a se' stesso.

COMMENTS ON — ARROWSMITH — by Sinclair Lewis[9]

Instalment Three

Board of Aldermen – La Commissione dei Dirigenti di Città.

Tabernacle – si dice così di una 'chiesetta' – in senso ironico.

Novel features – spettacoli di novità – intrattenenti.

Boy Scouts – Esploratori Giovani.

booth – una 'separèe' – recinto apposito.

dinky – piccolo – ridicolo

ground-up – macinato.

pie – torta americana – di vastissimo uso.

had fitted up – preparato – aveva messo sù – aveva combinato.

fireman – pompiere – 'pompista.'

licker – per – liquor – (liquore) americano parlato.

plain-clothes man – poliziotto in borghese – detective.

Have you picked? Hai scelto?

crackajack – per – cracker jack – esperto – in gamba molto.

9 No date on this third installment of comments on *Arrowsmith* (chapters XXIII–XL).

to wind up – winding, wound, wound – terminare – concludere.

kindling – legno da incominciare che vien preso da non si sa dove!

Pick-up candidate – Un candidato che vien preso da non si sa dove!

circus advance-agents – impresario dei circhi che vanno sempre in avanti del circo a combinare gli spettacoli. Come si fa anche con delle compagnie drammatiche – hanno uno che va da città a città a combinare le loro rappresentazioni.

Side-kick – slang per – aiutante – Compagno di lavoro.

crooked politics – politica storta – disonesta.

hot wienies – hot dogs – delle salsiccie calde.

Chapter XXIV

Lousy – da 'louse' – pidocchi.

D.B. – Dead Beat – Paga-niun – chi non paga mai.

'Hired-girl' – Persona di servizio. Da 'to hire, hiring, hired, hired' – noleggiare.

grocer – chi vende dei commestibili. Wholesale Grocer – Venditore di commestibili all'ingrosso.

suit – processo di diritto.

couch – specie di sofà.

rowdyish – faccia tosta – prepotente.

to monkey with the buzz-saw – a scherzare con la sega elettrica.

D.P.H. Department of Public Health.

pet cub – beniamino.

to dig up – cercare.

guts – slang – intestine.

fast – qui vuol dire – alla moda dei piaceri.

dunning letters – quelle che chiedono i pagamenti.

cop – . slang – poliziotto.

see their way clear – vedersi al chiaro delle cose.

to break someone in on something – Far fare la pratica a qualcuno.

Chapter XXV

fencing lesson – lezione di scherma.

split an infinitive – disgiungere un infinito (grammatica). Si sa che in inglese il verbo ha davanti a sè la particella 'to,' che è necessaria perché sia l'infinito. Ora l'avverbio per descrivere questo infinito deve trovarsi o prima dell'infinito oppure dopo, e non MAI fra la particella (preposizione) 'to' ed il verbo proprio.

Mr. Pavese gladly wants to learn slang. (regolare – giusto)
Mr. Pavese wants to learn slang gladly (regolare – giusto).
Mr. Pavese wants to gladly learn slang. (Disgiungere dell'infinito – splitting the infinitive.)

La quale cosa fa spesso Lewis!

soot – la polvere delle ceneri. Quello che viene dal tubo della stufa.

Better-bilt – per Better-built – Marca d'indumenti.

get stuck in a problem – impacciarsi con qualche problema.

buzzards – uc[c]elli di preda – che chi usasi come individui di preda.

Brer – per – Brother.

Chapter XXVII

Fumblingly – quando tutto scappa da mano – quando ogni cosa che si prende in mano deve per forza scivolare. Da 'to fumble, fumbling, fumbled fumbled' –

invoices – resoconti.

Tacking – Da 'to tack, tacking, tacked, tacked' – inchiodare – ma con chiodini solo!
'Tack' – (chiodino).

it drove him on – lo ha spinto in avanti.

peep – uno sguardino.

Duck this spread! – tralasciare questa cena! 'To duck, ducking, ducked ducked'— schiavare – 'Spread' – quello che è messo in lungo e in largo.

rented – affitato.

tear the carpet with his spare – Stracciare il tappeto con i suoi speroni.

to be up to something – stare per combinare qualcosa.

What are you up to now? Cosa stai facendo, combinando ora?

rubber – gomma.

Gottdamn – ironico per 'God damn' – bestemmia americana.

rabbicks – per – rabbits – coniglie – detto da 'carina – cretina.'

turtle – la tartaruga.

You're lawn-mowing and daisy-picking, not digging – Stai tagliando l'erba del cortile E stai raccogliendo i pensieri (fiori) e non che tu stia lavorando seriamente.

nix – niente – che viene dal tedesco – niente – (nulla).

math – matematica.

tenth-rater – decimo nella fila. – di qualifica – decimo.

M.P. – Military Police – come i carabinieri.

gunman – quelli che lavorano con la rivoltella – furto, assassino, ecc.

Portygee – per – Portugese – Portughese. .

Chapter XXVIII

M.R.C. Medical Reserve Corps – Corpo Medico di Riserva.

At the Institute telephone switchboard he plugged in wherever it seemed reasonable. – (letteralmente) – Al controllo dei telefoni dell'Istituto attaccava i fili ovunque gli sembrava ragionevole. – Sa bene, Pavese, che questo 'controllo' è zeppo di buchi – ogni buco corrispondente ad un numero di telefono; ebbene, siccome era di notte l'operatrice addetta non c'era di modo che Arrowsmith tentava egli di indovinare il numero per parlare con sua moglie. 'to plug in' qui vuol dire mettere nei buchi i fili corrispondenti per l'attacco.

Ring off! – Si dice così per dire – smetta la conversazione – smetta a parlare – Rimetta il telefono come era.

felt his way back – come fa il cieco che va in giro.

fagged – stanchissimo.

lip-stick – il 'lapis' del rosso per le labbra.

subway – tramway sotterraneo.

to sic it on someone or something – Come si fa quando si dà il largo ad un cane e che gli si fa vedere la preda, il bastone nell'acqua, o anche il ladro alla finestra. Allora noi diciamo 'Sic him.' che vuol dire prendilo – avanti – ammazzalo! Ecc.

a shave – un radersi della barba.

and to not sleeping – esempio di 'splitting the infinitive' – il disgiungersi dell'infinito – che già abbiam visto.

beeswax – L'alveare. – quello con cui le api fanno il miele. 'beeswax' (cera di api).

fake reports – dei rapporti falsi.

four-day tramp – four-day hike – un cammino di quattro giorni.

That he might pound on the faster – che egli potessi andare più infretta – – ragione per cui andava – solo –!

by sleeper – nel Pullman – treno a letti.

Chapter XXIX

nasty – di brutto.

coops – casuccie, come si fanno per i cani, le galline o gli uccelli.

windy – gonfiati – grandiosi.

Chapter XXX

a scad – un mucchio.

to back me – appoggiarmi.

I'd give him a lot more floor-space – che vale – Gli darei molto più della corda!

a sloop in her wake – una barca nella sua via davanti.

Wha's like – per – what's it like? – Come è?

wilence – per – violence – violenza.

den – camera privata – per sè – per star tranquillo.

butchers – macellai.

suit-cases – valigie.

Chapter XXXI

cane hands – lavoratori sulle piantaggioni di zucchero.

smuggler – contrabbandiere.

gang-plank – quello sul quale si scende e discende sulle navi da terra.

African bush – la giungla africana.

headhunters – I cacciatori di teste – tribù africana.

slot machines – delle machine nelle quali vi è una cosa la quale si può avere se si mette una moneta nel 'slot' (piccolo buco) e poi se si fà girare la maniglia. Di 'slot machines' vi sono per il 'chewing gum' per certi dolci, per sandwich, ecc.

Chapter XXXII

big – boom-boom – grande reclame.

to blow in a lot of money – Spendere molto denaro.

scut – pigrona.

jiggers – problemi.

What's biting you? – Cosa ti irrita? (Da 'to bite, biting, bit, bitten' — Mordere.)

Palm Beach Suit – abito tutto bianco, elegante – come indossano appunto i vi[l]eggianti di Palm Beach, Florida, durante la stagione di piacere.

round trip – andata e ritorno.

The Star Spangled Banner – Il nostro Inno Nazionale.

motor launch – piccola barca a motore.

gin sling – bibito [*sic*] di gin.

snooze – dormire

Chapter XXXIII

pouch – i sacchi grandi di posta.

to balk – opporsi – come fa il mulo quando non vuol andar avanti.

stank – da 'to stink, stinking, stank, stunk' – puzzare.

mess-sergeant – sargente [*sic*] di mensa.

topers – bevitori inveterate.

punch, fizz, swizzle – sono delle bibite di preparazione speciale.

Chapter XXXIV

COW-DUNG – Sterco di mucca.

I'm onto him! Io lo capisco – So da quale piede zoppica!

mammies – le mame negre.

burrows – buchi scavati nella terra.

curly gray mop – capigliatura grigia e ricciolata.

Rock of Ages – da un quadro raffigurando una donna che abbraccia una grande croce di pietra – La Fede dei Secoli!

slop-pails – secchie di ammondizia mescolata con dell'acqua sporca.

Chapter XXXV

the funnies – le caricature nei giornali – come il Corriere dei Piccoli.

To see someone off – dare l'addio a qualcuno alla partenza.

It's a go! – per dire – Ci sto! – È Combinato! Va benone! Ecc.

Hold your horses. – (Tenga i cavalli.) Si dice quando uno vuol fare o dire in fretta e furia, ch[i]ome i cavalli che si spaventano e che vogliono poi filare.

to skim through something – leggere, or fare, qualchecosa alla svelte.

Chapter XXXVII

piffling[10] – roba da ridere.

plus-fours – pantaloncini da 'golf.' Da scozzese!

Rolls-Royce – La più cara macchina di lusso! automobile.

shanty – capanna – a una camera sola, benchè qui sia di due camere.

Here's the layout! Ecco il piano! (Da combinare.)

topper – cappello a cilindro.

spats – quelli che si mettono sopra le scarpa – le ghete! Ha!

Chapter XXXVIII

frock – abito.

laundry – il lavaggio.

steak – la carne.

flu – influenza.

chimps – per – chimpanzees. – razza di scimmie grandi.

To sponge on someone – chiedere qualchecosa da qualcuno.

---

10 Next to this word an 'x' is marked in pencil.

to hold out on someone – tenere qualchecosa indietro – ritenere.

Where's the catch? – Dov'è il trucco? Dove è la cosa che non va?

Chapter XXXIX

to high-hat someone – Trattare da aristocratico – da 'high-hat' il cilindro!

Gen. Public – General Public – il pubblico in generale.

din-din – dinner (cena).

high-rollers – gente ricca.

hootch – liquore. – on prescriptions – su ordini dai dottori.

water-tight – stretto contro l'acqua – a prova d'acqua.

tootelus-bootelus – da 'to boot' (in più – (non è verbo) –). Parole fatte per l'occasione – uso Sinclair Lewis!

to rig up – combinare – preparare –

Bran-new – da – brand-new – nuovissimo.

Dee-ah – per – Dear – inglesizzato.

Teloddeling. – Andare – muoversi – slang fatto per l'occasione!

shake a hoof – ballare.

homey- grub-grabbing – A pescare del mangiare uso casa propria!

whole darn outfit – tutta la baracca.

pleezhure – per – pleasure.

Missus – per – Mrs. (signora).

Au Reservoir – per – Au Revoir – bel francese, eh? E un bel tipo!

to furnish – mobigliare [*sic*] – mettere i mobili.

valay – per – valet – il domestico.

was the cat's pajamas – modo di dire era tutto quello che si poteva desiderare. Abbiamo un sacco di questi mod[i], che poi vogliono dire la stessa cosa – per esempio

To be the cat's meow! cat's pajamas.

To be the snake's hips! To be the berries! ECC.

To put on the dog – darsi delle arie!

Didn't cotton to me – didn't take a liking to me.

Old Lady – slang per – Signora.

skirt – slang per – donna – da 'skirt' – vesta.

butler – domestico.

four-poster – letto a quattro colonne.

highfalutin' – per – highfaluting – aristocratico.

from the tall grass – dalla campagna.

Chapter XL

squabs – dei pigioni [*sic*] piccoli.

cash-registers – le casse per i soldi – come si usano nei negozi.

lumber interests – le aziende per il legno da costruzione.

a sideshow barker – L'annunciatore degli spettacoli di circo.

bob-sled – una slitta.

chip-littered snow – della neve coperta di pezzettini di legno.

Come for keeps – vengo per sempre. (Modo idiomatico.)

supply-toting – il portare dei rifornimenti.

to hum, humming, hummed, hummed – cantare a bocca chiusa.

FINIS

Chiuminatto's comments on William Faulkner's As I Lay Dying.[11]

***As I Lay Dying* – Faulkner**

Cigar store Indian – busto di pellerosso in legno che trovavasi sul marciapiede davanti al tabaccaio. Quasi sempre una figura di vecchio pellerosso austero, solenne. Da lontano si vedeva così il tabaccaio. La figura si usava allora forse perché nei primi tempi furono i pellirossi a fumare – che già conoscevano l'uso del tobacco.

say-so – il dire.

'On my say-so' (sul mio dire – sulla mia parola)

Swapped – da 'to swap' (fare lo scambio).

tom-boy – dicesi delle donne che hanno l'andamento maschile.

miscue – da 'cue' che è il bastone da bigliardo. 'Miscue' si dice quando il basto[ne] scivola dalla palla, facendo un colpo irregolare.

ourn – per 'ours' (il nostro)

sho – per 'sure' (sicuro!) detto alla maniera dei negri.

durn – per 'darn' – esclamativo come sarebbe 'accidenti,' ecc.

dassent – il volgare per 'to dare not' (non osare) i dassent – per 'I dare not.'

durn nigh – quasi, quasi!

to aim – to adopera qui nel senso di 'fare conto di' 'I aim to do it' (faccio conto di farlo).

holp – per 'help' (aiutare)

Laid-by – messo a posto!

11 These comments are found at the end of Chiuminatto's letter of 21 February 1932.

outen – per 'out of' (fuori di).

Old Master – Old Master (Vecchio Padrone) che sarebbe 'Dio' nel modo negro.

et – ate – (mangiato).

gittin' – per 'getting'!

hit – per 'it.'

That ere – per 'that there' (quello là)

keer – care (cura)

sich – such

sot – set (fisso)

Paw – Pa – (papà) alla moda del Sud.

kilt – killed – (ucciso)

Git – get – come imperative vuol dire ('va!')

hit want – it wasn't.

to hitch the team – metter la coppia dei cavalla [*sic*] al carro.

to give someone the creeps – dare i brividi. Far paura.

swole-up way – Swollen-up way (nel modo di gonfiato).

To dicker – pasticciare, litigare per certe piccolezze.

INDEX

www.ingramcontent.com/pod-product-compliance
Lightning Source LLC
Chambersburg PA
CBHW060944120726
47910CB00002B/485

* 9 7 8 1 4 8 7 5 8 7 1 9 2 *